When Daniel Boone goes by, at night,
The phantom deer arise
And all lost, wild America
Is burning in their eyes.

"Daniel Boone" by Stephen Vincent Benét

LOST WILD AMERICA

LOST
WILD
AMERICA

THE STORY OF
OUR EXTINCT AND VANISHING WILDLIFE

REVISED, EXPANDED and UPDATED EDITION

ROBERT M. McCLUNG

Illustrated by Bob Hines

M111554549

Linnet Books   1993

Library of Congress Cataloging-in-Publication Data

McClung, Robert M.
Lost wild America : the story of our extinct and vanishing wildlife /
Robert M. McClung : illustrated by Bob Hines.
Rev., expanded, and updated ed.
p.   cm.
Includes bibliographical references and index.
Summary: Traces the history of wildlife conservation
and environmental politics in America to mid-1993
and describes various extinct or endangered species.
1. Wildlife conservation—North America—History—Juvenile literature.
2. Wildlife management—North America—History—Juvenile literature.
3. Extinction (Biology)—North America—History—Juvenile literature.
4. Extinct animals—North America—History—Juvenile literature.
5. Endangered species—North America—History—Juvenile literature.
[1. Wildlife conservation.   2. Rare animals.   3. Extinction (Biology)]
I. Title.
QL84.M38   93-15657   591.52'9'0973—dc20
ISBN 0-208-02359-3 (alk. paper)

Illustration credits: All illustrations are by Bob Hines,
except for the following by Robert M. McClung: Snail Darter,
Bowhead Whale, Northern Spotted Owl, Puerto Rican Parrot,
Thick-billed Parrot, Golden-cheeked Warbler, Sockeye Salmon,
Schaus Swallowtail, Mission Blue Butterfly, Monarch Butterfly.

Grateful acknowledgment is made to Brandt & Brandt for
permission to quote from *A Book of Americans* by Rosemary and
Stephen Vincent Benét, published by Holt, Rinehart, and
Winston, Inc. Copyright 1933 by Stephen Vincent Benét;
copyright renewed 1961 by Rosemary Carr Benét.

The paper in this publication meets the minimum requirements
of American National Standard for Information Science
—Permanence of Paper for Printed Library Materials,
ANSI Z39.48–1984. ♾

Printed in the United States of America.

To the memory of my parents,
and for Gale
and the future of our children
and grandchildren

CONTENTS

*Like winds and sunsets, wild things were taken for
granted until progress began to do away with them.
Now we face the question whether a still higher
"standard of living" is worth its cost in things
natural, wild, and free.*

—Aldo Leopold,
A Sand County Almanac

FOREWORD

In 1967, when the first edition of this book was being prepared, then
Secretary of the Interior Stewart L. Udall listed seventy-eight different
vertebrate animals—mammals, birds, reptiles, and fish—that were in
imminent danger of extinction in the United States. All of them, he
warned, faced a bleak future or no future at all, unless their downward
plunge was reversed in time. "An informed public will help reduce the
dangers threatening these rare animals," he said. And it is true that
many effective programs have been put into practice in the years since
to aid endangered wildlife. These programs have helped some threatened
species to survive.

Others, however, have disappeared, in spite of all efforts in their
behalf, as the following pages show. While conservation causes gain
adherents, suitable living space for wildlife continues to shrink at an
alarming rate. Every year more and more people need more and more
homes, more developments, more factories, more roads, more food.
Inevitably the squeeze on endangered species becomes greater and
greater.

In 1990, nearly a quarter-century after that first list of endangered
species was compiled, the U.S. Fish and Wildlife Service listed 179
vertebrate animals and 54 invertebrates as either threatened or endangered. Unfortunately, this does not show the whole picture. Many
hundreds—even thousands—of other forms of American wildlife that
are also threatened or endangered still wait their turn to be listed.

The narrative that follows is an accounting of how we have treated
our wildlife since Colonial days: how we completely exterminated some
species; how we pushed others to the brink, only to give them a reprieve
at the last possible moment; how we harried many others to their present
perilous state; and, finally, what we are doing at this time to save these
currently endangered species.

Experiences of the past clearly show how human activities can threaten or destroy wildlife. Past experiences also demonstrate how proper conservation and management efforts can save endangered species.

Have we learned these lessons of history? More important still, do we care enough about our wildlife heritage to make the needed effort to preserve it?

ACKNOWLEDGMENTS

The first shadowy concept of this book was jotted down as a one-page outline in the spring of 1955. Since that time, many hundreds of books, periodicals, pamphlets, news items, and other references added their bits and pieces to the developing idea and work, and so did the ideas and generous advice of many individuals. I acknowledge my indebtedness to all of these contributions, which were of inestimable help in the writing of the original 1969 edition of this book.

During the twenty-four years since the publication of that edition, I kept my subject files current by adding new information and material as developments occurred. For this 1993 edition, the accounts of all the threatened and endangered species have been revised and updated, and additional accounts have been written for the following: bowhead whale, northern spotted owl, Puerto Rican parrot, thick-billed parrot, golden-cheeked warbler, sockeye salmon, Schaus swallowtail, mission blue butterfly, and monarch butterfly. Two new chapters, "Politics and the Environment, 1963 to 1993" (Chapter 8), and "Butterflies and Other Invertebrates" (Chapter 18), have been added. The final chapter, "Humanity, an Endangered Species" has been largely rewritten to bring humankind's present status into clearer focus.

I continue to be grateful to the late Lee S. Crandall, general curator emeritus of the New York Zoological Society and longtime secretary of the American Committee for International Wildlife Protection, and to the late Dr. William B. Sheldon, leader of the Massachusetts Cooperative Research Unit at the University of Massachusetts. Both of them reviewed the 1969 manuscript in its entirety and made a number of helpful suggestions.

Dr. Archie Carr of the University of Florida was kind enough to review the original chapter on reptiles and amphibians. Dr. Charles F. Cole, associate professor of fisheries at the University of Massachusetts, did the same for the chapter on fish, and Scott MacVay of Princeton University reviewed the chapter on whales. I thank them again for their interest and help.

Refuge managers, wildlife biologists, and field and other staff personnel of the U.S. Bureau of Sport Fisheries and Wildlife were invariably interested, helpful, and hospitable during the course of my original research—both on trips to many different refuges and in the Washington office. I am deeply indebted to Gale Monson and Philip DuMont, both of the Division of Wildlife Refuges, and to Harry A. Goodwin, Office of Endangered Species. Each of them also reviewed the 1969 manuscript and made many helpful suggestions and corrections.

In preparing the 1993 revised, expanded, and updated edition of the book, I received help and current information from many different sources. I particularly thank the following individuals: William E. Knapp, chief, Office of Endangered Species and Habitat Conservation, and Craig L. Rieben, chief, Office of Current Information, both of the Fish and Wildlife Service; and Patricia A. Montanio, Protected Species Management Division, National Marine Fisheries Service.

A number of wildlife and environmental specialists reviewed portions of the revised and updated manuscript and contributed many helpful suggestions. These include: John Green, biological technician, U.S. Forest Service; Don Kroodsma, professor of ornithology, University of Massachusetts, Amherst; Boyd Kynard, section leader, Fish Behavior/Ecology, Conte Anadromous Fish Research Center, Turners Falls, Massachusetts, Fish and Wildlife Service; James Sibbison, former press officer, Environmental Protection Agency; and Tom Tyning, master naturalist, Massachusetts Audubon Society. Jean Thompson, long-time friend and expert copyeditor, reviewed the bibliography. I thank all of these for their valuable contributions. Any mistakes that may remain are my own, as is the responsibility for all statements and expressed opinions.

Finally, heartfelt thanks to Bob Hines, whose attractive and expertly rendered illustrations add so much to the appearance of the book; to editor Connie Epstein and her staff for all they did in guiding the first edition through its many stages, from germinal idea to finished product; and to Diantha Thorpe, editor of this expanded and updated edition, for similar help. Last, but most important, I thank my wife Gale, whose encouragement and advice have been of immeasurable help throughout the work on both editions, and who patiently and painstakingly deciphered all my changes and additions for this current edition and put it all down on her word processor.

I

VICTIMS OF THE PAST

*Life for the Indian is one of harmony with Nature and
the things which surround him. The Indian tried to fit
in with Nature and to understand, not to conquer and
to rule. We were rewarded by learning much that the
white man will never know. Life was a glorious thing,
for great contentment comes with the feeling of
friendship and kinship with the living things about
you. The white man seems to look upon all animals
as enemies, while we look upon them as friends and
benefactors. They were one with the Great Mystery
and so were we. We could feel the peace and power of
the Great Mystery in the soft grass under our feet and
in the blue sky above us.*

—Ota K'te (Chief Standing Bear, Sioux),
My Indian Boyhood

And I brought you into a plentiful country,
To eat the fruit thereof and the goodness thereof;
But when ye entered,
Ye defiled my land,
And made mine heritage an abomination.

—Jeremiah 2:7

1

EXPLORERS AND PIONEERS:
America until 1800

A band of primitive hunters wandered across a grassy plain, heading toward the rising sun. They did not know it, but they were going into an unknown land—a land where man had never been before. Behind them lay the vast stretches of arctic Siberia, ahead the destiny of a New World. These were the first human beings to set foot in North America.

The time? Perhaps fifteen thousand years ago, perhaps two or three times that long in the past. Great ice sheets thousands of feet thick still covered much of North America during part of this period, and vast quantities of water were locked up in the frozen depths. The oceans were lowered as a result, and a broad land bridge lay exposed between Asia and America. Not only man but many kinds of animals passed back and forth across this connecting link between Siberia and Alaska.

The first nomads moved gradually southward through mountain passes, and other tribes followed in their footsteps. These early Americans hunted caribou and musk-oxen and woolly mam-

3

moths with fire-hardened spears of wood. They skinned their quarry with instruments made of stone and flint. They fought off the attacks of giant cave bears, dire wolves, saber-toothed cats, and many other Ice Age predators. Indeed, some scientists believe that early man, as a hunter, was largely responsible for the extinction of many of the big Ice Age mammals in North America: mammoths, long-horned bison, giant ground sloths, the saber-toothed cat *Smilodon*, and others. All these animals disappeared after man had come to the New World.

Generation succeeded generation, and still other bands of primitive men crossed over the land bridge into Alaska. Hundreds of generations succeeded each other as the first Americans spread out over the new land, advancing ever southward and eastward. Perhaps half a thousand generations passed before men reached the east coast of the continent and crossed to the islands of the Caribbean.

The primitive hunters found North America a land of many contrasts. In the north were vast stretches of arctic tundra; in the south, dry desert country cut by deep canyons of sculptured rock. In between were shining, snow-capped mountains and vast grasslands where bison ranged in uncounted millions. The endless eastern forests harbored deer and elk and many kinds of furbearers. Rivers teemed with fish; lakes and marshes sent up clouds of waterfowl. Adapting to these diverse areas, the early Americans split up into many tribes, which developed many different languages and cultures.

Tribes of the north shaped their way of life to the comings and goings of vast herds of caribou. Along the Pacific coast they became fishermen, hunting the abundant salmon, whales, and other gifts of the sea. The nomadic tribes of the Great Plains followed the bison. In the Southwest, some of the people eventually settled down in apartment houses built of sun-baked clay and cultivated fields of maize, beans, and melons.

In Mexico, first the Mayans and then the Aztecs developed advanced civilizations. These people mined gold and silver and other metals and created elaborate works of art. They laid out and built great cities, complete with roads and parks, temples and public buildings. In eastern North America, woodland Indians developed a culture based on hunting and primitive agriculture. By the year 1492 the Iroquois tribes were beginning to forge a military alliance or confederacy.

All together, the original Americans totaled little more than a million people north of the Rio Grande. In Mexico and the lands to the south, there were perhaps four million.

That year, 1492, a new invading force came to the New World—European or "civilized" man, with Christopher Columbus as the first representative. The meeting of whites and native Americans was a fateful encounter, since it marked the beginning of great changes for North America's original inhabitants—and for the land and wildlife as well.

For Glory, Gold, and Empire

After Columbus had shown the way, the invasion from Europe came thick and fast. Fleet after fleet of adventuresome Spanish conquistadors sailed to the New World to explore and conquer and search for treasure. By 1521 stout Cortez had subdued the mighty Aztec empire in Mexico and looted the capital city of its treasures. By 1542 Coronado and his army had explored the land far to the north and west. Some of his followers gazed into the awesome Grand Canyon, while others marched as far north as what is now Kansas in a vain search for the fabled seven golden cities of Cibola.

Representatives of other European nations were soon roaming about the new land, too. As early as 1497 John Cabot explored the coasts of Newfoundland for England. In 1534 Jacques Cartier, a French explorer, penetrated the same region and ventured into the St. Lawrence River, northern gateway to the interior of the continent. Sailing past the famed Bird Rocks off Newfoundland, he noted that "These islands were as completely covered with birds, which nest there, as a field is covered with grass . . . all the ships of France might load a cargo of them without perceiving that any had been removed."

The abundance of wildlife along these northern coasts

amazed all the explorers. They gazed on pods of whales frolicking far up the St. Lawrence River and saw huge walrus herds in the area too. The fabulous fishing on the Grand Banks of Newfoundland had been known and exploited by countless hardy European fishermen for many years before the first official explorers came along. By 1550, according to some estimates, at least a thousand vessels were coming to the Banks each year to fill their holds with cod, haddock, and other fish. Many temporary settlements for curing fish sprang up along the rugged northern coasts. These encampments were so numerous that one prophetic viewer remarked that the woods along the shore were "so spoyled by the fishermen that it is a great pity to behold them, and without redresse undoubtedly it will be ruine of this good land."

The French did not seek gold and plunder in the same direct way the Spanish did. They aimed to gain their fortunes by trading with the natives for furs. Year after year they probed ever more deeply into the northern forests and waterways. By 1603 Champlain and other French explorers had traveled up the St. Lawrence to the Great Lakes and beyond. The French rivermen, or voyageurs, lived with and like the natives. They made little mark upon the wilderness, except for the trading posts they built at strategic spots. Their main interest was in trading for furs and in controlling this great land for the glory of France.

The English, on the other hand, came to found permanent settlements. Their object was to tame the land and live in it, as close to the way they had lived in England as possible. Exploring Virginia for Sir Walter Raleigh in 1584, Arthur Barlowe found the country ideal for such a purpose: "Deere, Conies, Hares and fowls . . . in incredible abundance. . . . The soil is the most plentiful, sweete, fruitfull and wholesome of all the worlde." By 1607 an English toehold in this sweet land had been established at Jamestown.

Landing at Plymouth Rock in Massachusetts Bay in 1620, the Pilgrims looked at the country with a somewhat more jaundiced eye than Barlowe had. To many of them, the promised land seemed "a hideous wilderness, full of wild beasts and wildmen." The land was a wilderness all right, but it proved to be rich and abundant in its returns, once the tough, hardworking Puritans learned how to adapt to it and reap its harvest.

The New England rivers abounded with salmon, shad, and other fish, and beaver dams were plentiful on the smaller streams. Wild pigeons whistled by in vast flocks that darkened the skies. As for other game birds, there were ducks and geese, heath hens and wild turkeys almost for the taking.

The Dutch built a trading post on Manhattan Island and were so well established by 1626 that official Peter Schagan could write to the States-General of the Netherlands that "The *Arms of Amsterdam* . . . sailed from New Netherlands out of the Mauritius [Hudson] River on September 23; they report that our people . . . have bought the island of Manhattes from the wild men for the value of 60 guilders [about $24]. . . . The cargo of the aforesaid ship is: 7246 beaver skins, 178 half otter skins, 675 otter skins, 48 mink skins, 36 wildcat skins, 33 minks, 34 rat skins."

By 1664 the English had wrested New Amsterdam from the Dutch and renamed it New York. Busy establishing permanent settlements all along the eastern coast, they also vied with the French for control of Canada. In 1670 they established the Hudson's Bay Company, which was to become an incredibly successful and far-flung trading empire based on furs.

Cut, Burn, Plant, Destroy, Move On

Along the eastern slopes of the continent from Massachusetts to Georgia, the wilderness slowly gave way to pioneer settlements. Fanning out from the coastal towns and forts, settlers established interior trading posts and cut down forests to make way for farmlands. Like pioneering people anywhere, they gave no thought to the preservation of any of the abundant natural resources about them. They were too busy with the backbreaking work of making clearings and burning stumps, reaping their first meager harvests, and often fighting for their lives against an aroused and hostile native population.

The age-old virgin forests had to go before any farming could be started, so the settlers cut down the towering trees and let in the sunlight. They burned the fallen monarchs and used the trunks of smaller trees to build their log-cabin homes. "Cut, burn, plant, destroy, move on." That was the policy of the pioneers, as conservation historian Fairfield Osborn noted in his book, *Our Plundered Planet*. But such a policy was inevitable. The pioneers had to subdue and conquer the forest in order to survive.

Of course, no game laws existed in those days, unless one counts the early bounties on predators. The pioneers engaged in unrelenting warfare against wolves, panthers, wildcats, and all other "varmints." Wolves were a particular source of trouble nearly everywhere. These big wild dogs were abundant, and found pigs, sheep, and other livestock easy victims. In consequence, Massachusetts Bay Colony offered a one-penny bounty on wolves as early as 1630.

Useful game such as deer was plentiful too. Venison was a staple of the pioneer diet, and buckskin was a principal material for moccasins, breeches, and other clothing. Some idea of the extent of the traffic in deer can be gained from the fact that more than two million pounds of deerskins (nearly half a million deer) passed through the single port of Savannah, Georgia, between 1764 and 1773.

To many pioneers, game existed just to be killed, whether needed or not. Game drives were sometimes organized in pioneering communities with the object of killing as much wildlife as possible. One such drive was organized in central Pennsylvania in 1760 by Black Jack Schwartz, known as the Wild Hunter. As related by Colonel H.W. Shoemaker, a compiler of early Pennsylvania lore, the hunters in this one drive massacred "41 panthers, 109 wolves, 112 foxes, 114 mountain cats, 17 black bears, 1 white bear, 2 elk, 98 deer, 111 buffaloes, 3 fishers, 1 otter, 12 gluttons [wolverines], 3 beavers, and upwards of 500 smaller animals."

"The choicest hides were taken," Shoemaker continued, "together with buffalo tongues, and then the heap of carcasses, 'as tall as the tallest trees,' was heaped with rich pine and fired. This created such a stench that the settlers were compelled to vacate their cabins in the vicinity of the fort, three miles away."

Under pressure like this, the first serious impact upon the land and wildlife of North America began to be felt. By 1639 deer had become so scarce in Rhode Island that the colony passed regulations making it illegal to kill deer between May 1 and November 1 each year. Massachusetts had its first closed deer season in 1694. By 1776 every colony except Georgia had a closed deer season.

Once a person traveled inland past the settlements, however, deer and other game seemed as plentiful as ever. Canada and the interior of the continent were still vast treasure-houses of furbearers for the trapper and trader. In 1743 alone, French traders bartered with the Indians for about 170,000 pelts of beaver, marten, otter, and fisher. And in just one sale the flourishing Hudson's Bay Company disposed of the skins of 26,750 beaver, 14,730 martens, and 1,850 wolves.

From 1755 to 1763 archrivals France and England fought each other in the struggle known as the French and Indian Wars for the prized interior of the continent. England won that war, but below the St. Lawrence River the American colonists soon wrested the prize from the mother country in their own War of Independence. And once they had gained their freedom, the colonists faced westward. They scaled the Appalachians and floated down the Ohio toward the Mississippi River. They tramped into Kentucky, following the Wilderness Trail blazed through the Cumberland Gap by Daniel Boone, the famous scout. Kentucky was a fabulous region, incredibly rich in wildlife and other natural resources.

John James Audubon, the noted naturalist and artist, recounts how he met Daniel Boone during the early years of the nineteenth century. Boone, in a rare burst of talkativeness, told Audubon tales of Kentucky when Boone had first visited it—when the lower parts of the region "'were still in the hands of nature. . . .

"'But ah! Sir, what a difference thirty years make in a country! Why, at the time when I was caught by Indians, you would not have walked out in any direction for more than a mile without shooting a buck or a bear. There were thousands of

Buffaloes on the hills of Kentucky; the land looked as if it never would become poor; and to hunt in those days was a pleasure indeed. But when I was left to myself on the banks of the Green River, I dare say for the last time in my life, a few signs only of deer were to be seen, and, as to a deer itself, I saw none.' "

As Boone sadly noted, the plunder of North American wild-life had already started by 1800. But the opening of the great West, and much much more plunder, was yet to come.

Our lands were originally very good; but use and abuse have made them quite otherwise. We ruin the lands that are already cleared, and either cut down more wood, if we have it, or emigrate into the western country.

—George Washington

2

THE WESTWARD SWEEP, 1800 to 1880

In the eyes of Daniel Boone, the country east of the Mississippi had already been spoiled. But not the western wilderness! This land was vast, untouched, and largely unexplored when President Thomas Jefferson negotiated the Louisiana Purchase with France in 1803. By this act, the United States gained a huge territory drained by both the western tributaries of the Mississippi and the Missouri River.

Jefferson promptly sent Captains Meriwether Lewis and William Clark on their famous expedition (1804–06) to explore the western lands, to observe and record the wealth of wildlife and other natural resources, and, if possible, to map a feasible route to the Pacific. Who knew? They might even find living mammoths in the far wilderness!

Lewis and Clark saw no mammoths on their epic journey, but they did gaze on many other wildlife wonders, including "immense herds of Buffaloe, deer elk and Antelopes which we saw in every direction feeding on the hills and plains." They collected a

11

number of animal species hitherto unknown to science, and had hair-raising adventures with pugnacious "white," or grizzly, bears. As for valuable furbearers, Clark reported "beaver dams succeeding each other in close order, and extending as far up those streams as he could discover them."

Beaver was the main lure that drew the first ripple of western pioneers in the wake of Lewis and Clark. These were the fiercely individualistic mountain men—men like John Colter, Jim Bridger, Jedediah Smith, Hugh Glass, Kit Carson, and many others. In their heyday, roughly from 1820 to 1840, they were the hardy breed who disappeared into the wilds for years at a time to trap beaver, match wits with hostile Indians, and—above all—glory in the soul-stirring freedom of life in the wilderness.

Next came the organized fur companies, and soon many other kinds of pioneers were heading westward: farmers and ranchers, businessmen and women, land speculators, outlaws, dance-hall girls, young men and old men, long-suffering pioneer women and children—all of them searching for riches or adventure or a better life. They crossed the plains and headed for the shining mountains any way they could: in covered wagons, on horseback, and afoot. All of them, reaching their particular bits of the Promised Land, settled down to make their marks.

"A time would come," the historian Francis Parkman noted in the preface to his famous book *The Oregon Trail*, "when those plains would be grazing country, the buffalo give place to tame cattle, farmhouses be scattered along the water courses, and wolves, bears, and Indians be numbered among the things that were."

The West Coast region, however, was still relatively untouched in 1840, except for several Russian trading posts and a few Spanish missions and settlements. But in 1848, gold was discovered at John Sutter's mill on the south fork of the American River, and the California Gold Rush was on. The West was suddenly invaded with a vengeance, as untold numbers of fortune seekers swarmed to the West Coast. Homesteaders built log cabins and sod houses all along the way, and railroads began to extend their silvery rails westward as fast as they could. The avalanche was slowed a bit, first by the Civil War and then by Plains Indians fighting desperately for their homelands. But the flood of emigrants was stemmed for only a brief moment.

To the newcomers in the West, the great herds of bison seemed inexhaustible, just like the vast flocks of passenger pigeons in the East. A man could watch for days as the flood of dark, shaggy beasts passed in migration. Colonel R.I. Dodge, observing one such herd in 1871, in the valley of the Arkansas River, calculated that it was at least twenty-five miles wide and fifty long . . . perhaps four million bison in this one group.

With herds such as these there for the taking, hordes of buffalo hunters swarmed over the plains, and the greatest wildlife slaughter the world has ever known began. Railroads made it easy to transport the hides to eastern markets, and from Kansas alone, a million and a quarter were sent back in 1872 and 1873.

Market hunting for waterfowl, shore birds, deer, and other game was at its height in the seventies and eighties too. Game clogged the marketplaces of the cities—as if all America was determined to kill off its wildlife as quickly as possible.

"The United States in the 1880s was a nation on the move," conservation historian James B. Trefethen has remarked, "a lusty young giant concerned more with the pleasures of the present than with the security of the future. Blessed with a birthright of natural wealth greater than that of any nation on earth, it seemed bent on squandering its riches in a single massive binge. The American wilderness was not only being tamed; it, almost literally, was being beaten to death."

Something had to give before such pressures. What gave were the forests, the rich prairie soil, the watersheds, the wetlands— and the wildlife. Some animal species were massacred so merci- lessly—for market, for fur, for sport—that they never recovered their numbers. But they were the lucky ones, for they at least survived. Other forms of wildlife disappeared forever under the onslaught. They became extinct.

3

DEAD AS A DODO

The expression "dead as a dodo" has entered our language as a phrase denoting extinction. The dodo, which vanished about 1681, was the first fairly well-documented species to disappear as a result of man's influence. For this reason its story is worth telling, even though it did not take place on the American continent.

A huge, flightless bird related to the pigeon, the dodo (*Raphus cucullatus*) lived only on the island of Mauritius, one of the Mascarene Islands in the Indian Ocean. Twice as big as a goose, it had a compact body, heavy, fowl-like legs, stubby, flightless wings, and a short, curled tail. Its feathers were generally light gray or ash colored. The skin around the dodo's face and eyes was bare, and it had a huge beak that ended in a hook.

This luckless species built a bulky ground nest in which it incubated only a single egg at a time. It ate fruit and vegetable matter, and it prospered as long as the natural conditions on its island remained undisturbed.

The Portuguese discovered Mauritius in 1507 but did not colonize the island. In 1598, the Dutch landed and took possession, introducing pigs and pet monkeys, among other blessings of civilization. The settlers killed the dodos with clubs and ate their flesh and eggs. Foraging pigs and monkeys broke up the nests and ate the eggs too. The flightless dodo had no defense against such foreign dangers, and its numbers dwindled. The last recorded bird died in 1681. Today, all we have to prove that the species ever lived are a few skeletons and several body fragments in museum collections.

Thus, nearly three hundred years ago, the first documented victim of man's thoughtlessness and greed passed into extinction. Two close relative species of the dodo—one on Reunion and one on Rodriguez, the other principal islands of the Mascarenes— soon met a similar fate.

Man undoubtedly destroyed other species of wildlife even before the dodo. We have no clear record of the final days of most of these, however. One of them was *Aepyornis*, the elephant bird, a huge species that lived in Madagascar and weighed in the neighborhood of a thousand pounds. Others were *Dinornis*, the twelve-foot-tall great moa of New Zealand, and its smaller relatives.

The dodo, the elephant bird, and the great moa were all giant, flightless birds. All had descended from remote ancestors that could fly, but they gradually lost their powers of flight on island homes where food was plentiful, and where there were no predators to threaten them. Conditions changed when man came to their islands, and it was man who sealed their doom.

A number of other island species have disappeared in much the same way in more recent times—dozens of species of birds on the Hawaiian Islands alone. All in all, scientists estimate that a hundred or more different kinds of birds have become extinct the world over since the time of the last dodo less than three hundred years ago. As for mammals, reptiles, amphibians, fish, and invertebrates, no accurate estimate of extinction due to man can be made.

Extinction and Evolution

North America was one of the last of the world's great land masses to be discovered and exploited by civilized man. Yet it has one of the worst extinction records of all, having lost more than forty different kinds of mammals and birds during the last two hundred years. Dozens of species of vertebrates and invertebrates have disappeared in the United States during the past ten years alone. And just one state, Hawaii, has lost at least twenty butterflies and moths and more than forty other invertebrates during the same period. Not all of these, of course, were full species. Some were races or subspecies.

A *species* is a population of similar animals that under natural conditions breed freely among themselves but usually not with any other animal groups or populations. The white-tailed deer and mule deer, for example, are closely related but distinct species of deer. The robin and bluebird are two different species of American thrushes.

Common names, such as those given above, are very handy, but they can be quite misleading. The bird we know as a robin, for example, is one species, while the English robin is another. In order to avoid such confusion, scientists the world over give every species of animal and plant a Latinized two-part name, following a system first suggested in 1735 by Swedish scientist Carolus Linnaeus. First is the generic name, used to designate a group of closely related species, followed by the specific name. Under this system, the white-tailed deer is *Odocoileus virginianus*, and the mule deer, *Odocoileus hemionus*.

Many species include a number of more or less distinct subspecies or races. A *subspecies* is an integrated group which occupies part of the range of the species and whose members differ slightly in coloring, size, or other minor particulars from the rest of the populations of the species. A subspecies is designated scientifically by a third Latin name that follows the specific name. Thus the little Florida Key deer, one race or subspecies of the familiar white-tailed deer, is known scientifically as *Odocoileus virginianus clavium*.

Before Charles Darwin's important book *The Origin of Species* descended upon a doubting world in 1859, the general public considered that every animal species was a changeless and immutable creation. Today, with the ideas of organic evolution widely established and accepted, we know that species evolve and change through great periods of geologic time.

The natural life span of a species can be measured in millions of years, but eventually the species gives way to another form. It may either adapt to changing conditions, or become increasingly specialized to exist in a particular habitat or on one particular kind of food. If the species becomes too highly specialized, it may be unable to adjust to changes in its environment and then it dies out. If it continues to adapt successfully, however, it eventually becomes a new species.

Subspecies, or races, can be considered new species in the making. If one race becomes isolated from neighboring races or if it adapts in a new direction, the differences between it and its relatives widen. It gradually becomes distinct from the parent species and no longer interbreeds with it.

Such evolutionary changes have been going on ever since the dawn of life on earth. Thus, over great periods of geologic time, amphibians evolved from fish, reptiles from amphibians, and birds and mammals from reptiles. Thus rose and fell a mighty host of dinosaurs, pterodactyls, titanotheres, and countless other forms of prehistoric life. Man, of course, cannot be held responsible for the disappearance of these. They passed on naturally in the evolutionary parade.

Extermination at the Hands of Man

But mankind *can* be held responsible for the disappearance of many life forms within historic times. Man upset the precarious natural balance for species after species so that they were snuffed out before their allotted time. And as Robert Porter Allen has observed, "There is a vast difference between the slow extermination of a species as a result of natural selection, and an abrupt, callous, and unthinking extermination at the hands of Man."

Humanity tips the balance against wildlife in many ways, causing some species to disappear by altering their natural habitat—cutting forests, draining wetlands, spraying poisonous pesticides over areas that wildlife needs for food and living space—or introducing unnatural predators, such as the pig and the monkey against the dodo. Sometimes, as in the accounts that follow, reckless slaughter—for food, for fur, for feathers, or just for fun—causes a species to vanish.

STELLER'S SEA COW
Hydrodamalis gigas

In the summer of 1741 Commander Vitus Bering, a Dane in the employ of the imperial Russian government, set out from Petropavlovsk, on Siberia's Kamchatka Peninsula, on one of history's most important voyages of discovery. He led the expedition in his flagship, *St. Peter*. A second ship, *St. Paul*, was under the captaincy of a Russian, Alexei Chirikof. Their object: to discover and explore *Bolshaya Zemlya*, the "Great Land," which Russian geographers suspected lay somewhere to the east of Siberia.

Sailing eastward into the unknown, the two vessels became separated in a summer storm and the *St. Paul* had the honor of sailing on to catch the first glimpse of the new land. On July 15, 1741, her men discovered the island of Sitka. Just a day later Bering and the crew of the *St. Peter* sighted the Alaskan mainland in the vicinity of what is now Cape St. Elias.

Chirikof and the *St. Paul* sailed back to Kamchatka that fall, but Bering and the *St. Peter* were not so fortunate. For four long months the ship was battered by storms as she tried to beat her way back to Siberia. Food and water began to give out, and many members of the crew sickened and died of scurvy and other ailments. On November 4, the little ship foundered on a submerged reef near the shores of a previously unknown island. Now known as Bering Island in honor of its unfortunate discoverer, it is one of the Commander, or Komandorskie, Islands. Making their way ashore, the survivors dug underground shelters and began to battle for their lives against the bitter arctic winter.

Starving, they killed sea otters, seabirds, and an occasional seal for food. They were constantly beset by hordes of blue arctic foxes that slunk about the camp like starving dogs. Never having seen men before, the foxes were so bold that they invaded the shelters and snapped at whatever was lying about, including sick and sleeping men.

Commander Bering died on December 8, 1741, and was buried in a rude grave on the island that bears his name. Many others died that winter too, but German naturalist Georg Wilhelm Steller and others managed to survive.

Steller recorded the horrors of that winter in his journal. A trained zoologist and the official naturalist of the ill-starred expedition, he also wrote detailed descriptions of a number of species then new to science. Today, most of them are known by his name: Steller's jay, Steller's eider, Steller's sea eagle, Steller's sea lion, and Steller's sea cow. All except the last are with us still. But

Steller's sea cow, a giant manatee that Bering's marooned crew hunted for food, has long since become extinct.

Looking something like a huge seal, this remarkable mammal measured twenty-five to thirty feet in length and weighed an estimated four tons. It had no hind limbs, and its tail was flattened from side to side like that of a whale. The small, paddle-like forelimbs were bent under, so that the animal supported itself on its "knuckles." The inch-thick skin was dark brown or blackish, much wrinkled and tough, and the lips and cheeks bristled with heavy whiskers. "To the navel it resembles a land animal," Steller observed, "from there on to the tail, a fish."

Living in herds, the sea cow "does not stay far out at sea," Steller recorded, "but keeps close to shore. Its back is above water, and with the flood tide it moves toward the shore to feed on the sea cabbage. As the tide goes out, the sea cow goes along so as not to get stranded, being such a large animal." From all reports, it evidently inhabited only a very restricted area in the northern seas, mainly around the Commander Islands. Steller did comment that it was also known along the coast of Kamchatka, where the natives called it "cabbage-eater."

Slow-moving, defenseless giants, Steller's sea cows were lifesavers for the shipwrecked men of the *St. Peter*. The crew hunted the huge creatures by harpooning them from a whaleboat as they browsed in the shallows. The mountain of blubber and flesh was hauled ashore at low tide and cut up for food. Steller waxed enthusiastic over the result: "The meat, when cooked, although it must boil rather long, is exceedingly savory and cannot be distinguished easily from beef."

In the late summer of 1742 Steller and the other survivors built a makeshift forty-one-foot boat from the wreckage of their old vessel. Loaded down with some seven hundred sea otter skins they could not bear to leave behind, they set sail on August 3, and after a harrowing twenty-three-day voyage, they limped into the harbor of Petropavlovsk. Their return was hailed as a miracle, for they had long since been given up as dead.

The return of the Bering party with their precious sea otter skins marked the beginning of Russian activity in North America. Sea otter pelts were especially valuable for trade with the Chinese, and during the next half-century, Bering Island and its near neighbors became regular ports of call for Russian fur hunters. They killed the giant sea cows enthusiastically, for they prized them as quick, easy, and apparently limitless sources of food. Defenseless, the Steller's sea cow quickly plunged down the path to extinction.

In 1755 a Russian geologist named Jakovlev visited the Bering Sea islands and foresaw the inevitable fate that awaited the sea cow unless it was protected. He urged government officials in Kamchatka to provide such protection, but nothing was done. So, in 1768, a brief twenty-six years after the species had been discovered and described by Steller, the last recorded sea cow was killed. Some say a few may have survived until the early years of the nineteenth century, but there is no proof of this. Steller's sea cow was almost certainly the first species within historic times to be killed off by man out to explore and exploit the continent of North America.

SPECTACLED CORMORANT
Phalacrocorax perspicillatus

Another species that helped sustain the marooned crew of the *St. Peter* was the spectacled, or Pallas', cormorant. A large, almost flightless bird, its range was very restricted, and it apparently lived only on the Commander Islands.

Weighing close to fifteen pounds, this handsome species had bronzy-green plumage with steel-blue reflections on its head and neck, and large white spots on its flanks. Its head was decorated with two jaunty crests, or tufts of feathers. The wings were small, and the bird seldom even attempted to fly.

It may very well have nested on small offshore islets; otherwise the hordes of blue foxes on Bering Island could have wiped it out even before Steller's arrival. The shipwrecked party caught these large, clumsy birds easily, and Steller relates that "one single bird was sufficient for three starving men."

After 1741 the Russian sea otter hunters that came to Bering

Spectacled Cormorant

Island hunted the spectacled cormorant regularly for food. So did the native Aleut hunters they brought with them. The species dwindled and finally disappeared about 1850. Today the only proof that it ever lived are six mounted specimens in museums.

GREAT AUK
Pinguinus impennis

At about the same time that the spectacled cormorant became extinct, the great auk was exterminated off the opposite shores of North America. In contrast to the cormorant, the auk had a wide range and had been known to man for many centuries.

In May 1534, explorer Jacques Cartier stopped at Funk Island, a rocky dot of land off the northeast coast of Newfoundland, and found huge flocks of great auks, or "garefowl," as they were known to Europeans. Delighted with this fresh meat after the long voyage, his crew filled two of the ship's boats with the birds and salted them down in casks.

The great auk was ridiculously easy to capture on land, for it was totally unable to fly. Standing two-and-a-half- feet high, it looked very much like a penguin, and many early writers called it the "northern penguin." Its back and head were glistening black, while its breast and underparts were white. In breeding plumage, there was a large white spot in front of each eye. Rather clumsy ashore, it could dive and swim with startling speed, propelling itself through the water with stubby, paddle-like wings.

In prehistoric days, as determined from bony remains, the great auk had ranged the coastal waters of the North Atlantic from the shores of North America to Iceland, the British Isles, Scandinavia, and Spain. Its single six-inch-long egg was usually laid on the bare rock of offshore islands. By the time of Cartier's explorations, its range had already decreased a great deal. Funk Island harbored one of the largest breeding colonies, and others inhabited various offshore islands near Iceland.

After the settlement of the New World, the Grand Banks of Newfoundland were increasingly frequented by fishermen, whalers, seal hunters, and others. Many visited Funk Island to replenish their food supplies with a harvest of great auks. At about the time of the Pilgrims, Captain Richard Whitbourne of England noted the ease with which the auks could be captured. "Men drive them from thenes [sic] upon a board into their boats by hundreds at a time," he related, "as if God had made the innocency of so poor a creature to become such an admirable instrument for the sustension of man."

By the time of the American Revolution, great auk hunting expeditions were spending several months at Funk Island every summer. Stone compounds were built into which whole flocks of the big birds could be herded, then slaughtered with clubs. Feathers and down were plucked and the carcasses were rendered over fires for the oil they contained. Under such persistent exploitation, the colony of garefowl on Funk Island had almost vanished by the early years of the nineteenth century.

The last known breeding areas were a few islands off southern Iceland. The principal one was a barren outcropping known as Geirfuglasker (Gare Fowl Skerries) near Cape Reykjanes. About 1830, Geirfuglasker sank beneath the sea in a violent volcanic upheaval, and from then on the great auk was a very rare bird indeed. Its final nesting place was nearby Eldey Rock.

A mass of volcanic rock, Eldey rises like a rugged and forbidding skyscraper out of the cold green waters of the North Atlantic. On its western side a ledge slopes gradually to the sea—the only possible landing place for boats. It was here, at dawn of June 4, 1844, that three Icelanders scrambled out of a longboat and climbd up the volcanic slope in search of great auks. A collector from Reykjavik, Iceland, had offered 100 crowns for every specimen brought to him.

Ahead, the men spied two auks hopping clumsily from rock to rock, using their wings as balancers. Swiftly the men overtook them and clubbed them to death. One man found an egg too, but it was cracked, so he smashed it against a rock. On this note, a species that had lived in the Atlantic community for thousands of years disappeared forever from the face of the earth. For a dozen years or so after 1844, reports came in from one barren shore or another of the sighting of a surviving great auk. Perhaps authentic, they were impossible to verify.

Today the American Ornithologists' Union calls its official journal *The Auk*, in remembrance of the first bird, whose range included part of continental North America, that became extinct at the hands of man.

EASTERN BISON
Bison bison pennsylvanicus

In 1612 the English navigator Sir Samuel Argall sailed up the
Potomac River "about sixty-five leagues" and then marched inland. There he saw "great store of Cattle as big as Kine, of which,
the Indians that were my guides, killed a couple, which wee found
to be very good and wholesome meate. . . ."

In Colonial days these eastern bison ranged from western
New York, Pennsylvania, and Virginia south as far as Georgia.
Judging from eyewitness reports, they were somewhat different in
appearance from the Plains bison and may have been a distinct
subspecies. It was said that they had little or no hump, and their
hind legs, unlike those of the Plains animal, were about as long
as their front legs. Their color tended to be very dark, and their
horns flared upward like the horns of Ayrshire cattle. On the basis
of this hearsay evidence, Colonel H.W. Shoemaker gave them the
subspecific name *pennsylvanicus*.

Traveling in bands that sometimes numbered several hundred
animals, eastern bison made annual migrations north and south,
often following well-worn trails from summer feeding grounds to
sheltered wintering areas. These trails frequently led past salt

springs, where the bison gathered to drink and to lick the salty earth.

One of the early settlers of western Pennsylvania built his log cabin near just such a salt spring that the bison were accustomed to visiting. As the settler told the English traveler Thomas Ashe, the bison "sought for no manner of food, but only bathed and drank three or four times a day and rolled in the earth. . . . In the first and second years this old man, with some companions, killed from six to seven hundred of these noble creatures, merely for the sake of the skins, which were worth only two shillings each.

"The simple story of this spring is that of every other in the settled part of this western world—the carnage of beasts was everywhere the same."

In another section of his *Travels in North America*, Ashe comments that "the first settlers, not contented with this sanguinary extermination of the animals, also destroyed the food to which it [*sic*] was most partial, which was the cane, growing in forests and brakes of immeasurable extent. To this the unsparing wretches set fire in dry seasons in order to drive out every living creature, and then hunt and persecute them to death."

In such manner the numbers of the eastern bison were greatly reduced by the last decades of the eighteenth century. By 1799 the Pennsylvania population had been reduced to about 400 animals, which wintered in the Seven Mountain area of Union County.

The winter of 1799–1800 was a particularly severe one, and the bison, imprisoned high in the Seven Mountains by the settlements in the valleys below, could not get enough to eat. Desperate with hunger, they came down in December, led by a giant black bull that the settlers had nicknamed "Old Logan" after a well-known Indian chief.

As related by Colonel Shoemaker, the buffalo invaded the barnyard of one Martin Bergstresser and broke through the stump fence surrounding a haystack and some domestic stock. In the resulting struggle to reach the hay, a number of domestic calves and sheep were crushed to death. Then, frightened by shots from the settler, the bison stampeded and ran toward the nearby

McClellan homestead. McClellan shot into the herd, and in the furor that followed, the fear- crazed bison broke down the door of his log-cabin home and began to crowd into it, as many as could. Trapped inside, McClellan's wife and children were crushed and stampeded to death. After this tragic incident the bison retreated to the mountains.

Aroused, the pioneers organized a bison hunt. A howling blizzard delayed their start for several days, but finally fifty hunters with many dogs followed the trail of the herd up into the mountains. According to local legend the date was December 31, 1799—the last day of the eighteenth century.

The hunters found the herd at last, neck-deep in snowdrifts in a hollow called "The Sink" near the present town of Weikert in Union County, Pennsylvania. Half-frozen and weak from hunger, the animals were practically immobilized in the crusted drifts. The hunters shot some but killed many more simply by cutting their throats with bear knives. By the time they were finished, the field was crimson with blood. After cutting out the tongues of the bison, the hunters left the carcasses where they lay. Thereafter the place came to be known as "The Buffalo Field."

That was almost the last of the Pennsylvania bison. In the fall of the next year a famous Indian fighter, Colonel John Kelly, saw three animals—a bull, a cow, and a calf. He shot the calf but the other two escaped. The next winter he came upon the bull again and shot him. That, as far as anyone knows, was the last native bison killed, or even seen, in Pennsylvania.

In less settled states, some eastern bison lingered on for a few years longer, but gradually they too were all killed. By 1832 bison had disappeared entirely east of the Mississippi. But to the west, vast herds of plains bison still roamed the grassy prairies. Their turn was yet to come.

SEA MINK
Mustela macrodon

Redder than the ordinary mink and almost twice as big, the sea mink lived on the rugged coasts and offshore islands from Newfoundland to Massachusetts. The Maine islands may have been its

Sea Mink

stronghold, for most of its recorded remains come from Indian shell heaps and village sites in this area.

A century and more ago, the hunters and trappers of this region prized the sea mink especially, for its pelts usually brought higher prices than skins of the smaller mainland mink. Surprised, or flushed from its hiding place, the lithe, reddish-colored mink often sought refuge in a burrow or some crack in a ledge or rock. The hunters might first try to dislodge it with crowbars and shovels. If this wasn't successful, they often shot charges of pepper into the shelter hole, or used brimstone to smoke out their quarry. Once in the open, the sea mink was quickly killed by dogs or hunters.

In much this way, soon after the Civil War, the last of the sea minks may have met its fate.

Never plentiful, the sea mink received scant recognition—except for its valued fur—while it was alive. It was first described as a distinct species in 1903, from bones uncovered near Brooklin, Maine. It had already been extinct for some years.

LABRADOR DUCK
Camptorhynchus labradorius

From time immemorial, gray-green rollers have swept in from the cold Atlantic to crash against Long Island's winter beaches in foamy fountains of salt spray. Hardy beachcombers on these shores can still hope to glimpse diving ducks—eiders, scoters, golden-eyes, and others—riding the swells out beyond the breakers. But never again will they be able to see the Labrador duck, a close relative. It vanished nearly a century ago.

One of the prettiest of the sea ducks, the male Labrador had a black body with contrasting white wing patches. His head and neck were white too, except for a velvety-black collar and a black streak running back across his crown. His mate and young were brownish-gray.

Never plentiful, Labrador ducks ranged America's East Coast during fall and winter, from Nova Scotia to New Jersey and perhaps as far south as Chesapeake Bay. They frequented shallow bays, where they probed for shellfish and other seafood in the sandy bottoms. Hunters and fishermen sometimes caught them on hooks baited with mussels. Shy birds, they took off in swift, whistling flight when approached too closely. Sometimes they traveled in small groups of five or ten birds, but often only a single bird or a pair were seen.

They were tempting targets, and hunters shot them whenever they had the opportunity. Although their flesh wasn't very good eating, they were frequently offered for sale at marketplaces in New York and other eastern cities. There they often hung unbought until they spoiled and had to be thrown away.

So little is known about the habits of this vanished bird that we aren't even sure where it nested. The breeding grounds supposedly lay somewhere on the southern coast of Labrador. Perhaps it nested on small offshore islands, as its relative the eider duck still does.

Even before the American Revolution, many New England seafarers made regular summer voyages to Labrador to harvest eggs and feathers of waterfowl and other seabirds. They came during and just after the nesting season, when the birds were moulting and most vulnerable. The yearly plunder continued through the first half of the nineteenth century, and by the time of the Civil War, the Labrador duck was a rare bird.

The last recorded specimen was shot in the fall of 1875 on Long Island, and its skin now reposes in the collections of the Smithsonian Institution in Washington, D.C. Three years after that, a boy reportedly shot another specimen on the Chemung River in New York State, but it was not saved. Since that time the Labrador duck has never been seen alive again.

CAROLINA PARAKEET
Conuropsis carolinensis

In Colonial days, brightly colored birds streaming over the treetops in rapid, undulating flight were a familiar sight to southern farmers. A dense flock of Carolina parakeets would circle an orchard, making the air ring with their shrill repeated cries of "Qui, qui, qui!" Finally settling on a fruit tree, the little parrots— each about the size of a mourning dove—would climb from limb to limb and attack the fruit. By then the farmer usually had gotten his gun.

Besides its destructiveness, the Carolina parakeet had other characteristics that made it tempting to kill. Its feathers were prized by Indian and white man alike, and its bright plumage made it an easy mark for hunters. The bird's body was mostly a vivid green, but the head was yellow, with orange-red markings around the bill, on the crown, and behind the eye.

"When they alighted on the ground," naturalist Alexander Wilson noted in 1808, "it appeared at a distance as if covered by a carpet of richest green, orange, and yellow: they afterwards settled, in one body, on a neighboring tree . . . covering almost every twig of it. . . . Having shot down a number, some of which were only wounded, the whole flock swept repeatedly around their prostrate companions, and again settled on a low tree, within twenty yards of the spot where I stood. At each successive discharge, although showers of them fell, yet the affection of the survivors seemed rather to increase. . . ."

This flocking together, this unwillingness to abandon wounded members of the band, made the parakeets easy targets for farmers. The species was prized as a cage bird as well, and was often taken alive for this purpose. Pioneers frequently called it "gabby bird," for like other parrots it could be taught to say a word or two. Because flocks often roosted in hollow trees, the whole band could be captured merely by placing a sack over the hole in the tree.

Ranging farther north than any other member of its family, the Carolina parakeet originally lived from Florida to Virginia, and westward to Texas, Kansas, and Nebraska. Sometimes it wandered as far north as Pennsylvania and the Great Lakes. Richly timbered bottomlands bordering streams were favored habitats. So were cypress swamps. Usually from two to five eggs were laid in a tree-hole nest.

As the country became more settled the birds gradually

declined—evidently not so much from destruction of their habitat as from shooting. By the dawn of the twentieth century the vivid little parrot had vanished nearly everywhere. The noted ornithologist Frank Chapman recorded the last flock, thirteen birds that he spied in 1904 near the northern shores of Lake Okeechobee, Florida. Another small flock was supposedly seen in the same state in 1920, but this record remains uncertain. We *do* know that the last captive parakeet died in 1914, the same year in which the last passenger pigeon on earth died too.

In 1938 a great hope thrilled conservationists when a group of experienced ornithologists reported a flock of parakeets in the swampy wilderness of the Santee River basin in South Carolina. Most ornithologists doubted the sighting, however, and the birds were not seen again. Soon thereafter, a large part of the Santee wilderness was destroyed to make way for electric power lines.

PASSENGER PIGEON
Ectopistes migratorius

In numbers, they seemed as inexhaustible as drops of water in the ocean or grains of sand on the shores. In vast flocks they swept through the skies, blotting out the sun, their roaring wings stirring up a mighty gale. Hour after hour they passed overhead, an awesome sight of wildlife abundance the likes of which we will never again see. This was the passenger pigeon in its heyday.

Ornithologist Alexander Wilson viewed a Kentucky flight in 1810 that he figured to be at least a mile wide and 240 miles long. Considering the birds' speed of flight and the length of time it took for them to pass, Wilson calculated that there were more than two billion passenger pigeons in this flock alone. Judging from all accounts, they were probably the most abundant bird of one species in America at that time. Yet in the course of a century, this seemingly inexhaustible population was completely wiped from the face of the earth.

Colonists and pioneers knew the bird simply as pigeon, wild pigeon, or wood pigeon. The Narragansett Indians called it *wuskowhan*, or "wanderer," because of its migratory habits. This same habit gave the species its scientific name, *migratorius*, as well as the common name we remember it by today—passenger pigeon.

Streamlined and graceful, the passenger pigeon had a long tapering tail and narrow wings that equipped it for swift flight. A beautiful and elegant bird, it had a bright red eye, a sleek blue head, and a nape that gleamed with metallic iridescence. The upper parts of the body were mostly slate gray, while the throat and breast were rich russet, shading to white on the abdomen.

The wild pigeons originally ranged over most of eastern North America, from southern Canada to the southern United States, and as far west as the Dakotas. They inhabited areas of great hardwood forests, where there were abundant supplies of beechnuts, chestnuts, acorns, berries, and seeds. Every year they migrated in huge flocks from southern wintering areas to northern nesting grounds. The vast breeding colonies had sharply marked boundaries. For many miles there might be dozens or hundreds of nests in each tree, yet some invisible barrier marked where the nesting stopped, and neighboring trees had no nests at all. One egg was usual in a flimsy nest platform balanced precariously on a forked branch.

The birds did not always breed in the same locality every

year. Whenever their food supply was exhausted, they sought new areas. And after the nesting season they broke up into small flocks that fanned out over large areas in daily search of food, then gathered together again each evening in roosting areas. John James Audubon described one of these: "The Pigeons, coming in by thousands, alighted everywhere, one above another until solid masses, as large as hogsheads, were formed on every tree, in all directions."

These flocking habits, the need to nest and roost in close proximity to each other, made the pigeon an easy victim. The carnage at roosts or breeding areas was almost unbelievable. Congregating from every direction, gunners and netters would take up advantageous positions and start sulfur fires smoldering beneath the roosts to stupify their victims. They then knocked the birds down with poles and clubs, shooting and netting them. Pigeons died by the millions. When the hunters were finished, droves of hogs were often turned into the woods to fatten on discarded bodies of adult birds, and on helpless young that had fallen from their nests.

From earliest days, pigeons were a staple on the food market in nearly every city, and their abundance and ease of capture made them cheap. "In August, 1736, pigeons fell in Boston to two pence per dozen (not a penny, lawful) and many could not be sold at that." Year after year the slaughter went on, and the supply seemed as plentiful as ever. In the spring of 1851, for example, the Erie Railroad brought seventy-four tons of birds to New York City, all of them taken in two upstate counties. "There's no killing them all," was the common attitude.

That's what the Ohio senate thought in 1857, when it voted against a proposed law that would have given some protection to the species. "The passenger pigeon needs no protection," the lawmakers stated confidently. "Wonderfully prolific . . . no ordinary destruction can lessen them or be missed from the myriads that are yearly produced."

But this was no ordinary destruction, even by the standards of that day. A mere twenty-one years later the birds staged their last great nesting in a strip of land fifteen miles wide by about seventy-five miles long near Petoskey, Michigan. There were an estimated 136 million pigeons at Petoskey in that spring of 1878, and market hunters joyfully descended on the area to engage in one last big killing spree.

Ten years later the wild pigeon had practically vanished from the face of the earth. But in 1881 there were still enough of them left for hunters to remove 20,000 squabs from their nests and ship them to New York, to be shot down by participants in a Coney Island pigeon shoot. This "sporting" affair was sponsored, ironically enough, by the then New York State Association for the Protection of Fish and Game!

By 1890 the wild pigeons were rare birds—and no wonder. Time and events had caught up with them at last. But many people simply would not believe that they were gone for good. Some said they must all have flown to Australia, while others chose Canada or South America. The last recorded wild passenger pigeon was gunned down in 1899 or soon thereafter, and the last living individual, an old female named Martha who lived in the Cincinnati Zoo, died on September 1, 1914. Even then, some hopeful souls could not believe that the wild pigeons were really extinct. For some years rewards were offered for the location of wild individuals, nesting areas, or flocks—all to no avail.

What *really* caused their extinction? Was it market hunting? Disease? Lack of food? Or cutting down of the great hardwood forests? The flocking and colonial nesting habits of the birds certainly contributed to their downfall, but the downfall itself was the direct result of wholesale slaughter, year after year.

At Wyalusing State Park in Wisconsin, that state's Society for Ornithology has erected a bronze memorial, "Dedicated To The Last Wisconsin Passenger Pigeon. Shot At Babcock, Sept. 1899. This Species Became Extinct Through The Avarice And Thoughtlessness Of Man."

It was a sad and shameful ending for a mighty host, yet perhaps it would help the future course of conservation. A. W. Schorger, whose book on the passenger pigeon stands as another memorial to the species, believes so. "The wanton slaughter and extinction of this bird," he writes, "did more than all the laws put together to focus the attention of the American people on the necessity of protecting what we have before it is too late."

HEATH HEN
Tympanuchus cupido cupido

The heath hen was the eastern race of the greater prairie chicken. A plump, square-tailed game bird with long tufts of feathers on either side of its neck, it looked and acted very much like its western relative, which still roams over suitable territory in the prairie states.

In Colonial days the heath hen ranged from New England to Virginia, and possibly to the Carolinas. Every springtime cocks assembled on communal "booming grounds" during the breeding season and performed elaborate courtship rites before gatherings of hens. They "boomed" by inflating orange-colored air sacs on either side of their necks, then expelling the air forcefully with a resultant hollow sound.

At that time heath hens were abundant throughout their range. Around Boston they were so plentiful that "servants stipulated with their employers not to have Heath Hen brought to the table oftener than a few times a week." The plump birds were hunted so eagerly that, by the time of the Revolution, they had declined drastically in many areas. Their numbers became so reduced in New York State that "an Act for the preservation of the heath hen and other game" was introduced in the legislature in 1791.

In spite of this and other measures, the heath hen continued its steady decline throughout the East as the result of a combination of pressures: unrestricted shooting, market hunting, and widespread destruction of its habitat and nesting places by the ax and plow. By 1850 it was a rare bird nearly everywhere on the mainland, and by the early seventies it had been completely exterminated, except for a last stand on the island of Martha's Vineyard. Even here an 1890 census revealed only 200 birds. By 1906 only seventy-seven could be counted: the heath hen was almost gone.

During 1907 and 1908 a sanctuary of about 1,600 acres was established for the surviving remnant. Under the protection of a warden who controlled cats and other predators, the population slowly but surely increased. By 1916 there were close to 2,000 birds on the island, and it appeared as though the heath hen was on its way back.

But that same spring disaster struck. A fire burned over nearly twenty square miles of the best nesting territory, destroying nests and eggs and killing many adult birds and young. The following spring a plague of goshawks reportedly descended on the remnants and wrought havoc among them. From a total of 2,000, the population shrank to about a hundred birds.

The heath hen never recovered from these hard blows. Confined as it was to one small area, its existence depended on that one colony. The surviving population was too small, too susceptible to disease or catastrophe. Under strict protection the population did increase to nearly 600 birds in 1920, but from then on it dropped yearly despite every conservation effort. By 1925 only an estimated twenty-five birds were left, the majority of them males. The heath hen was doomed.

One lone bird, an old male, survived until 1932 and was last seen on March 11 of that year. After that—none.

Henry Beetle Hough, editor of the island's *Vineyard Gazette*, mourned the passing of the heath hen with an editorial that has been quoted again and again all over the world. Its words serve as an epitaph, not only for the heath hen, but for all other vanished species as well:

> *We are looking upon the utmost finality which can be written, glimpsing the darkness which will not know another ray of light. We are in touch with the reality of extinction.*

The nation behaves well if it treats the natural resources as assets which it must turn over to the next generation, increased and not impaired in value.

—Theodore Roosevelt

4

SOME CAME BACK:
The Start of Wildlife Conservation,
1880 to 1920

The years immediately following the Civil War, the 1870s and 1880s, were probably the high tide of wildlife slaughter in the history of North America. The guns of buffalo hunters boomed throughout the West, cutting the great herds into ribbons. Armies of professional market hunters flourished as never before, shooting wild pigeons, waterfowl, and shorebirds by the carloads. Plume hunters pillaged every rookery of wading birds they found.

Now, almost for the first time, there was a stirring of alarm over the excessive slaughter. Already a few farsighted people had seen the handwriting on the wall and had begun to campaign for the protection of wildlife and other natural resources. Among their first accomplishments were the enactment of closed seasons on big game such as bison, deer, elk, and pronghorn in several western states, and the creation of Yellowstone as our first national park in 1872. Four years after that, the first Forest Reserve Bill was passed, giving protection to federal forests around river sources. In 1878 California and New Hampshire established the first state game departments, and the next year Congress created a Public Lands Commission to codify and bring order to all the myriad and conflicting land laws. All of these were steps in the right direction. But they were just a beginning in resource conservation.

In 1883 a group of ornithologists who were alarmed at the mass slaughter of birds for flesh and feathers, founded The American Ornithologists' Union. Established with the purpose of promoting bird study and protection, this organization—called the AOU for short—has grown steadily in stature and influence.

It was largely due to the influence of the fledgling AOU that a Branch of Economic Ornithology and Mammalogy was created in the Department of Agriculture in 1885. This official government department was the forerunner of the Bureau of Biological Survey, which in turn eventually became the Fish and Wildlife Service.

In 1885 George Bird Grinnell—a well-known scientist, hunter, publisher, and conservationist—sparked the founding of a private organization to fight against the slaughter of birds for food and plumes. From this beginning stemmed the National Audubon Society, which has long been a militant and vigilant force in the battle to protect wildlife and other resources.

In December, 1887, Grinnell teamed with Theodore Roosevelt to start the Boone and Crockett Club, which quickly became a powerful voice for wildlife conservation, especially of big game, and for the establishment of various national parks and wildlife refuges.

In the 1890s these and other conservation organizations were engaged in almost hand-to-hand combat with the forces of destruction. With their support and backing, a Forest Reserve Act was passed in 1891, permitting the President to set aside designated public lands as Forest Reserves. Under this act, Presidents Harrison and Cleveland earmarked forty million acres of public domain as Forest Reserves by the end of the century.

During this last decade of the nineteenth century, the deer population had hit its all-time low, and the once seemingly inexhaustible hordes of passenger pigeons and bison were almost gone. When poachers attacked the tiny Yellowstone Park herd of a couple of hundred bison—the only wild herd left in the United

States—even the general public began to realize the danger. As a result, the government took action to add teeth to the regulations protecting wildlife in the National Parks. The Lacey Act—the first general act to protect wildlife and regulate its killing and sale—followed in 1900.

The tide was at last beginning to turn. The effort was too little and too late to save the passenger pigeon and the Carolina parakeet. But it would help save the bison and various other species from almost certain extinction.

In 1901 Theodore Roosevelt became President of the United States—and the wildlife protectors had a friend in power. An enthusiastic sportsman and conservationist, Roosevelt was one of the few men of his time who recognized the interdependence of forest, water, soil, and wildlife, and that wildlife needed suitable living space as well as protection from unlimited hunting.

In 1903, by presidential proclamation, Roosevelt created our first national wildlife refuge—Pelican Island, a small area of mangrove and sand off the Indian River in Florida, where brown pelicans nested. Two years later he oversaw the organization of the U. S. Forest Service, with Gifford Pinchot, a professionally trained forester and conservationist, as its chief.

Other national wildlife preserves soon followed Pelican Island, and the start of our present extensive system of national wildlife refuges was well under way. The Wichita Forest and Game Reserve in Oklahoma, now called the Wichita Mountains Wildlife Refuge, was set aside in 1905, and the National Bison Range in Montana, in 1908.

Conservation causes continued their steady progress through the second decade of the twentieth century. In 1911 the United States, Great Britain, Russia, and Japan signed a treaty to control the take of fur seals and sea otters in the waters of the northern Pacific. Five years later another important treaty was negotiated—with Great Britain this time—to protect the migratory birds that flew over Canada and the United States. And after years of struggle, the plumage trade was finally outlawed.

The wildlife protectors were making good headway at last, and their efforts helped to save a number of endangered species.

BEAVER
Castor canadensis

More than any other animal, the beaver influenced the opening up of North America to exploration and settlement. The animal was of value for its thick, velvety fur, which was used for making beaver hats. Durable, cool, easy-fitting, and handsome, this style of headgear was the height of European fashion during the period of America's colonization.

In New England, early settlers found beaver dams on practically every stream, row upon row of them. William Bradford, in his *History of Plimoth Plantation*, listed seven sailings from the colony between 1631 and 1636 that carried a total of more than 12,500 pounds of beaver fur to the Old World, with a value of about 10,000 pounds sterling. The Dutch of New Amsterdam built up a similar thriving trade.

In seventeenth- and eighteenth-century Canada, the French traveled far and wide through previously unexplored waterways, trapping beaver and trading with the Indians for beaver skins. They established trading posts at Quebec, Detroit, Mackinac, and many other strategic spots, largely built upon the lucrative trade in this fur. And England established the powerful Hudson's Bay Company for very much the same reason. In those early days, beaver fur was just as good in business transactions as coin of the realm. Twelve beaver skins or "plews" were the usual price of a good gun; six of them would buy a Hudson's Bay red blanket.

By 1800 beavers had been hunted so long and so hard in the eastern half of the continent they were becoming scarce in many areas. But there were still plenty of them in the West. Lewis and Clark found this vast new territory "richer in beaver and otter than any other country on earth." With reports such as this coming back, it wasn't long before the beaver trappers were on their way.

The pioneering mainstays of the western fur companies were the mountain men, accustomed to the danger of having their scalps lifted by hostile Indians at any time, accustomed to wading chest deep in the icy waters of Rocky Mountain streams for hours at a time as they set and inspected their traps. By the 1840s, however, the brief era of the mountain men was just about finished. For one thing, the West was becoming too settled for their taste. And for another, silk hats were gaining favor and supplanting the "beaver" as the epitome of what the well-dressed gentleman wore. The demand for beaver skins dwindled as a result, and the whim of fashion gave the species a partial reprieve.

The breathing spell came just in time. After centuries of exploitation, the beaver was sore pressed throughout North America. In Pennsylvania the thick-furred dam builder was almost completely exterminated by 1865. Only ten of them, according to the best estimates, existed in all of New York State in 1895. By this time the beaver had disappeared nearly everywhere in the East, and was disappearing from many Western states as well.

Acting at last, most of the states passed strict laws, either giving the beaver total protection or establishing beaver-trapping seasons and control of the number permitted each trapper. The species was too valuable a furbearer to let it disappear completely. By this time some people also realized that the beaver, because of its dam-building activities, was a potent ally in flood control and the creation of wetland habitats. Under protection, the beaver began very gradually to recover and reoccupy much of its former territory.

To speed up this process in recent years, surplus beaver have often been live-trapped in areas where they are plentiful, then transported to wilderness areas in former beaver territory and released. In rough or mountainous country, they are sometimes flown in by plane. The beaver, enclosed in cages designed to open on contact with the ground, are dropped by parachute at the desired release spot. Such transplant programs have worked well, and beaver are now found over most, if not all, of their old range.

Thanks to regulation and management, it is still possible to walk alongside a wilderness pond or stream and, if we are lucky, come upon a beaver dam and lodge. Watching the big furry rodents swim back and forth, hearing the loud whack of a flat tail against the water, gives us some sense of what the mountain men glimpsed in former days.

PLAINS BISON
Bison bison bison

In frontier days, the Kiowa were one of the proudest and most warlike of all the Indian tribes of the Southwest plains. In *The American Bison*, Martin Garretson records their legend of creation as the Indians told it to an old scout many years ago, when millions of buffalo roamed the plains:

> *The first day the Great Spirit planted by the side of the waters the Great Way Tree whose boughs extended into the Heavens, by way of which all creatures were sent down upon the Earth, and lastly a Kiowa man and woman who walked about the creation, but in the evening*

they returned to the Great Way Tree, and there they met
the buffalo, and the Great Spirit descended and said:
"Here are the Buffalo. They shall be your food and your
raiment, but in the day you shall see them perish from
off the face of Earth, then know that the end of the Kiowa
is near—and the Sun set."

The dire prophecy of that legend turned out to be all too accurate, not only for the Kiowa but also for the Comanche, the Cheyenne, the Sioux, and all the other Plains tribes as well. "Buffalo Indians," these groups followed the great herds and depended upon them for all their needs. When the animals vanished, the way of life of the Plains Indians vanished as well.

The Indians ate buffalo flesh raw or cooked; they dried it for winter use. They fashioned tepees and clothing from buffalo hides, and used the woolly robes as sleeping spreads and floor coverings. They made soup ladles of the horns, tools and weapons from the bones. Very little of the animal was wasted.

Before the coming of the white man, Indians hunted buffalo on foot, and killed them with spears or arrows. Sometimes skilled hunters draped themselves in animal skins and crept close to a herd undetected. Or, if conditions were right, a whole group of hunters surrounded a herd and stampeded the animals over a cliff, thus harvesting a large supply of meat and skins at one time. With the advent of the Spaniards, the Indians gained the horse. Mounted, the Plains Indians could gallop into the midst of a herd of buffalo and shoot them easily.

Cortez and his doughty band of conquistadors were probably the first Europeans ever to see the American bison. Invading the capital of the Aztecs in 1521, they are said to have visited the menageries of Montezuma, the Aztec ruler, where they recorded they encountered "the Mexican Bull; a wonderful composition of divers Animals. It has crooked Shoulders, with a Bunch on its Back like a camel . . . its Neck covered with Hair like a Lion. It is cloven footed, its Head armed like that of a Bull, which it resembles in Fierceness, with no less strength and Agility."

Probing into the southwestern plains, the Spaniards soon saw many other bison and marveled at their abundance. But they never saw more than a tiny portion of the whole population. At that time, an estimated sixty million bison ranged the continent, from northern Mexico to central Canada and from the Rockies almost to the eastern seaboard.

Indians followed the buffalo and lived off their bounty. Bands of huge buffalo wolves trailed the herds too, preying on stragglers, calves, or old and weakened individuals. Winter blizzards took their toll of buffalo, and so did droughts, diseases, and mass drownings when the animals were crossing spring-swollen rivers. But no matter what the losses, there were always plenty of bison left.

The balance changed after the Civil War, however, when the white man invaded the West in force. The broad prairies and plains began very quickly to fill up with settlers, as well as with fortune hunters of every stripe. Everywhere they went the newcomers slaughtered bison for food, for hides, for profit, or simply for sport. Once the railroads began to creep across buffalo country, the numbers of the great herds declined with unbelievable rapidity.

"Buffalo Bill" Cody got his start as a hunter for the Kansas Pacific Railroad, killing 4,120 buffalo in a year and a half as food for the railroad construction crews. The first trains west were sometimes stopped for hours at a time as they waited for a big herd of buffalo to cross the tracks—so the railroad companies promoted buffalo hunts for sport. Soon, hide hunters by the thousands were fanning over the West, and buffalo hunting became the chief industry of the Plains. After skinning their victims, and perhaps taking the tongues, the hide hunters usually left the rest of the carcasses where they fell. In later years, after the buffalo were all gone, some people made their fortunes by collecting the whitened bones and selling them to be ground up as fertilizer.

By the early 1870s, the millions of buffalo in the Southwest had been wiped out, except for a few stragglers. The prophecy of the Kiowa legend had at last come true, for soon the Kiowa were reduced to living on reservations and depending on the questionable charity of the white man for a subsistence existence.

Struggling to avoid a similar fate, the Indians of the northern plains—the powerful Sioux, the Cheyenne, and their allies—fought back desperately against the invading whites. In 1876 the Indian leaders Crazy Horse and Sitting Bull united the northern tribes to annihilate General George Custer and most of his command at the famous Battle of the Little Bighorn. But the great Indian victory was a hollow one. Within a year most of the scattered tribes were subdued and herded onto reservations, and the white hunters were free to attack the buffalo without fear of retaliation. It took just five years to complete the destruction.

The last sizable herd, perhaps 75,000 animals in the Yellowstone area, was slaughtered in the summer of 1883. Now, except for a few scattered remnants, the buffalo was truly a thing of the past. During the next several years, most of the small surviving bands were hunted down one by one, and destroyed.

In 1890 the disillusioned but powerless Indians danced the Ghost Dance on their reservations and prayed to the Great Spirit—in vain—to bring back the buffalo. By now there were no more than several hundred wild bison left in the United States, most of them in the Yellowstone Park area. These were theoretically protected, but regulations were not enforced. Poachers continued to kill buffalo in the park, and some taxidermists did a thriving but illegal business making buffalo robes and mounting heads for wealthy patrons. By 1894 there were only twenty or twenty-one buffalo left in the Yellowstone area—the last wild buffalo remaining in the United States, except for an equally small band in Lost Park, Colorado.

At last the public was aroused to something approaching either shame or conservation consciousness, and Congress enacted a law providing stiff penalties for killing buffalo in Yellowstone National Park. The few animals in Colorado continued to be preyed upon by trophy hunters, however. The last four—two bulls, a cow, and a calf—were shot and killed in February 1897. Buffalo in the United States had reached their lowest ebb.

Luckily, a number of them had been preserved in small captive herds under private control. There were still several hundred wild buffalo in Canada too, in the almost inaccessible wilderness around Great Slave Lake. These Canadian bison were recognized as a distinct race, known as wood bison (*B.b. athabascae*). By preserving and breeding these surviving buffalo, perhaps the species could be saved after all.

With this in mind, a group of public-spirited conservationists formed the American Bison Society in 1905, with William Temple Hornaday, a militant crusader for wildlife, as its president. Hornaday was also the director of the New York Zoological Society, which had about forty captive bison in its animal collections. Fifteen of these were donated to the government in 1907 to form a nucleus herd for the newly created Wichita Forest and Game Reserve in Oklahoma. In 1908 the American Bison Society was largely responsible for establishing the National Bison Range in Montana and stocking it with thirty-four bison. During the next ten years, additional protected herds were established at Wind Cave National Park in South Dakota, and Fort Niobrara Reservation in Nebraska. The buffalo was on its way back in the United States. By the 1930s even Alaska boasted a small herd of several hundred, all descended from twenty-three animals transported there in 1928.

The Canadian government did its part by purchasing a privately-owned Montana herd in 1906 and transporting the animals to Alberta, where they were kept for propagation purposes in a 200-square-mile enclosure near Wainwright and a smaller enclosed area at Elk Island National Park. By the 1920s the Wainwright herd had increased to 8,000 or more, close to the carrying capacity of the range. In order to keep the herd at a manageable size, about 6,000 young buffalo were taken from Wainwright during the three-year period from 1925 to 1927 and released in the wilderness area south of Great Slave Lake—the traditional home of the wood bison. By this time the wood bison herd had increased to about 2,000, and the Canadian government had officially designated their range as Wood Buffalo National Park.

Unfortunately, the plains bison transplanted from Wainwright interbred with the wood bison. As a result, the pure strain of wood bison was thought to be extinct by the 1940s. In 1957, however, a

band of about 200 pure wood bison was discovered near the
northern boundary of the park, and some of these were moved to
a new area, known today as the Mackenzie Bison Sanctuary, north
of Great Slave Lake. The bison have prospered there, and in 1989
numbered about 2,000.

All in all, an estimated 120,000 buffalo now roam wildlife
ranges and national parks of Canada and the United States and
many private holdings as well. They have flourished so well that a
number of the animals have to be slaughtered and sold for their
meat every year to keep the herds in manageable proportion to the
range available. Canada permits a limited number of wild bison to
be taken by hunters, almost in the same manner as in the old
days.

Bison will never again roam the western plains and prairies
in unnumbered millions, as they once did. But, thanks to conservation measures taken in the nick of time, their survival is
assured.

PRONGHORN
Antilocapra americana

"Hurra for the prairies and the swift antelope," John James
Audubon exuberantly wrote in his journal after seeing the animals
on a trip up the Missouri River in 1843. "They fleet by the hunter
like flashes or meteors. . . ."

Equipped with slender, flying legs and powerful muscles, the pronghorn, or prongbuck, is America's fastest mammal. Adults have been clocked at more than fifty miles an hour. With its streamlined form, cinnamon-brown coat, snowy rump, and distinctive horns, the pronghorn is also one of our most beautiful animals.

The only surviving member of a unique family of mammals which evolved in North America—the Antilocapridae—which evolved in North America, the pronghorn probably once numbered many millions. They ranged the plains, prairies, and deserts of the West, from northern Mexico to Canada. Unlike the true antelopes of Africa and Asia, the pronghorn has hollow, branched horns that are shed each fall, new ones growing the following spring.

Like the bison, the pronghorn flourished until the white man invaded its territory. Settlers killed the fleet animals for meat and sport; they stocked their grazing lands with cattle and sheep; and eventually they posted their farms and ranches with fences. As a result, by 1908 the pronghorns had dwindled from perhaps thirty or forty million to an estimated twenty thousand animals north of Mexico.

But now people had learned the lesson of the bison. Most of the western states gave their remaining pronghorns a breathing space by enacting closed seasons on antelope hunting. In 1931 the Boone and Crockett Club and the National Audubon Society acted together to purchase some 34,000 acres of land in northwestern Nevada as the Sheldon National Antelope Refuge. Five years later, President Franklin Delano Roosevelt set aside an additional half-million acres of adjacent public lands as the Charles Sheldon Antelope Range. These two refuges are named to honor the conservation accomplishments of Charles Sheldon of the Boone and Crockett Club. At the same time, Roosevelt created the Hart Mountain National Antelope Refuge in nearby southeastern Oregon. Together, these three areas provided needed breeding, fawning, and wintering areas for the pronghorns of the region.

The 1930s, the decade of the Great Depression, brought hard times and many changes to the Great Plains. A combination of years of overcultivation, the drainage of natural wetlands, and a prolonged drought created a vast dust bowl throughout the region. Countless numbers of farmers and ranchers lost everything they had, and much of the land was rendered unfit for either people or wildlife.

Acting vigorously in the wake of the disaster, the federal government initiated a highly successful program of soil conservation, wetlands preservation, and tree planting that gradually restored much of the ravaged land to its former usefulness and made it once again a suitable habitat for the pronghorn and other wildlife of the Plains.

In the years since, the pronghorn has responded unbelievably well to protection, restoration of suitable habitat, and a trap-and-transplant program to bring the species back to parts of its original range. By 1939 its population in the United States alone had increased to about 200,000 animals.

Today, a half-century later, nearly a million pronghorns roam North America, about half of them in Wyoming. Many western states and two Canadian provinces now permit yearly regulated pronghorn hunting, and the take in Wyoming and Montana alone is more than 50,000 animals each year. The sustained population justifies that harvest, too. If pronghorn numbers were to drop significantly, the hunting would be restricted.

Only the Sonoran pronghorn (*A.a. sonoriensis*) is in present danger. Inhabiting deserts of extreme southern Arizona and northwestern Mexico, this race is legally protected in both countries, but its population is declining.

AMERICAN ELK OR WAPITI
Cervus elaphus canadensis **and its relatives**

In Colonial days elk were one of the most widespread species of big game on the North American continent, ranging in half-a-dozen different forms from southern Canada into Mexico, and from the Pacific coast almost to the Atlantic. All of these were once classified as distinct American species, but today they are usually considered races of one cosmopolitan species, the Old World red deer (*C. elaphus*).

European settlers called these huge New World deer "elk,"

American Elk or Wapiti

after a familiar species from their homelands. But the European elk is the same animal that Americans today know as the moose. A better name for the American elk is "wapiti," the name given it by the Shawnee Indians and meaning "light rump."

Settlers hunted the eastern wapiti (*C.e. canadensis*) so enthusiastically that by the time of the Civil War it had been exterminated nearly everywhere east of the Mississippi. A few years after that, the race was extinct. With the rapid settlement of the Rocky Mountain and Pacific coast states, the elk of these regions were soon threatened with the same fate.

The tule elk (*C.e. nannodes*), a small form that inhabited the San Joaquin and Sacramento valleys of California, was ruthlessly slaughtered during the California Gold Rush. By 1885 only twenty-eight known survivors were left in a tiny remnant band on the Miller-Lux Ranch in Kern County. The Arizona, or Merriam's, elk (*C.e. merriami*), a large-antlered, pale-colored form that lived in the mountains of Arizona and New Mexico, was not so fortunate. It became extinct about 1906, when the last band was killed in the Chiricahua Mountains. The Roosevelt, or Olympic, elk (*C.e. roosevelti*), a large, dark-colored form with heavy antlers, survived in coastal areas from northern California to Vancouver Island.

By 1910, however, the only sizable elk herds left in the United States were those of the Rocky Mountain race (*C.e. nelsoni*) that inhabited the Yellowstone Park-Jackson Hole region of Wyoming and Montana. The Rocky Mountain race had formerly ranged widely and abundantly over all the states of the mountains and high plains, but now their numbers were dwindling nearly everywhere, except in such isolated pockets of wilderness as Yellowstone. Here, evidently, they were making their last stand.

Yellowstone elk traditionally summered in lush mountain meadows and high slopes. After the fall mating season, when bulls gathered harems of cows, the bands of elk formed larger herds and streamed down from the high elevations to winter in the open valleys and grasslands of the Jackson Hole area, or even further south.

As Wyoming and Montana became more settled, the herds were forced to run an ever-increasing gauntlet of hunters every fall. Thousands of elk were slaughtered for their canine teeth alone, which sometimes brought ten dollars a pair. The Benevolent and Protective Order of Elks had a membership millions strong at this time, and elk teeth mounted in gold as a weighty watch fob were prized as the unofficial badge of the group.

But the slaughter of the elk was not the only symptom of a species on the wane. The real trouble was that their old wintering areas were now largely denied to the elk by miles of range fences, and by ranches and barns. The wild grasslands were disappearing under the plow or being used for domestic stock, and farmers and ranchers naturally resented the fact that elk competed with cattle for available fodder.

Without their age-old wintering grounds, the Rocky Mountain elk suffered, and in hard winters they died by the thousands. As early as 1892, at least 5,000 of them starved to death in the Jackson Hole area alone. A few ranchers and state officials took pity on the animals and attempted to supplement their winter food by putting out hay for them.

This feeding offered no final answer, however, and local, state, and federal officials were all concerned. In 1912, through their combined efforts, a National Elk Refuge was created on

2,760 acres of the Teton valley north of the town of Jackson, Wyoming. A regular program of supplementary feeding was started for the elk that crowded into the area every winter. Thanks to additions financed by the Izaak Walton League, the Benevolent and Protective Order of Elks, and the state and federal governments, the National Elk Refuge now covers about 24,000 acres. Every fall thousands of elk pour into the refuge for the winter, and one of the greatest spectacles for wildlife enthusiasts in America today is the sight of sleds going forth daily in late winter to scatter hay for the hordes of hungry animals.

Spectacle or not, the whole thing illustrates the fact that conditions are obviously very wrong for the Jackson Hole elk. "Artificial feeding of game animals is now rightly looked upon as the last resort in wildlife management," wildlife biologist Olaus Murie, author of *The Elk of North America*, observed years ago, "a practice to be adopted only when all efforts to provide suitable winter range have failed."

In fact, elk that must be fed are not true wild animals; they are only a step removed from livestock. And today there are just too many elk in the Yellowstone-Jackson Hole area for the limited winter range still available to them. So many members of the northern herd winter in Yellowstone that they have long threatened to overgraze parts of the park.

Officials of the Park Service have struggled energetically with this problem for years. As early as 1892 they started a program of trapping surplus elk and shipping them for release in other areas where elk had long since disappeared. From that date until 1939, more than 10,000 elk were shipped out in this fashion, and the practice continues today. As a result, nucleus bands of elk have been transplanted to at least thirty-six states and a number of foreign countries. Many of them have taken hold in a very satisfactory way.

Colorado, for example, began transplanting elk from Jackson Hole to suitable areas within its borders in 1912, and these have flourished. Now the state boasts an elk population of well over 100,000. Other transplants of Rocky Mountain elk now thrive in the mountains of Arizona and New Mexico, where the extinct

Merriam's elk once roamed. Today, the elk population throughout the United States has increased to more than 900,000 animals.

The continuing live-trapping program at Yellowstone and on the National Elk Refuge at Jackson does not begin to take care of all the surplus stock there. Neither does selective shooting by regular park rangers. In the winter of 1989, some 7,000 animals starved to death in the region. Controlled public hunts in Yellowstone and Grand Teton National Park have been used in recent years to help reduce the herds. Another control measure has been suggested—the reintroduction of traditional elk predators such as wolves into remote areas of the parks. But surrounding stockmen would certainly object.

Rocky Mountain elk, as exemplified by the burgeoning population in the Yellowstone region, are by far the most abundant race today. A Canadian race, the Manitoba elk (*C.e. manitobensis*), ranges Manitoba and Saskatchewan in much smaller numbers. The Roosevelt, or Olympic, elk is protected in Washington's Olympic National Park, as well as on the Madison Grant Forest and Elk Refuge in California. This elk has also been introduced on Afognak Island, Alaska.

Under strict protection, the several dozen tule elk that survived in California in 1885 had increased to about 500 by 1970. One band led a fenced-in existence in Tule State Park near Tupman, California. Another ranged over the Owens Valley Wildlife Refuge, created by authorization of the Los Angeles City Council in March 1967. But even this small protected band competed with livestock for available food, and some neighboring ranchers and farmers pressed for its reduction.

By 1993, under wise management and the transplanting of surplus elk to other suitable areas, the statewide population of tule elk has increased to about 2,500 animals, dispersed in more than twenty different herds.

The sad truth seems to be that there is no room in the United States anymore—except in Alaska—for sizable herds of free-roaming big game such as bison and elk. Given adequate forest habitat and winter pasturage, however, America's elk will flourish.

SEA OTTER
Enhydra lutris

After the wreck of the Bering expedition ship *St. Peter* in November 1741, as naturalist Georg Wilhelm Steller was making his way to Bering Island, he observed that "a number of sea otters came toward us, which from a distance some took for bears, others for wolverines."

Marooned all winter on the desolate shores of the previously unknown arctic island, the hard-pressed survivors of the *St. Peter* killed many sea otters—or "sea bears," as they called them—for food. Not the tastiest of fare, the flesh did help to keep the weakened men alive, and it had the added virtue of being easy to obtain. The animals were plentiful on Bering Island, and on land they could easily be run down and killed.

Comparatively slow and clumsy ashore, the sea otter is swift and graceful in its native element, the sea. Lithe and streamlined, it propels itself through the water with strokes of its flipper-like hind limbs, while its forelimbs trail close to the body. A full-grown male sometimes measures four or five feet in length and weighs close to seventy-five pounds. Females are considerably smaller.

Only one young is usually born at a time. Over a foot long,

fully furred, and with its eyes wide open at birth, it is a cuddly and appealing youngster. The mother otter cradles the young one in her arms and is very reluctant to abandon it in the face of danger.

For food, sea otters hunt mollusks, crabs, and sea urchins. In California waters, abalone is a favorite meal. Diving to the bottom to pick up its prey, the sea otter often brings a flat rock to the surface too. Floating on its back, the resourceful animal places the rock on its belly and uses it as a pounding board for breaking the hard shell of its dinner.

The sea otter's fur is probably the most beautiful and lustrous the world has ever known. The gleaming blackish-brown undercoat is as soft and plush as two-inch-thick velvet. A frosting of longer guard hairs creates a faint silvery sheen. Valued more than any other fur, sea otter pelts brought untold riches to a few hunters, and death and disaster to many others.

When Steller and his surviving companions made their way back to Kamchatka in 1742, they carried several hundred sea otter pelts with them, as well as tales of the hordes of otters they had left behind in the newly discovered lands to the east. The news spread quickly, and before long swarms of hunters were sailing across the storm-tossed North Pacific toward Bering Island and the Aleutians. Ruthless and determined, these Russian fortune hunters conquered and enslaved the natives whenever they could and forced them to hunt sea otters for them. The Aleut hunters sometimes netted the animals on reefs but usually speared them from walrus-hide *bidarkas* or canoes. Hunted as never before, sea otters had practically disappeared from the Commander and Aleutian islands by the 1780s. The Russians' next target was the otter population of Alaska's coastal islands.

In order to tighten their claim to Alaska and to exploit the profitable sea otter trade more efficiently, the Russians organized the Russian-American Fur Company in 1783. By now, Spain and England were investigating the region too. When the great English explorer Captain James Cook visited Vancouver Island in 1778, he and his crew were quick to appreciate the profits to be gained in trading with the coastal Indians for sea otter skins. "A dozen large glass beads were enough to purchase six of the finest skins," one of the men wrote.

Just ten years later, Boston skipper Robert Gray sailed his ship *Columbia* into Alaska's Nootka Sound and started to trade with the natives too. At one stopping place, according to the historian George Bancroft, "Gray received 200 sea otter skins, worth no less than $8,000, in exchange for an old iron chisel." Sailing on to Canton, China, Gray exchanged his rich cargo of furs for silks, spices, and other exotic Oriental products. Then he proceeded back home to fame and fortune.

The competition for furs continued for years, and the sea otter population gradually dwindled throughout its range. When the United States bought Alaska from Russia in 1867, the trade seemed to be on its way out. Unrestrained by the government, however, enterprising American hunters pursued the sea otter with renewed vigor. Between 1881 and 1890 a total of nearly 48,000 skins were taken.

After that, the fur fleet searched for its quarry in vain, for the sea otter was truly on the verge of extinction.

In 1900 the entire take was just 127 skins. The price of pelts skyrocketed, but there were practically none to be had at any price. In 1910 a single skin sold for $1,703.33. The next year the United States, Great Britain, Russia, and Japan all signed a treaty giving absolute protection to the animal. At the time, it seemed a case of locking the barn door after the horse had been stolen.

Several decades passed, and nothing was seen or heard of the sea otter, even though it was "protected." Pessimists considered it surely extinct, while optimists thought perhaps a few individuals survived in outposts of the Aleutians or other lonely islands. A single skin, quietly offered in the London fur market, sold for close to $2,500.

Then, on March 19, 1938, a couple walking near the mouth of Bixby Creek, on California's Monterey Peninsula, sighted some animals in the waters offshore that aroused their curiosity. When game wardens were called in, they identified the creatures with the sleek, bobbing heads as sea otters—no fewer than ninety-four of them. In California waters, at least, the prized furbearer was still living. There were also survivors in Aleutian waters.

At present, after nearly a century of protection, the sea otter has gradually repopulated most of its old territory. Today, an estimated 150,000 or more of them range through the coastal waters of the Pacific, from the Kuril Islands and Kamchatka eastward to the storm-tossed Pribilof and Aleutian islands and southward to the coast of California. Many of these inhabit the seventy islands and more than 2,700,000 acres of the Aleutian Islands National Wildlife Refuge.

The species has done so well, in fact, that in 1967 Alaska revived the sea otter trade as a state monopoly. The next year 826 skins were offered for sale to the fur trade, and some of the best skins were sold for $2,300 apiece.

But even in the remote sanctuary of the Aleutian Islands National Wildlife Refuge, civilization still poses a threat to the otters, although in a form somewhat different from the old days. In the fall of 1965 the U.S. Atomic Energy Commission set off an underground test blast of a nuclear weapon (Project Long Shot), on Amchitka, one of the main islands of the refuge. Precautions were taken to protect the otters and other wildlife as much as possible, but who can predict the long-range effects of nuclear explosions?

Shock waves from another atomic blast in 1971 killed an estimated twelve hundred otters by concussion. As partial repayment for its misdeeds, from 1969 to 1972 the Atomic Energy Commission helped to transplant eighty-nine Alaskan sea otters to favorable bays and inlets of Canada's Vancouver Island, where the species had been practically extinct for a century or more.

Another human hazard for sea otters and other marine animals is oil discharged from ships, accidentally or otherwise. Floating and spreading widely over the surface of the water, oil forms a deadly layer on the fur of sea otters and the feathers of seabirds. Unable to swim effectively, and with the insulating properties of their fur or feathers destroyed by the coating of oil, the animals soon die.

The disastrous effects of a really big oil spill were demonstrated on March 24, 1989, when a huge tanker, the *Exxon Valdez*, ran aground on a reef in Prince William Sound, Alaska, spilling eleven million gallons of crude oil, which quickly spread, bringing death and desolation to hundreds of miles of formerly pristine shoreline. Seabirds and sea otters died by the thousands, and the loss of other marine life was incalculable.

Today, nearly 2,000 southern sea otters (*E.l. nereis*) range along some 230 miles of California coast, from just north of Santa Cruz southward to San Luis Obispo. Commercial shellfishermen think there are too many sea otters for the area, and declare that the species' fondness for abalone and other shellfish poses a threat to pocketbooks and jobs. They protested efforts of state and federal wildlife officials to extend the otters' range to a new area in 1987, when more than a hundred of them were transplanted to San Nicolas Island, some sixty miles southwest of Los Angeles. These otters had colored plastic tags attached to the webs of each hind foot, and fifteen of them carried surgically implanted radio transmitters so that their travels and activities could be monitored. Many of these animals have disappeared, and others have returned to their old areas. About a dozen remained, at last count. Hopes are high, however, that the new colony will eventually succeed.

Having survived a century and a half of hunting exploitation, the sea otter has proved a hardy breed. Perhaps it can also survive the many present dangers posed by human technology, oil spills, habitat destruction, and greed.

NORTHERN FUR SEAL
Callorhinus ursinus

Some 250 miles north of the Aleutians, five small, rocky islands rise from the fog-misted waters of the Bering Sea. These are the Pribilofs, where hundreds of thousands of northern fur seals come each spring to breed.

First to arrive are mature bulls, seven to fifteen years old, some of them weighing 600 pounds or more. Clambering ashore, each one immediately stakes out a section of beach as his own. A pugnacious beach-master, he roars and threatens and fights rival bulls to protect his claim. A couple of weeks later, immature males arrive. They do not dare to challenge their elders but go meekly off to bachelor quarters on other beaches or hauling

grounds. Pregnant females are last to put in their appearance. They arrive in late June.

As the females appear along the shores, each big bull gathers as many as he can onto his hard-won strip of territory. Constantly on guard, he prevents wayward females of his harem from wandering off onto a rival's territory, and he fights off raids by neighboring bulls. Within a very few days after she comes ashore, each female gives birth to a blackish, ten-pound pup, and within a few more days, she mates with the bull. Her next pup will be born fifty-one weeks later.

In July, thousands of bawling pups dot the rocky shores. From time to time the nursing mothers swim as far as a hundred miles out in the open sea to hunt fish for themselves. Each female unerringly finds her way back through hordes of pups to her own particular infant. The harried bulls, however, remain on station on the beaches throughout most of the summer. For six weeks or more during the height of the pupping and breeding season, they neither eat nor drink.

In late summer the harems begin to break up. Pups are weaned and quickly follow their mothers into the water to learn how to catch fish for themselves. Their breeding responsibilities over, the bulls put out to sea as well. By the time November storms crash against the Pribilofs, the beaches are completely deserted until the next spring. Bulls sometimes spend the entire winter in the open reaches of the North Pacific, but females and young range as far south as the coastal waters of California.

The breeding grounds of the fur seal were unknown until 1786, when Gerasim Pribilof, a navigator with the Russian Navy, discovered the islands that now bear his name. The fur seal population at that time may have been as much as three million or more, and fur hunters soon descended on the Pribilofs in droves. By 1834, a half-century after the islands' discovery, the hunters had harvested two million pelts. The herds were noticeably reduced, and the Russians thereafter restricted the shore killings— no females were to be taken. As a result, only 600,000 pelts were harvested during the next thirty years. In 1867, when the United States took possession of the Pribilof Islands along with Alaska, an estimated two and a half to three million fur seals still hauled out on the beaches every year.

But hunters from the United States pursued the seals even more vigorously than the Russians had. The government leased hunting rights ashore to private firms, which between them accounted for 100,000 skins a year until 1890. At the same time, seal hunters of many nations pursued the animals in the open ocean. In 1892 about 120 vessels were engaged in this activity in the North Pacific.

Open-ocean sealing did not discriminate between the sexes, and as a result many pregnant and nursing female seals were killed. Ashore, thousands of orphaned pups starved and died. Attacked on both land and sea, the herds dwindled year after year. By 1910, instead of millions, there were only about 300,000 fur seals coming ashore on the Pribilofs each spring. Unless something was done, the northern fur seal would soon be extinct.

Rescue came in 1911, with the same international treaty that gave protection to the sea otter. Sealing on the open seas was outlawed, and five years of grace was given to the breeding seals ashore. After that, the country owning the breeding grounds was to harvest and manage the herds on its own islands.

Under these terms, the Pribilof herds had increased to nearly two million animals by 1950, a total that seal experts considered the optimum number for the breeding grounds available. Each year 60,000 or more three- and four-year-old bachelor seals were harvested by the Bureau of Commercial Fisheries or the National Marine Fisheries Service, which took over the seal management in 1972. The USSR managed two smaller rookeries, totaling perhaps 200,000 animals that bred in the Commander Islands and on tiny Tiuleni Island in the Sea of Okhotsk. Canada and Japan, the other two signatories of the treaty, each got a percentage of the American harvest every year.

In an experimental management move, a quota of female seals as well as the bachelor seals were killed from 1956 to 1968. Whether because of this or for other reasons, the Pribilof fur seal population began a steady decline. By the early 1980s it was less than half of what it had been thirty years before. The commercial seal harvest was just 22,000 in 1984, the year that marked the end of the fur seal convention of 1911. The renewed version of the treaty failed to win U.S. Senate approval because of intense lobbying against it by various animal welfare groups, and that signaled the end of commercial sealing in the Pribilofs. Thereafter, no seals were to be taken, except for research or to meet the subsistence needs of the Aleuts.

In spite of this, the fur seal population has continued to decline, and in 1988 the National Marine Fisheries Service designated the Pribilof herd as "depleted"—its population a million or less. The cause of this downward slide is uncertain. Some blame commercial fishermen for taking too many of the fish that the seals need for food, but there is little or no evidence to support this theory. Others believe that the seals are being killed off by chemical poisoning, DDT and PCBs ingested with their food, or as the result of oil spills. One clear cause, however, is the dumping of plastic junk and discarded netting into the waters of the North Pacific and Bering Sea, some 1,830 tons of it yearly. According to one estimate, at least 50,000 seals die annually after being ensnared and drowned in scraps of nets. The majority of these are young seals of both sexes.

In 1987 the U.S. Senate ratified an international agreement to prevent ocean dumping of garbage, including plastics, but until all seafaring nations prohibit such dumping and strictly enforce the regulations, the seal decline is likely to continue.

NORTHERN ELEPHANT SEAL
Mirounga angustirostris

The visitor to Mexico's Guadalupe Island or California's coastal islands has an excellent chance these days of seeing a herd of gigantic seals snoozing on the sandy beaches. Their crusty hides are tattered with shreds of peeling skin, and each adult male has a flabby proboscis that droops over his jaws like a wrinkled leather bag. The size of those males has to be seen to be believed. Large individuals often measure fifteen or sixteen feet long—the record is close to twenty-two feet—and weigh three tons or more.

A century and a half ago elephant seals by the thousands roamed the waters off the coasts of California and Baja California. Each springtime they hauled up on the Channel Islands, off the coast of southern California, to snooze, to mate, and to bear their ninety-pound pups. They bellowed and fought and shed outer layers of skin, then humped their way back to sea to hunt for fish, squid, and other marine tidbits.

Russian fur hunters, probing southward from Alaska, discovered the elephant seals and found them easy to kill. So did the Spaniards and the enterprising seamen of England and the United

States. Whalers of all nations stopped at the islands to kill the big seals too. The oil that could be rendered from their blubber was considered even better than that from the sperm whale, and a big male yielded as much as 200 gallons. Under such exploitation, the elephant seal had almost vanished by the late years of the nineteenth century.

In 1892 a group of U.S. scientists landed on Guadalupe Island, 180 miles west of central Baja California, the last outpost of the elephant seal. They found only nine of the big beasts there, and promptly collected seven of them. At least they would have some museum specimens all properly labeled and available for study. Afterward, for the next fifteen years, the elephant seal was all but officially pronounced extinct.

In 1907, however, the Rothschild scientific expedition visited Guadalupe and—much to the members' surprise—found forty elephant seals hauled up on the beaches. Fourteen of these were promptly killed as specimens. Four years later a third scientific expedition came and this time found a herd of about 150. That same year the Mexican government put the species under complete protection. Since then, it has come back—slowly at first, then faster and faster.

By the late 1960s the elephant seal population had increased to 10,000 animals or more, and by the early 1980s—with numbers doubling every five years—the total was at least 90,000. Today it has jumped to more than 130,000, and the expanding herds have reoccupied most of their old haunts, including the Farallon Islands, just thirty-five miles west of San Francisco's Golden Gate Bridge, the Channel Islands, and South Coronado Island, a mere twenty-one miles from San Diego.

TRUMPETER SWAN
Cygnus buccinator

The world's largest waterfowl, the trumpeter swan weighs nearly thirty pounds and carries itself aloft on wings that spread seven feet from tip to tip. Its plumage is glistening white, its bill solid black. Its call is powerful, low-pitched, and distinctive, somewhat resembling the triumphant bugling of a French horn.

Trumpeter Swan

In pioneer days the trumpeter swan ranged over much of the interior of the continent, flying northward to nesting grounds each springtime, then southward each fall to sheltered wintering areas in the Ohio and Mississippi valleys and the Rocky Mountain states. As people settled ever more thickly in its territory, the trumpeter's numbers inevitably declined. The huge white bird was a tempting target, and its flesh was a welcome change from venison, buffalo steak, and beef. Wing quills made fine pens, and the soft swansdown was ideal for featherbeds, pillows, and powder puffs.

More than 17,000 swanskins were sold between 1853 and 1877 by the Hudson's Bay Company alone. Add to this the number of swans shot by other commercial organizations and individual hunters, and some idea of the grand total of swans killed in those years becomes apparent. Many of the victims were whistling swans, a somewhat smaller and more abundant species, but the trumpeter was the more highly prized target.

By the start of the twentieth century the trumpeter had disappeared from almost all its old haunts in the United States. The species seemed to be on the way out, as well-known ornithologist Edward Howe Forbush sadly noted in his 1912 work, *A History of the Game Birds, Wild-Fowl and Shore Birds of Massachusetts and Adjacent States*: "The trumpeter has succumbed to incessant persecution in all parts of its range, and its total extinction is now only a matter of years."

The Migratory Bird Treaty Act of 1918 gave legal protection for the first time to both the trumpeter and the whistling swan, but many people continued to shoot them illegally. By 1930 the trumpeter swan's entire U.S. population was concentrated in the Yellowstone region of Wyoming and the neighboring Red Rock Lakes area of southwestern Montana. Both of these areas boast thermally heated springs and ponds, some of which remain open and free of ice all winter long.

In 1933 at least seventeen trumpeter swans were shot and killed in this region, and a census the next year revealed only seventy-three birds south of the Canadian border. Then tthe crusading new chief of the U.S. Biological Survey, J.N. (Ding) Darling, a noted political cartoonist and conservationist, swung into action. Largely through his efforts, some 40,000 acres of trumpeter swan habitat around Montana's Red Rock Lakes was made a national wildlife refuge in 1935. For the first time in history the swans had an inviolate breeding territory.

The trumpeters responded so well to protection that by 1958 a census revealed 735 of the big birds south of Canada—310 of them on the refuge. This number represented the saturation point at Red Rock Lakes, for every pair of breeding trumpeter swans needs a sizable nesting territory. How to increase the flock? The answer was a program whereby birds would be captured at Red Rock Lakes, then introduced into other refuges.

The swans were usually captured in late summer, when they had molted their flight feathers and were temporarily unable to fly. Wing-clipped and kept in enclosures at the new areas during the winter, the birds were then released the next spring. If everything went as planned, they would adapt to the new surroundings, stay there, and breed.

In this way, trumpeter swans were introduced to a number of suitable refuges, including Malheur in Oregon, the National Elk Refuge in Wyoming, Ruby Lake in Nevada, Turnbull in Washington, and Lacreek in South Dakota. On each of these the swans successfully nested. Pairs of swans have also been loaned to about fifty zoos for captive breeding.

By 1971 the trumpeter swan population totaled about 5,000

birds, including nearly 3,000 in Alaska. The species was removed from the federal list of endangered and threatened wildlife, for it seemed to be out of danger and well on the way back. In the 1980s there was a significant increase in the number of swans wintering in Montana, Wyoming, Idaho, and the Pacific coast, and in 1985 the first flock to winter on the Atlantic coast in 180 years was recorded.

WOOD DUCK
Aix sponsa

Many people consider the male wood duck the most beautiful of all waterfowl. His crested head and back glint with iridescent dark-greens, blues, and purples, interrupted by bold scallops of pure white. His breast is a deep wine color, and his eyes are ruby red. His mate, in contrast, is garbed in delicate shades of brown and gray mixed with white.

A century and more ago wood ducks were quite common over most of temperate North America. They were prime hunting targets, for their flesh was tasty and their feathers were ideal for use in making trout flies or trimming millinery. The drake, mounted in a lifelike pose, made a splendid ornament for the Victorian sitting room. Few states had any effective limitations on waterfowl shooting in those days, and the beautiful little duck was killed at any season of the year.

Shooting, however, was not the only factor working against the wood duck. The species nests in tree holes, and widespread lumbering and land-clearing operations reduced the suitable sites. In addition, the constant drainage of wetlands for agricultural use took away much of the bird's best habitat. By the first decade of the twentieth century the wood duck was disappearing everywhere at an alarming pace.

In order to save it, the Bureau of Biological Survey called for a closed season on the species in 1901. A number of states responded, but there was still no general federal protection. This legislation was delayed until 1916, when the United States and Great Britain negotiated their treaty regulating the take of all migratory waterfowl. Both governments gave complete protection to the endangered wood duck in 1918 and kept it on the prohibited list until 1941. The species came back so well under protection that since that time a limited wood duck season has been permitted in the United States each fall.

Today the wood duck is once again a common bird in many areas, but it still needs all the help we can give it. Many waterfowl enthusiasts do their bit by building and erecting wood duck nesting boxes which encourage the species to nest in areas where there are no longer enough natural tree holes.

WILD TURKEY
Meleagris gallopavo

When Cortez and his conquistadors occupied the capital of the Aztecs in 1521, they saw a number of wild turkeys that had been domesticated by the Indians. So did the soldiers of Coronado's army when they explored the Southwest a few years later. The Pueblo Indians, they noted, kept "cocks with great hanging chins."

Along with many other treasures, the Spaniards sent some of these domesticated fowl back to Spain. Such was their popularity there that after several generations they had been introduced into most of the countries of Europe. Confusion about their place of

Wild Turkey

origin gave these splendid New World birds their common name, since they were mistakenly considered to have been imported from some part of the Turkish empire. As a result, they have been called "turkey" ever since.

Sailing for America, the first English settlers brought some turkeys with them, little dreaming that they would encounter wild turkeys in abundance in the new land. The Pilgrims found a "great store of wild Turkies" in Massachusetts Bay Colony and are said to have feasted on them at their first Thanksgiving. Wild turkey helped to sustain the colony during its first difficult years, for a hunter was almost sure to get a bird or two whenever he went out.

Some idea of the turkey's abundance—and rapid decline—can be gained from the quote of one New England traveler in the year 1674: "I have also seen three-score broods of young turkies on the side of a marsh, sunning themselves in a morning betimes. But that was thirty years since; the English and Indians having now destroyed the breed, so that 'tis very rare to meet with a wild turkie in the woods." Already—before settlement was well under way—the wild turkey was threatened with extermination in the Northeast. But in many other regions it was still abundant.

"The high forests ring with the noise, like the crowing of the domestic cock, of these social sentinels," the naturalist William Bartram remarked in the 1770s, describing a Florida trip, "the watchword being caught and repeated from one to another for hundreds of miles around. . . ."

At this time, wild turkeys ranged over much of the continent, from New England and the Rockies in the north to Florida and southern Mexico in the south. Many of these early birds were splendid specimens—cocks, according to report, frequently weighed as much as forty or fifty pounds. Acorns, chestnuts, and beechnuts were among the wild turkey's principal foods, although tubers, bulbs, grubs, and weed seeds all went into its crop as well. A great wanderer, it traveled miles searching for the best feeding areas. Wary and elusive, it roosted high in the trees at night, and on the ground it could just about outrun a man.

"I wish the bald eagle had not been chosen as the representative of our country," lamented Benjamin Franklin. "For in truth, the turkey is in comparison a much more respectable bird . . . a bird of courage." This judgment may be somewhat biased against the eagle, but history has amply honored both species. The bald eagle is our national bird, while the turkey is universally acclaimed as the official bird for Thanksgiving dinner.

Under civilization's relentless heel, the wild turkey soon declined in many areas, due to overshooting and lumbering operations that steadily whittled away at prime turkey habitat and food supply. In 1730, for example, the wild turkey was so common that, dressed and ready for roasting, it sold for one-and-a-half cents a pound in Northampton, Massachusetts. A century later, it was seldom available at any price, for the wild turkey had disappeared almost entirely throughout the Northeast. Connecticut lost its last wild turkey in 1813, and Massachusetts in 1851.

By the 1920s the species had been wiped out in eighteen of the states it had once lived in and had disappeared from nearly three-quarters of its original range. The spreading chestnut blight added impetus to the disappearance, for this catastrophic tree disease destroyed the source of one of the turkey's most important foods.

Wildlife experts now began to pay attention to the turkey problem, the state game department of Pennsylvania being a pioneer in research. Wild turkeys raised on state game farms were released in suitable habitat, but many of these birds were too tame, and not hardy enough to withstand the northern winters. Then the Pennsylvania wildlife managers set up an experiment that put pinioned, half-wild, half-domestic turkey hens in fenced enclosures in the mountains where there were still a few wild birds in the surrounding woods. Wild cocks winged their way over the fences to mate with the hens, giving invigorating new blood to the resultant offspring. Domestic weaknesses were gradually strained out in this way.

The most successful management technique, however, has been to catch completely wild stock with cannon nets. These are nets propelled by powder charges over birds lured to an area baited with food. The netted birds are then taken to suitable new areas and released. This capture-and-release method is being used today over most of the turkey's original range, and it even serves to introduce the species into some areas where it has never occurred before.

Thanks to such management practices, the wild turkey population in the United States has increased almost beyond anyone's wildest dreams. Today this splendid game bird can be found in every state except Alaska, and its numbers have increased from a total of perhaps 30,000 birds in the 1930s to more than four million in the 1990s.

EGRETS AND THE PLUME TRADE

Feathers were the crowning glory of ladies' hats in the early years of the twentieth century—and that didn't mean just a feather or two. Whole birds were sometimes mounted precariously atop the crown of a hat, giving, one would imagine, a rather top-heavy effect when good-sized specimens were used. London, Paris, and New York were the centers of the millinery trade in those days, and bird skins by the millions flowed through these cities: the skins of herons and egrets, parrots and hummingbirds, birds of paradise and many others. Every colorful bird was fair game for

Snowy Egret

the plume hunters. In just one season, 1892, a single "feather merchant" of Jacksonville, Florida, shipped 130,000 bird skins to New York for the trade. In that year, many other similar shipments were being assembled in North America, South America, Africa, Asia, Australia, and New Guinea as well. The plume trade was vast, well-organized, and well-financed.

In North America, the principal victims were the snowy egret (*Egretta thula*) and the great egret (*Casmerodius albus*), beautiful herons that had at one time been familiar birds with a widespread distribution. The two species bred in colonies, with hundreds of nests often built close beside each other in low-branched trees in southern swamps. During the breeding season the adults developed special courtship plumes called aigrettes, which were especially prized. Descending on a nesting colony, plume hunters could utterly destroy it in a day or two. They killed all the adult birds for their feathers, then left the eggs and young birds to die. Under such assaults, the egret population went into a rapid decline.

By the turn of the century, egrets had disappeared nearly

everywhere in Florida, their former stronghold in the United States. In other southern states the story was about the same, with one notable exception: Louisiana. Here a sizable flock of egrets still nested in comparative security at the Avery Island Preserve, a private sanctuary established by E.A. McIlhenny, an enthusiastic and affluent conservationist. He and a few other ardent champions of embattled wildlife were fighting to preserve the plume birds in every way they could.

The various Audubon clubs that had sprung up around the country since 1885 were among the organizations that led the battle. They secured their first notable success in 1901 with the passage of a Florida law protecting nongame birds, including all of the species especially valued for their plumes. That same year the clubs banded together in a loose federation, the National Committee of the Audubon Societies of America, with militant conservationist William Dutcher as chairman. Four years later the federation evolved into a truly integrated organization, the National Association of Audubon Societies for the Protection of Wild Birds and Animals, with Dutcher as its first president.

The Audubon clubs came to the fore just in time, for in 1903 only eighteen specimens of the common egret could be discovered in the entire state of Florida. These were gathered in the Cuthbert rookery in the Everglades.

The fledgling National Audubon Society promptly employed four wardens to patrol and protect the remaining rookeries of water birds in the state. Young Guy Bradley was one of the four, and his territory was Monroe County, which covered Florida's lower keys.

On July 8, 1905, Bradley heard shots coming from the direction of the Oyster Keys, near his home. Getting into his boat, he set out to investigate and was never seen alive again, except by the poachers who killed him. The murderers were never punished for their act, for there was no concrete legal evidence against them. But they were known, and some of their cronies learned what had happened. As Bradley had approached the poachers' anchored schooner, two of the plume hunters had also been returning to it in a small boat loaded with dead birds. Bradley attempted to arrest the men and was shot by a third poacher, who was standing on the deck of the schooner. The raiders promptly sailed away from the area, and some hours later Bradley's body, a bullet hole in the neck, was found in his drifting boat.

"Every movement must have martyrs," William Dutcher declared when he heard the news, "and Guy Bradley is the first martyr to bird protection."

A wave of indignation over the murder swept the country, and the feeling against plume hunters became even more pronounced in 1908 when a second Audubon warden was shot and killed as he attempted to protect a rookery in South Carolina. Because of the widespread resentment over such acts and the resultant publicity campaign launched by the National Association of Audubon Societies, an Audubon Plumage Bill was pushed through the New York State legislature in 1910. This act banned the sale of wild-bird plumage anywhere in the state, including New York City, the center of America's millinery trade. In 1913 the federal government reinforced this law with an act barring the importation of wild-bird plumage of any sort into the United States. After that, state after state followed the lead of New York in prohibiting any commerce in plumage—and the fight was won.

After their near brush with extinction in the United States, the plume birds' recovery was almost miraculous. "Once the plume hunting was stopped," Alexander Sprunt IV, director of research for the National Audubon Society, noted in a 1987 article in *Audubon* magazine, "the wading birds bounced back and reached a peak in the 1930s, more than a million in the Everglades alone."

Since that time, however, these species have experienced a sharp decline in southern Florida—as much as 90 percent in the Everglades—due to extensive land clearing, loss of habitat, and diversion of vitally needed water from the Everglades for intensive agricultural irrigation.

The snowy and great egrets responded to this threat by expanding their ranges to other areas. Today these two beautiful plume birds are common throughout the South and much of the East during the breeding season, and during their post-breeding flights they can be seen widely throughout much of the rest of the country.

Conservation is a state of harmony between men and land. By land is meant all the things on, over, or in the earth. Harmony with land is like harmony with a friend; you cannot cherish his right hand and chop off his left. That is to say, you cannot love game and hate predators; you cannot conserve the waters and waste the ranges; you cannot build the forest and mine the farm. The land is one organism.
—Aldo Leopold,
A Sand County Almanac

5

THE DEVELOPING SCIENCE OF WILDLIFE MANAGEMENT, 1920 to 1940

As the country moved into the 1920s, conservationists could take justifiable pride in what had been accomplished for wildlife protection during the preceding couple of decades. The worst excesses of market hunting had been brought under control and plume hunting abolished. The fur seals were protected by international treaty, and so were waterfowl and other migratory birds. Protected by stricter hunting laws, some of the endangered big-game species were also making remarkable recoveries.

Deer were one example. Down to their all-time population low at the turn of the century, practically exterminated in vast areas, they had responded immediately to protection. Now they were coming back nearly everywhere. All any species needed to prosper, it seemed, was legal protection and regulation—plus control of predators, of course. At least that's what many game protectors believed.

A few dark clouds marred the conservation horizon, however,

clouds that cast some doubt on such a simple philosophy. Game management as a science was still in its infancy, and many of the factors controlling wildlife populations were either unknown or not generally accepted. But several things were happening to prove that the easy answer was not always the right one. The case of the Kaibab deer was one of them.

In 1906 President Roosevelt had set aside the Kaibab Plateau, a high, semi-arid area of about a million acres on the northern rim of the Grand Canyon in northern Arizona, as a national game preserve. Its chief purpose was the protection of a herd of about 3,000 mule deer that lived in the area. A vigorous predator-control campaign was quickly launched, and by 1923 a total of 674 mountain lions, 120 bobcats, 11 wolves, and about 3,000 coyotes had been killed in the Kaibab. The deer, protected from both human and animal hunters, responded by increasing to at least 30,000 head by 1924—local opinion said 100,000. Whatever their numbers at the height of the population explosion, there were far too many of them for the area to support, especially during hard winters. Without enough food, the deer became weakened by malnutrition. Disease swept through the herds, and during the next few winters the animals died by the thousands.

Another consequence of the overpopulation was that the starving animals also stripped the Kaibab bare of food plants. "The whole country looked as though a swarm of locusts had swept through it," one observer remarked, "leaving the range . . . torn, gray, stripped, and dying."

In spite of such evidence, uninformed animal lovers still protested any attempts to trim the size of the herd by selective hunting. Even worse, the official policy of killing predators continued.

A few people recognized the fallacies of such a program, however, and worked hard to introduce a more enlightened approach. Two of the leaders were George Bird Grinnell and Charles Sheldon, of the Boone and Crockett Club. Another was Aldo Leopold, an assistant district forester stationed in Albuquerque, New Mexico. Long fascinated by the network of factors influencing wildlife populations, he had followed the fortunes of the Kaibab deer at close hand. In 1925 he recorded some of his theories in an article, "New Developments in Game Management," in the *Bulletin* of the American Game Protective Association. "We have learned that game, to be successfully conserved, must be positively produced, rather than negatively protected . . . ," he noted. "In short, we have learned that game is a crop, which Nature will grow and grow abundantly, provided only we furnish the seed and suitable environment."

"Suitable environment" was the key to the situation, as Leopold realized. Anything that changed the balance of a particular environment also affected the fortunes—for better or worse—of various wildlife species living there. And when any wildlife population increased out of bounds, trouble was sure to follow.

In 1929 Leopold was invited to give a series of lectures on game management at the University of Wisconsin. Four years later his book *Game Management* was published—still the acknowledged bible of that science. In 1934 the University of Wisconsin appointed him as its—and the nation's—first professor of the subject. Leopold's teachings have been spread widely since then, and today he is recognized as the "father of modern wildlife management."

Today, using many of the wildlife management techniques advocated by Leopold, the mule deer population on the Kaibab Plateau has gradually been brought back into a better balance with the available food supply.

The Land and Water Crisis of the Thirties

The kind of problem represented by too many deer on the Kaibab wasn't the only one that faced conservationists in the late twenties. There was also the perplexing matter of the continent's dwindling waterfowl populations. In the early twenties, ducks and geese had increased very encouragingly. The Migratory Bird Treaty Act protected them during the vital breeding season and regulated their take during the fall shooting season. But in spite of such protection, waterfowl populations started an alarming downward trend during the late twenties and early thirties. Why? It almost seemed like the problem of the Kaibab deer in reverse.

The reasons, however, were not very hard to discover. Every year drainage projects were turning more and more vital waterfowl-breeding areas in the northern states and Canada into agricultural or grazing lands. Every year irrigation canals were siphoning more and more water from western rivers, drying up many of the marshes that waterfowl needed if they were to prosper. It was in just this way that the Bear River marshes of Utah, once one of the continent's most productive waterfowl areas, were destroyed.

Waterfowl soon began to feel the scarcity of living space, and disease added its toll as birds by the thousands crowded into the dwindling areas left to them. Over the years, millions of waterfowl died in the stagnant remnants of the Bear River marshes, many of them victims of botulism, a deadly disease caused by an anaerobic bacteria that flourishes only in polluted or deoxygenated waters.

Acknowledging that the Bear River marshes had become a death trap for waterfowl, the federal government in 1928 established the area as a refuge and took immediate steps to build impoundments that would restore the marshes as suitable waterfowl habitat. What's more, Congress passed the Migratory Bird Conservation Act the next spring, authorizing the acquisition of wetlands all across the nation as refuges for waterfowl and other migratory birds. These were steps in the right direction.

But the fall of 1929 witnessed the stock market crash that ushered in the Great Depression. With its economy suddenly in tatters, the nation had little interest in acquiring refuges for waterfowl. People needed refuge too, and the primary concerns of the moment were basic human requirements—jobs, security, hope.

As the thirties began, the Great Depression settled over the country like a chronic illness. But there was even worse to come, for now nature played a cruel trick on the nation too. The year 1931 was a dry one, with less than average rainfall over the prairie and plains states. In this way began a great drought that endured for four long years—searing and killing the crops and drying out the rich topsoil. Vast dust storms swirled over millions of acres that had been overcultivated and overgrazed without any thought of practical soil conservation. Prairie land, formerly the breadbasket of the nation, was fast becoming its dust bowl.

Inaugurated as the nation's thirty-second president in March 1933, Franklin Delano Roosevelt immediately set in motion a whirlwind of programs and activities designed to help the poor and needy, the hard-pressed farmer—and the parched and mistreated land as well. "By 1934," historian Arthur Schlesinger, Jr. noted, "a massive national effort was at last under way, aimed at checking erosion, at strengthening the soil and purifying the water, at securing the physical bases of American civilization."

By this time the continent's waterfowl population—victims first of drainage projects and then of the great drought—had fallen to an all-time low. In all of North America, according to best estimates, there remained only about twenty-seven million waterfowl of all species, less than a fifth of the 1900 population.

Acknowledging the crisis, President Roosevelt appointed a special "duck committee," consisting of Aldo Leopold, Ding Darling, and Thomas H. Beck, the editor of *Collier's Weekly*, to investigate the problem and suggest a solution. They quickly came up with the same answer that had been put forward in 1929: waterfowl needed more wetlands for breeding, and as feeding and resting areas during migration. This time, however, immediate steps were taken to solve the problem.

To get the program launched, the president appointed Darling chief of the Bureau of Biological Survey. Darling immediately brought in a dedicated young assistant, J. Clark Salyer II, as head of the Bureau's refuge unit. Salyer was determined to do his utmost for any wildlife species that needed help, and to that end he toured tirelessly from one end of the country to the other, inspecting likely areas that might be acquired as refuges. Many years later Salyer observed, "There's an old Quaker proverb saying that any great humanitarian movement gets started only if someone is concerned. Well, we were all concerned."

Congress did its bit in 1934 by passing a Migratory Bird Hunting Stamp Act, which imposed a tax on licenses for hunting waterfowl and directed the revenue to be used for purchasing refuge lands. Soon the New Deal had battalions of men of the CCC, the Civilian Conservation Corps, hard at work on thirty-two of the newly acquired refuges, as well as in many national forests and parklands. CCC workers built access roads and headquarters buildings, constructed dams and levees, and dug canals and fishponds and reservoirs. They planted trees and food crops for wildlife and performed a host of other vital conservation jobs that had been too long neglected. The CCC served a double purpose: it put idle and hungry men to work, and it helped to conserve the nation's natural resources.

Further government aid for waterfowl came in 1937, when another migratory waterfowl treaty was negotiated with Mexico. That same year Congress passed the Pittman-Robertson Act, imposing a sales tax on sportsmen's ammunition. Ever since, the resulting revenue has been allotted to the individual states for the administration and improvement of state game and wildlife areas.

New Conservation Organizations

Meanwhile, Darling had the Bureau of Biological Survey humming with all sorts of new ideas and projects. One of these was the Cooperative Wildlife Research Unit program, whereby federal wildlife research would be carried on at various land-grant colleges in cooperation with the schools' own wildlife departments. Conservation and game management programs were being organized at a number of colleges and universities, and the science of natural resources and their conservation and management was at last coming into its own.

"In a single decade, conservation has become a profession and a career for hundreds of young technicians," Aldo Leopold was to observe a few years later in his book, *Round River*. "Ill-trained, many of them; intellectually tethered by bureaucratic superiors, most of them; but in dead earnest, nearly all of them."

Along with the developing science of conservation came a host of new organizations, many of them with confusingly similar names, that helped to further the conservation cause. In 1934 the Wilderness Society was organized, dedicated to the proposition "that wilderness is a valuable natural resource that belongs to the people and that its preservation—for educational, scientific, and recreational use—is part of a balanced conservation program essential in the survival of our civilized culture." In 1935 the American Wildlife Institute was founded to "promote and assist in the coordination of the wildlife conservation, restoration, and management work of existing agencies in the Western Hemisphere." It continues today as the North American Wildlife Foundation. That same year saw the launching of Ducks Unlimited, an organization devoted to the preservation and restoration of waterfowl-breeding areas. To date it has purchased or effectively preserved more than a million acres of waterfowl habitat, most of it in Canada.

The next year, 1936, saw the birth of the National Wildlife Federation as an outgrowth of the first North American Wildlife Conference, convened in Washington by Ding Darling. Today the conferences are annual events, and the federation is recognized as one of the largest and most effective conservation organizations in the world.

In 1937 the Wildlife Society was started as an organization for professional wildlife workers. It publishes the *Journal of Wildlife Management*, which from the beginning has been an invaluable reservoir of management techniques and wildlife research.

Through the efforts of these and many other organizations, a vast amount of needed information has been gathered during the past half-century. A great deal has been learned about the host of interrelated factors that influence wildlife survival—often quite different for each species and for each environment. These new facts and new techniques are today coming to the aid of beleaguered wildlife in every state. For a few species, however, they may have come too late.

They left the skyways and the wooded lands,
Forsook the winds, the glory of the sun,
And Time entombed them in his silent sands,
Their race was over and they had not won.

—A. Kulik,
The New York Times
(November 21, 1965)

6

ON THE BRINK

On a wall of the Great Apes House at the Bronx Zoo in New York hangs a mirror. Beside it, for the visitor to read after he has looked at himself, is this sign:

> *You are looking at the most dangerous animal in the world. It alone of all the animals that ever lived can exterminate (and has) entire species of animals.*

How true! Yet man stands apart from his fellow inhabitants of the earth because of his more advanced brain. He alone can learn and profit from the lessons of the past—if he will. And while there is life, there is hope.

A half-century ago, at least five species of American wildlife were already on the brink of extinction. These were the Eskimo curlew, the ivory-billed woodpecker, the black-footed ferret, the California condor, and the whooping crane. The combined living populations of these five may have totaled no more than two hundred remaining individuals at that time. They hung on to survival by the most slender of threads, and it seemed to many conservationists that no matter what we might do to help them in their struggle, we were probably too late.

Today, however, thanks to intensive management programs and techniques, populations of the whooping crane, California condor, and black-footed ferret have all increased very encouragingly. Hopes are now high that they have passed the crisis stage in their long road to recovery. Unhappily, the same thing cannot be said of the Eskimo curlew and the ivory-billed woodpecker. They may have already joined the passenger pigeon and the Carolina parakeet as extinct American birds.

ESKIMO CURLEW
Numenius borealis

A graceful brown shorebird, the Eskimo curlew was almost unbelievably abundant a century ago. Nesting on the arctic tundra of northwest Canada, it migrated eastward to Labrador each fall, then southward in dense flocks off the East Coast of the United States and across the ocean to South America. There it wintered on the pampas of Argentina and Chile. In springtime it traveled a different migration route, northward across South America and the Gulf of Mexico, then on through the prairie states and provinces to its far-north breeding grounds.

Gregarious, it gathered in vast springtime flocks on newly plowed prairie fields to feed on insects. There it was a favorite target of market hunters, who often killed a dozen or more birds with one blast from a muzzle-loading shotgun. Slaughtered by the thousands, the curlews were shipped by the wagonload to market where they often sold for as little as six cents a bird. The curlew was hunted just as avidly during fall migration, when it was so fat from feasting on berries that New Englanders called it "dough-bird." John James Audubon described the flesh as "tender, juicy, and finely flavored."

By 1890 the curlew was already a rare bird. Year after year its numbers dwindled, until one last lonely victim was shot in Labrador in 1932. A few scattered sightings were reported for the next five years. After that, there was nothing at all for seven years.

Then, in the spring of 1945, two curlews were reported to have been sighted at Galveston Island, Texas. A mistake? No one knew, but for the next fourteen years there was no further trace of the species. It almost certainly was extinct.

In 1959, however, a group of experienced ornithologists sighted a lone individual at Galveston Island. A similar sighting was recorded in 1960, and again in 1961. Then two individuals were seen in 1962. The known population had doubled.

In 1963 another Eskimo curlew was reported near Rockport, Texas, during spring migration. That same fall a shorebird shot during fall migration in Barbados, West Indies, was subsequently identified as an Eskimo curlew—the first one recorded as taken by a gunner since 1932. Was this one really the last? Only time will tell.

There have been a number of reported sightings in recent years from Texas, arctic Canada, and other areas, but none of these has been confirmed. In April 1987, Craig Faanes of the U.S. Fish and Wildlife Service claimed to have seen a lone bird along the Platte River in Nebraska. This, together with a flurry of other possible sightings, has led biologists from the United States and Canada to form an Eskimo Curlew Advisory Group to study and correlate such reports.

AMERICAN IVORY-BILLED WOODPECKER
Campephilus principalis principalis

The largest of American woodpeckers, the ivorybill is a striking bird. In both sexes the bill is bone- or ivory-colored and the plumage gleaming black, with large white patches in the wings. The male has a scarlet crest. The slightly smaller pileated woodpecker is sometimes mistaken for the ivorybill. The pileated does not have as much white in its wings, however, and its bill is largely black.

In Colonial days the ivory-billed woodpecker ranged through the cypress swamps and hardwood forests of the southern states, from North Carolina to eastern Texas. Its principal food was wood-boring insects, which it found in the inner bark of mature trees that had recently died. With such specialized requirements, the ivorybill was evidently tied to the virgin forests, and each pair needed a large territory in which to search for food.

Never plentiful, the ivorybill was prized by hunters even in the earliest days, as Audubon noted, "because it is a beautiful bird, and its rich scalp attached to the upper mandible forms an ornament for the war-dress of most of our Indians, or for the shot pouch of our squatters and hunters."

The bird's real downfall, however, came about as the result of extensive logging operations that destroyed the vital hardwood forests on which the species depended for food. By 1885 the ivorybill had disappeared from the northern part of its original range. And thirty years after that, only a tiny remnant population survived in scattered localities in South Carolina, Louisiana, and Florida. By 1925 some ornithologists considered the bird already extinct, until a few specimens were spotted in the Singer Tract in northern Louisiana, and the Santee River Swamp in South Carolina.

With the ivorybill almost gone, the National Audubon Society engaged Dr. James T. Tanner to undertake a detailed life-history study of the bird with the hope that with the information gained enlightened measures could be taken to save the species. At this time there were thought to be no more than twenty-five birds left—a half-dozen or so in the Singer Tract, where Tanner conducted his investigations from 1935 to 1939, and most of the rest evidently in Florida. The forests of the Singer Tract were cut over during World War II, and the birds there disappeared along with the trees.

The Florida population also dwindled after World War II, and after 1950 there were no more confirmed reports from that state. Nearly everyone considered the ivorybill extinct. Rumors of sightings persisted, however, and in both 1961 and 1966 there were more-or-less reliable reports of several ivorybills observed in eastern Texas.

In 1966, first the World Wildlife Fund and then the Bureau of Sport Fisheries and Wildlife contracted with John V. Dennis, a professional ornithologist and woodpecker expert, to search for the species and try to determine whether it had indeed survived or not. Searching the Big Thicket country of eastern Texas during the winter of 1966–67, Dennis reported seeing at least one ivorybill in the Neches River valley, and had found enough evidence of the species to convince him that at least five pairs of the birds were in the area. Without further proof, many ornithologists remained unconvinced.

Others, however, had their hopes rekindled that a few surviving ivorybills might still live in localized wild areas of several states in the deep South. One of these was Dr. George H. Lowery, Jr., a noted ornithologist and director of the Museum of Natural History at Louisiana State University. After examining photographs brought to him by a trusted individual, he stated that on May 22, 1971, "a pair of ivory-billed woodpeckers was seen and photographed somewhere in Louisiana." The birds in the photographs were indeed ivorybills, but other experts claimed that the pictures could have been faked, using a stuffed and mounted bird. Dr. Lowery, however, was convinced they were authentic.

There have been many unconfirmed sightings since, and the search continues. Some ornithologists—Michael Harwood is one—believe that although beetle larvae are the food of choice for the species, the ivorybill will eat other insects, fruit, and nuts when it must. With the destruction of the hardwood forests that were its prime habitat, the ivorybill may have become a nomadic species, moving from place to place and living in a variety of habitats. As evidence, Harwood argues that many of the "possible" sightings of recent years have occurred utterly by chance, in many different places.

The Cuban ivorybill (*C.p. bairdii*), another subspecies, still survives in limited numbers in the mountain forests of eastern Cuba, sighted and confirmed in 1986 by Lester Short, an ornithologist with the American Museum of Natural History, and Cuban scientists.

WHOOPING CRANE
Grus americana

During the last half-century, the whooping crane more than any other species has symbolized the cause of wildlife conservation, the plight of all endangered species in the modern world. Counted down and out more than seventy-five years ago, this splendid bird has fired the imaginations of people everywhere with its courageous struggle to survive against great odds.

Part of the attention it receives is due to its regal appearance. Standing a full five feet tall and weighing about twenty-five pounds, the whooping crane is our largest wading bird. Its plumage is

snowy white, except for black wing tips, a crimson crown, and a dashing black moustache. Mature birds of both sexes are identical.

Never abundant, whooping cranes once ranged widely over interior North America, from Mexico to the arctic regions, and from the Rockies into several eastern states. The northern prairies were its breeding grounds, the coastal marshes along the Gulf of Mexico its favored wintering area.

As the West began to fill up with settlers after the Civil War, the whooping crane's long migration flights through the center of the continent became increasingly hazardous. The big white bird was an almost irresistible target, and many of them were shot. An even more ominous threat was the rate at which man began to take over the species' ages-old nesting grounds. Year after year more of the prairie sloughs were being drained for agriculture and more of the rich prairie wilderness was disappearing under the plow.

The number of cranes nesting in the old haunts dwindled steadily. The last Iowa nest was recorded in 1883, the last in Minnesota in 1889. After 1907, no one was able to find a single whooping crane nest anywhere in the United States. The same could be said for Canada after 1922, when one last nest was reported in Saskatchewan. After that, for more than thirty years, no whooping crane nests were discovered at all. The few surviving whoopers, perhaps thirty or forty birds, were still nesting, but no one knew just where. Sorrowful conservationists made ready to add the whooping crane to the list of extinct birds.

In 1937 the expansion program for waterfowl refuges was in full swing, and a new national wildlife refuge, Aransas, was created on the Texas Gulf Coast near the mouth of the San Antonio River. Covering 47,000 acres of coastal marshes and islands, Aransas was the winter home of the last tiny flock of migrating whooping cranes—some fourteen to eighteen birds, as counted by the newly appointed manager in the spring of 1938.

In addition to these Texas whoopers, there was also a small flock of perhaps a dozen nonmigratory whooping cranes in the White Lake coastal area of Louisiana. These birds were not protected as at Aransas, and all of them disappeared during the next decade.

Prospects did not seem very bright for the Texas whoopers either. Even though the birds were protected at Aransas, conditions were far from ideal. Oil drilling was permitted on parts of the refuge, and extensive dredging operations were being conducted in the Gulf Intracoastal Waterway, which ran through the refuge. Another harassment was the training program for Air Force pilots, which used nearby Matagorda Island for photoflash bombing practice. By 1942 the cranes were at their lowest ebb. Just fifteen birds left Aransas that spring for the long journey to the unknown nesting grounds.

In spite of everything, the flock had increased to twenty-two birds by the end of World War II in 1945. It was at this time that the U.S. Fish and Wildlife Service, the Canadian Wildlife Service, and the National Audubon Society organized the Cooperative Whooping Crane Project—an all-out effort to help the surviving birds in their tenacious struggle.

The primary goals of the project were to find out everything possible about the life history and requirements of the species, and to conduct an intensive search for the unknown nesting grounds. Robert P. Allen, research ornithologist for the National Audubon Society, was soon deeply involved in both of these goals.

Moving to Aransas, he started a life-history study of the birds there. As part of his work, he bred two birds, both captured because they had been injured, in a large enclosure at Aransas. One youngster was hatched but quickly disappeared, presumably a victim of raccoons.

During the next few years the number of whooping cranes fluctuated from a low of twenty-one to a high of twenty-eight. For several years an intensive search had been made for the nesting grounds, with no success. Then, in the summer of 1954, came a lucky break. Canadian fire observers in a small plane spotted a pair of whooping cranes and their young in a remote area of Wood Buffalo National Park in Canada's Northwest Territories. The whoopers' nesting area had been discovered at last.

Robert Allen went into the area himself the next year and made a thorough study of the birds' nesting habits and environment. Wood Buffalo Park is a protected wilderness Eden, home of the last truly wild buffalo in North America and still undisturbed by man. Here the surviving whooping cranes had found the solitude they needed for nesting.

With the goals of the Cooperative Whooping Crane Project largely accomplished, a whooping crane conference was held in 1956 to determine the best way of protecting and preserving the species. No unanimity of opinion existed. On one side were aviculturalist proponents who wanted to capture some of the wild cranes with the aim of starting a captive breeding flock; on the other side were those—National Audubon officials among them—who thought that a species that survived only in captivity was little better off than if it were completely extinct.

In 1957 the big whooping crane news was that Josephine and Crip, a captive pair of whooping cranes at Audubon Park Zoo in New Orleans, had succeeded in hatching two youngsters. With a great deal of human help, these were successfully raised. In 1958 Josephine and Crip raised a third youngster, and the wild birds did their part by bringing nine young back to Aransas that fall. The whooping crane seemed to be on the upswing.

By the spring of 1962 the flock at Aransas totaled thirty-eight wild cranes, and there were seven birds in captivity as well. But now the whooping crane's fortunes took a frightening downward plunge. Ten adult birds were lost from the wild flock that year, and for the first time in years the survivors did not bring a single young one back to Aransas with them in the fall.

But once again the species showed its tenacity and fighting qualities. Seven wild youngsters accompanied their parents back to Aransas in the fall of 1963, and in 1964 a record ten young were produced, bringing the total to forty-two at Aransas.

The U.S. Congress took cognizance of the whooper's courageous struggle in 1965 and voted $350,000 to start an endangered wildlife research program under the auspices of the Bureau of Sport Fisheries and Wildlife. Facilities for threatened species, with whooping cranes at the top of the list, were built at Patuxent Wildlife Research Center in Laurel, Maryland. Dr. Ray C. Erickson was appointed leader of the endangered species facilities, and he immediately instituted an expanded program of keeping and breeding sandhill cranes in captivity, an experimental project that had been started several years earlier at Monte Vista National Wildlife Refuge in Colorado. By working with sandhill cranes, experts might devise methods for raising their close relatives—whooping cranes.

In 1967 developments came thick and fast. The research at Patuxent demonstrated that sandhills could be raised successfully in captivity, and officials felt that it was time to try the same methods with whooping cranes. In May, a long-planned Operation Egg Hunt was conducted in Wood Buffalo Park, in cooperation with the Canadian Wildlife Service. Ernie Kuyt of the Canadian Service located eight whooping crane nests by helicopter, and in June Dr. Erickson and Canadian Wildlife workers gathered six eggs, one each from six different nests. Whooping cranes usually lay two eggs but successfully raise only one youngster each year. The men hoped that if they took only one egg from each nest, the wild cranes would lay another egg and go ahead with their nesting as if nothing had happened.

The six whooping crane eggs that had been collected were sped back to Patuxent by plane. One of the eggs hatched en route, and the newborn young one died. The other five eggs were placed in incubators at Patuxent, and all of them hatched successfully. By November, four of these youngsters had been raised without any complications. A pair of captive whoopers at the San Antonio Zoo hatched and raised a youngster too. The captive flock now numbered a dozen birds—with a very bright breeding potential for the future.

Best of all, November 1967 found forty-eight wild whooping cranes—nine young among them—winging their way back to Aransas. The total now stood at sixty whoopers in all, the highest population in more than half a century!

In a repeat performance of the year before, United States and Canadian wildlife officials removed nine eggs and one newly hatched young bird from ten different nests in Wood Buffalo National Park in late May 1968 and sped them by special jet to the research center at Patuxent. All of the eggs hatched successfully, and by midsummer eight chicks were flourishing—making a total of twenty captive whoopers and an overall population of at least sixty-seven birds.

By 1974 Operation Egg Hunt had yielded a total of fifty eggs and one newly hatched chick for Patuxent, and twenty cranes had been successfully reared from these eggs. In 1976, two pairs of these captive cranes mated and laid eggs, and one second-generation young bird was successfully reared. Subsequent years saw further breeding and rearing of young in the captive flock, some of them by artificial insemination.

In 1975, with the aim of establishing a second wild flock of whooping cranes, fourteen eggs were transported to Grays Lake National Wildlife Refuge in Idaho and placed in the nests of wild greater sandhill cranes from which the original eggs had been removed. Nine young were raised by their foster parents that year at Grays Lake. The same egg-transfer operation continued year after year, until close to forty whooping cranes had been raised at Grays Lake by their foster parents. These whoopers accompany the sandhill cranes each year to their wintering grounds in the Bosque del Apache National Wildlife Refuge in New Mexico. So far, however, none of these whoopers has reproduced. Some aviculturists believe that they have been "imprinted" on their sandhill crane foster parents and will not reproduce with each other. Only time will tell.

By 1990 the world's population of wild and captive whooping cranes totaled at least 210 birds—probably the greatest number in the past century. Twenty-two of the captive flock at Patuxent were transferred to the International Crane Foundation at Baraboo, Wisconsin, to form the nucleus for a second captive flock. The Baraboo Foundation had been started in 1973 by Cornell University graduates George Archibald and Ronald Sucey. Since its beginning, it has bred thirteen of the world's fifteen species of cranes. A second flock of captive whoopers would cut the risk of an epidemic or other natural disaster wiping out all of the captive birds. In 1993 six Patuxent whoopers were sent to the Calgary Zoological Society in Canada to establish a third flock.

In the fall of 1992 the Fish and Wildlife Service announced plans to reintroduce whooping cranes into the Kissimmee Prairie region of south-central Florida, thus starting a third wild flock— this time of nonmigrating whoopers. The flock would be made up of captive-reared birds, and a "soft-release" technique would gradually condition them to life in the wild. According to plan, fourteen young cranes were released in protected prairie habitat in Florida in February 1993. Further releases were to follow.

The population of whooping cranes, both wild and captive, now totals about 250 birds. Judging from the encouraging developments of the past few years, the species has turned an important corner in its precarious struggle for survival.

Wild whoopers still face many dangers, however—hurricanes, hailstorms, collisions with power lines, and shooting by duck hunters who mistake them for snow geese. Also, as Tom Stehn of Aransas Wildlife Refuge warns, the refuge itself—the vital wintering area for the main wild flock—is being threatened by erosion. The heavy ship traffic in the Gulf Intracoastal Waterway causes wakes that over the years have washed away vital habitat for the cranes. The ships transport more than fourteen million tons of petroleum products and toxic chemicals past the Aransas Refuge every year, and a leak or spill could devastate much of the cranes' wintering grounds.

If both the whooping crane and people of goodwill have their way, however, the species will be with us for a long time to come.

BLACK-FOOTED FERRET
Mustela nigripes

In 1851 John James Audubon and John Bachman, then hard at work on the paintings and text for their monumental work on mammals, *The Viviparous Quadrupeds of North America*, were delighted to receive the skin of a weasel-like animal collected near the Platte River, close to Fort Laramie in present-day Wyoming. Recognizing it as a previously unknown species, they were the first to describe the animal known as the black-footed ferret.

About the size of a mink, the ferret had creamy-buff body fur. Its feet and tail tip were black, and so was a broad mask across the eyes. After Audubon and Bachman, twenty-five years were to pass before the species was even reported again. As late as 1896, when mammalogist C. Hart Merriam, chief of the Bureau of Biological Survey, undertook a detailed study of the weasels of North America, there were less than a half-dozen ferret skins available for examination. The black-footed ferret has evidently always been rare.

The original range of the ferret was the Plains country from northern Texas and New Mexico to Montana and North Dakota. The species has nearly always been found in the vicinity of prairie dog towns. Prairie dogs are the ferret's principal food, and their burrows furnish it ready-made shelter.

In their heyday a century ago, prairie dogs were extremely abundant. The naturalist Ernest Thompson Seton estimated that there must have been at least five billion of them. The hordes of rodents competed with livestock for available forage, and for that reason they have been systematically exterminated over vast areas of their former range during the past fifty years or more. Now there are few dog towns left, and prairie dogs themselves are becoming threatened species. With their reduction, the always-rare ferret almost disappeared as well.

An extensive survey conducted by the American Committee for International Wildlife Protection came up with only forty-two reports of black-footed ferrets in the United States for the period 1946 to 1953. These reports indicated perhaps fifty to seventy ferrets in all.

Pitifully few black-footed ferrets were sighted during the next twenty years, and the species was generally assumed to be extinct, or at least past the point of no return. A small population of the animals was discovered in South Dakota in 1964, but by 1974 these too had disappeared. Before this happened, however, Fish and Wildlife Service biologists captured six for captive breeding. Four of these soon died of canine distemper. Several more were captured in 1973, and all of the survivors were taken to the Patuxent Wildlife Research Center at Laurel, Maryland, to attempt a captive breeding program. The lone female of the group twice became pregnant, but all her young either were stillborn or died within several days. By 1978 all the surviving adults had died as well. As far as anyone knew, the species was extinct.

In 1981, however, a dog killed a ferret near Meeteetse, in north-central Wyoming. A subsequent search by wildlife biologists revealed an estimated population of at least 100 ferrets in the area. In 1984 a surprising total of 128 was recorded.

During the next couple of years disaster struck, as canine distemper killed off many of the ferrets and sylvatic plague swept through the prairie dog colonies in the area. Reacting to the crisis, biologists with the Wyoming Fish and Game Department trapped six presumably healthy ferrets in 1985 to start a captive breeding program, but these soon died of distemper. Later that year, six others were captured and taken to breeding facilities that had been prepared at the Sybille Wildlife Research and Conservation Education Unit near Wheatland, in southeast Wyoming.

The frightening die-off of wild ferrets at Meeteetse continued, and by 1986 only about twenty remained. At this point the decision was made to capture all of the survivors. As a result, 1987 saw eighteen black-footed ferrets held in captivity at the Sybille facilities. All were vaccinated against distemper. Several Siberian ferrets, close relatives of the American species, were also held at the station. Since Siberian ferrets breed readily in captivity, biologists considered that they would be useful for research in captive breeding techniques and artificial insemination—research which could then be applied to the native species. That year finally saw two successful litters of black-footed ferrets born and raised in captivity.

In 1988 there were thirteen litters, with a total of thirty-four young. Seven of them were transported to the National Zoo Research Facility at Front Royal, Virginia, and eight more to the Henry Doorly Zoo in Omaha, Nebraska, to form new breeding colonies. A number of other zoos were slated to receive captive breeding populations as well.

By 1991 there were no fewer than 325 black-footed ferrets in captivity, all of them born at Sybille except the first wild-caught specimens. Forty-nine of them were released that fall in south-central Wyoming. Wildlife biologists made plans to release fifty or more ferrets annually for several years, with the aim of establishing self-sustaining wild populations at a number of suitable western sites.

In the summer of 1992 several wild young produced by the released ferrets were spotted, and that fall another ninety-one captive-bred individuals were released in the Shirley Basin of Wyoming.

CALIFORNIA CONDOR
Gymnogyps californianus

Soaring higher and higher on outstretched wings that measure nearly ten feet from tip to tip, a huge vulture scans the ground beneath it for food. Most of the bird's plumage is black, but under each wing is a large white area. The head is bare of feathers, the naked skin orange. Finally spotting the carcass of a deer far below, the bird, a condor, glides down to a landing.

Lucky visitors to this bird's sanctuary in southern California can catch a glimpse of a soaring condor today and be as filled with awe as was early man when he gazed at a great thunderbird thousands of years ago. In prehistoric days, judging from fossil remains, the condor evidently ranged as far east as Florida. But within historic times it has been known only in the West Coast region, where it ranged over mountains and foothill country from Baja California to the Columbia River basin of Washington and Oregon.

During the California Gold Rush, prospectors used the hollow stems of condor quills as handy receptacles for carrying gold dust. Ranchers and homesteaders shot the big vultures for sport or because they thought that condors would attack their stock. By 1860 the birds had been exterminated in the northern part of their range. And by 1910 they were gone everywhere, except for a few survivors in Baja California and about sixty birds in the lower San Joaquin valley of southern California. After a few years the condors in Baja California disappeared too. Only the sixty California condors were left.

What caused the condor to decline? A number of factors seem to have been been at work. For one thing, although condors may live forty years or more, they are very slow breeders. They do not mature until they are six years old, and then each pair nests only every other year, laying one egg on a rocky shelf on a mountainside. Incubation takes about fifty-six days, and the downy and helpless young must be fed and looked after for at least seven months. Any outside interference may break up the nesting, since the birds are shy and easily disturbed.

For another thing, many condors have undoubtedly been killed during the years by eating poisoned bait used in predator control. Many others have been shot by individuals who either are prejudiced against all birds of prey or cannot resist firing at such huge, soaring targets. Despite stories to the contrary, condors feed only on carrion and never attack living prey.

By 1950 most of the condors—still numbering about sixty—were confined to nesting in two small mountainous areas of Los Padres National Forest some seventy miles northwest of Los Angeles. In the late forties Dr. Carl Koford had made a thorough life-history study of the birds there for the National Audubon Society. As one result of this study, the U.S. Forest Service had established the 53,000-acre Sespe Wildlife Range in that area as a condor sanctuary. Another smaller sanctuary was subsequently established some fifty miles to the west.

Through the years the National Audubon Society has been in the forefront of the fight to save the condors. Audubon, together with the National Geographic Society and the University of California, sponsored another study of the birds in 1963 and 1964. This work indicated that, despite all efforts, only about fifty condors were left—a disheartening decrease of about ten individuals in fifteen years.

At this time nine South American condors were captured in the Andes Mountains of Argentina and taken to the Patuxent research center for captive breeding experiments. By 1978 nine young had been successfully raised from eggs laid by these birds, and it had been determined that if the first egg laid by a nesting female was removed, she would lay a second egg, and sometimes a third. Three years later, four of these captive-reared Andean condors were released in the Andes, demonstrating that they could be successfully reconditioned for life in the wild.

By 1978 no more than thirty California condors were left, and a Condor Advisory Panel set up by the American Ornithologists' Union recommended that most of them be captured for a captive breeding program. The condor recovery team set up by the U.S. Fish and Wildlife Service several years before had recommended that at least seven condors be trapped. These, with the addition of one bird that had been abandoned by its parents and taken to the Los Angeles Zoo, would make four captive pairs. Many ardent birders and conservation organizations had bitterly opposed this plan when it was first suggested.

Nevertheless, in 1982 a young wild condor was taken from its nest and transported to the San Diego Wild Animal Park where it was reared. A few months later a second bird was captured and kept for captive breeding. In 1984 four eggs were taken from wild nests and the young raised at the San Diego Zoo. By now there were only fifteen remaining wild birds, including five breeding pairs. Two years later, the Fish and Wildlife Service decided to capture all the surviving birds, about seven of them. The last wild condor was trapped the following year, making twenty-seven captive birds in all.

Soon there were encouraging developments in the captive breeding program. A pair of condors at the San Diego Wild Animal Park hatched an egg in 1988. In 1989, with thirteen condors at San Diego and an equal number at the Los Angeles Zoo, four young were hatched, and the following year eight young were reared from sixteen eggs laid. By fall 1992 the condor population numbered sixty-four individuals, all of them in captivity except two which had been freed in Sespe in January of that year. These had been kept in a cave cage at a high elevation and conditioned to return to the cage for feeding. Six others were scheduled for release in that winter.

Some ornithologists criticized the manipulation of the condor's natural behavior pattern in the release program, charging that these condors were not truly wild birds, even though free to come and go. Others said that condors with changed behavior patterns were better than no condors at all. In any event, hopes for the survival of the California condor, once so dim, are looking brighter every year.

*America today stands poised on a pinnacle of wealth
and power, yet we live in a land of vanishing beauty,
of increasing ugliness, of shrinking open space, and
of an overall environment that is diminished daily by
pollution and noise and blight. This, in brief, is the
quiet conservation crisis of the 1960s.*
—Stewart L. Udall,
The Quiet Crisis

7

THE GROWING ENVIRONMENTAL CRISIS, 1940 to 1963

In December of 1941 the United States suddenly found itself in the midst of the life-and-death struggle of World War II. The nation immediately focused all of its attention on the war effort, and conservation, along with nearly all other civilian interests, took a temporary backseat.

Yet great strides had been made in resource management during the previous eight years, under Roosevelt's New Deal. Like the earlier President Roosevelt, FDR loved the land deeply and believed that stewardship of America's natural resources—land, water, forests, wildlife—was one of his most important duties. In 1936, as he laid the cornerstone of an imposing new building to house the various bureaus of the Department of the Interior, he had voiced this belief: "As I view this serviceable new structure, I like to think of it as symbolical of the Nation's vast resources that we are sworn to protect, and this stone that I am about to lay, as the cornerstone of a conservation policy that will guarantee to future Americans the richness of their heritage."

Roosevelt's secretary of the interior was Harold L. Ickes, a proud, stubborn, and opinionated man who was also as dedicated and effective a conservationist as one could hope to meet. Serving in office until 1946, Ickes labored tirelessly to build up the power and effectiveness of the Department of the Interior, and to make it known as the Department of Conservation. Through the years he tried one maneuver after another to wrest the Forest Service and the Bureau of Biological Survey away from the Department of Agriculture, and the Bureau of Fisheries from the Department of Commerce. He never did gain control of the forest organization, but in 1939 he succeeded at long last in getting the two bureaus of Biological Survey and Fisheries for the Department of the Interior. The following year these two bureaus were merged to form the new Fish and Wildlife Service.

For years the better-publicized and therefore more glamorous Forest Service and National Park Service had consistently up-staged the old Bureau of Biological Survey in the never-ending jockeying for government appropriations and influence. Perhaps the newly formed Fish and Wildlife Service could compete on a more nearly equal footing.

World War II finally ended in the fall of 1945, and under President Harry Truman the nation settled into the uneasy peace of the nuclear age and the cold war. But all too soon the United States found itself in a hot war again, as Communist armies invaded South Korea in 1950. For its next president, the nation turned in 1953 to Dwight D. Eisenhower, its trusted military leader of World War II. Eisenhower was committed to trying everything in his power to end the Korean War—and this he succeeded in doing. A conservative in comparison to the two presidents who preceded him, Eisenhower was also committed to consolidating—not advancing—the social gains of previous years.

His first secretary of the interior was Douglas McKay, a former governor of Oregon. Like many cabinet members in almost any administration, McKay was a political appointee, and had little experience in resource conservation. Hostile to the growing philosophy of federal control of the nation's resources, he tended to back the virtues of private enterprise in exploiting the natural

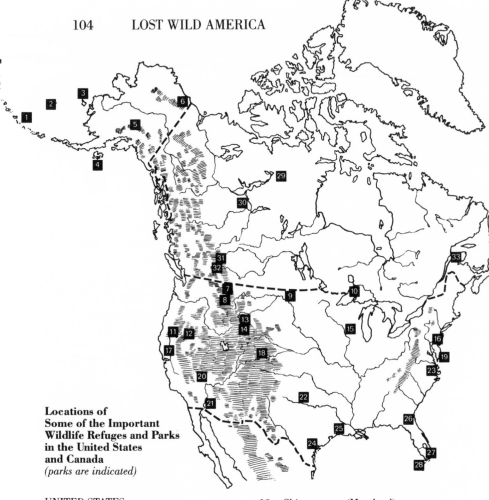

**Locations of
Some of the Important
Wildlife Refuges and Parks
in the United States
and Canada**
(parks are indicated)

UNITED STATES
1 Aleutian Islands (Alaska)
2 Pribilof Islands (Alaska)
3 Nunivak Island (Alaska)
4 Kodiak Island (Alaska)
5 Mt. McKinley National Park (Alaska)
6 Arctic (Alaska)
7 Glacier National Park (Montana)
8 National Bison (Montana)
9 Upper Souris (North Dakota)
   J. Clark Salyer (North Dakota)
10 Isle Royale (Michigan)
11 Lower Klamath (California)
12 Charles Sheldon (Nevada)
13 Yellowstone National Park
    (Wyoming)
14 Grand Teton National Park
    (Wyoming)
    National Elk (Wyoming)
15 Upper Mississippi
    (Illinois, Iowa, Minnesota, Wisconsin)
16 Brigantine (New Jersey)
17 Sacramento (California)
18 Rocky Mountain National Park
    (Colorado)

19 Chincoteague (Maryland)
20 Desert Game (Nevada)
21 Kofa (Arizona)
22 Wichita Mountains (Oklahoma)
23 Mattamuskeet (North Carolina)
24 Aransas (Texas)
25 Sabine (Louisiana)
26 Okefenokee (Georgia)
27 Everglades National Park (Florida)
28 National Key Deer (Florida)

CANADA
29 Thelon Game Sanctuary
    (Northwest Territories)
30 Wood Buffalo Park (Alberta)
31 Banff National Park (Alberta)
    Jasper National Park (Alberta)
32 Glacier National Park
    (British Columbia)
    Kootenay National Park
    (British Columbia)
    Yoho National Park
    (British Columbia)
33 Gaspesian Park (Quebec)

riches of the American earth. During his two-year reign as secretary of the interior, he granted almost as many commercial leases on federal wildlife refuges as had been granted in the whole previous history of the refuge system. Political appointees replaced career officers in the Fish and Wildlife Service, and morale hit a new low. As a result, some of the best-trained wildlife staff resigned.

Conservation: Down and on the Way Out

"Conservation: Down and on the Way Out" was what fiery Bernard DeVoto labeled Douglas McKay's policies in an article in *Harper's* magazine in August 1954. "In a year and a half," DeVoto charged, "the businessmen in office have reversed the conservation policy by which the United States has been working for more than seventy years to substitute wise use of its natural resources in place of reckless destruction for the profit of special corporate interests. . . . Every move in regard to conservation that the administration has made has been against the public interest—which is to say against the future—and in favor of some special private interest."

These were harsh words, and perhaps not entirely fair. In the long history of the abuse of natural resources in the United States, both major parties could check off their moments of glory and their moments of shame. "The worst enemies of wildlife are the Republicans and Democrats," was the way Ding Darling, a Republican working under a Democratic administration, put it, according to author Peter Matthiessen in *Wildlife in America*. His deputy, J. Clark Salyer, expressed it to a colleague even more generally: "*Homo sapiens* is the real problem! Ninety percent of any wildlife management job is controlling man."

McKay retired from office in 1955, and under Fred Seaton, who followed him as secretary of the interior, the resource-management outlook immediately took a turn for the better. In 1956 Congress upgraded the status of wildlife resources by passing the Fish and Wildlife Act, which created an assistant secretary for fish and wildlife in the Department of the Interior. The service was reorganized once again, to form a new U.S. Fish and Wildlife

Service, with both a Bureau of Commercial Fisheries and a Bureau of Sport Fisheries and Wildlife.

Nuclear Fallout

A new era in conservation began in 1961 with the inauguration of John F. Kennedy as president. Like both Roosevelt presidents before him, Kennedy was convinced of the vital importance of resource conservation. As his secretary of the interior he brought in Stewart Udall, under whose vigorous and visionary leadership the people of the United States were made aware as never before of the importance and the problems of conservation.

Surveying the wildlife scene in the early sixties, the average conservationist would have conceded that there was much to be thankful for. Most of the ruthless killing and game hogging was gone for good, and the general public stoutly backed whatever regulations were necessary to protect and conserve wildlife. The federal system of wildlife refuges had been expanded to include more than 300 units, extending from Alaska and the Aleutians to Hawaii and the Florida Keys and including more than twenty-eight million acres. And every year the sciences of ecology and wildlife management were supplying more and more of the detailed knowledge necessary for the protection of various threatened species.

In spite of all of these plusses, America's wildlife was in greater danger in the sixties than ever before in history. And, as might be expected, the responsibility lay directly at man's door. Wildlife, and man himself, were being increasingly threatened by four new dangers: nuclear fallout from bomb tests; the mass use of deadly insecticides; industrial waste and pollution on a huge scale; and a burgeoning human population that was fast taking over and destroying much of the remaining natural environment.

Starting in 1945, the nuclear powers—principally the United States and the Soviet Union but also France, England, and China—had been conducting repeated tests of their suicidal new weapons, and deadly rains of radioactive fallout had repeatedly drifted around the world. As a result, radioactive residue fell on every continent and ocean. What the ultimate effect on life will be, no one can foretell. The only certainty is that it will not be good.

Silent Spring

Much of the world had also been drenched by another kind of deadly fallout since 1945—pesticides. First developed and used in World War II, DDT (dichloro-diphenyl-trichloroethane) and its many deadly chlorinated hydrocarbon derivatives were being increasingly used to combat insect pests throughout the world. They poured "an amazing rain of death upon the surface of the earth," in the words of one ecologist, and their indiscriminate use became one of the most serious threats to wildlife in world history. Dr. George Wallace, an early investigator of the effect of DDT on songbirds, predicted in an address to the 1958 annual convention of the National Audubon Society that, unless the public did something about curbing the use of such poisons, "We shall have been witness, within a single decade, to a greater extermination of animal life than in all the previous years of man's history on earth."

In 1962 the late Rachel Carson voiced the same warning in her famous and controversial book, *Silent Spring*. Pesticide manufacturers and many responsible and sincere scientists immediately decried such views as alarmist, stating in no uncertain terms that such pesticides were necessary and beneficial allies in the human struggle to control disease and produce the crops needed to feed a rapidly growing population. The controversy raged on, even as the evidence of the hydrocarbon compounds' deadly effects on wildlife and mankind itself continued to mount. As with nuclear fallout, the ultimate damage that may occur is unknown. We do know, however, that DDT residue has been found in Antarctic penguins and arctic caribou, and in countless other forms of wildlife between the two ends of the earth.

The dangers inherent in nuclear fallout, pesticides, and the ever-increasing pollution of the environment with toxic industrial wastes were serious enough. But in the 1960s wildlife and man faced the greatest threat of all: the human population explosion.

In 1800 the United States had a population of only about five million. By 1900 it was 75 million, and in the late sixties more than 200 million. In 1992 we numbered nearly 250 million. At the same rate of increase, our population will be more than 300 million by the year 2000. And the human population of the rest of the world has been increasing at the same rate—or faster. From 3.5 billion specimens of *Homo sapiens* ("thinking man") in the 1960s, the world may well be crowded with 8.5 billion by the year 2020. With at least half the world's population already undernourished or, in many regions, facing famine and starvation, try to imagine what conditions will be like in the twenty-first century. Farmlands, forests, wetlands, prairies, any remaining pockets of wild lands—all will eventually be ravaged and destroyed by the ever more frantic efforts to feed and support our struggling descendants.

The Quiet Crisis

In 1963 Secretary Udall's *The Quiet Crisis* was published. His book discussed the increasing rate at which man was fouling and destroying his natural surroundings. With more and more people, the pressures against land and wildlife were becoming greater and greater every year. More land was needed for housing, for factories and airports and superhighways. Urban sprawl engulfed once-rural areas. Wetlands continued to dwindle as they were drained for use as croplands, or filled in for housing developments.

Millions of cars jammed our highways, belching exhaust fumes into the atmosphere as they sped past dreary wastelands of auto junkyards and municipal dumps. Pollution and industrial waste were being spewed into our streams and rivers, and into the air. Atmosphere and water pollution had joined other conditions in creating increasingly serious hazards for all life.

In the process, wildlife was being pushed into smaller and smaller pockets of suitable living space. With such pressures, much of our native wildlife had retreated just about as far as it could go. What then? A zoo, perhaps, for a few survivors. The rest would probably join the passenger pigeon and the dodo in museum cabinets.

But Americans need to be convinced that preserving the environment makes good economic sense as well as social sense; and a real environmental president could even make a solid case that a worldwide drive to preserve the environment offers limitless economic opportunity.

—Tom Wicker,
Audubon magazine

8

POLITICS AND THE ENVIRONMENT, 1963 to 1993

Conservationists had effectively sounded the alarm about our threatened environment, and both the federal government and countless concerned individuals were taking heed. But would the new awareness of the need for action continue to grow and gather strength?

In the fall of 1963 the nation reeled with the tragic news of President Kennedy's assassination. All the bright dreams of "Camelot" and a better life for America and the world dimmed in the shock and disillusionment of the moment. Taking over the reins of government, Lyndon B. Johnson retained Stewart Udall as his secretary of the interior and continued the positive policies of his predecessor.

Under their leadership, a number of important bills designed to protect America's land, waters, air, and wildlife were successfully ushered through Congress. In 1963 the Senate ratified a treaty banning nuclear tests anywhere except underground. That same year millions of fish were killed when industry dumped endrin, a toxic insecticide, into the Mississippi River. Such discharges were subject to abatement under the provisions of the Federal Water Pollution Control Act, and the government took steps to reinforce and strengthen the act's provisions. The Clean Water Restoration Act of 1966, granting aid for pollution abatement studies and programs, was another positive step in helping to clean up our waters. The Wilderness Act of 1964 and the Wild and Scenic River Act of 1968 gave vital protection to millions of acres of unspoiled natural areas.

To spotlight the danger to wildlife from poisons, pesticides, and loss of vital living space, the Bureau of Sport Fisheries and Wildlife in 1964 published a list of threatened American species. In his annual report the next year, Secretary Udall warned that "we are still losing the overall battle to save America's endangered species of fish and wildlife from extinction. . . . Unless the nation as a whole soon becomes aroused over the environmental crisis which threatens these species, we run the risk of further damaging these and other forms of life as well."

The Endangered Species Act

Congress responded in 1966 by passing the Endangered Species Preservation Act, which authorized the secretary of the interior to acquire habitat for endangered species but did little else for their protection. In 1969 Congress passed another measure, the Endangered Species Conservation Act, which increased the allotment for the purchase of vital habitat and also prohibited the import into the United States of any wildlife species under threat of worldwide extinction.

It was not until four years later, however—during the presidency of Richard Nixon—that Congress passed an endangered species law with real teeth in it. This was the Endangered Species Act of 1973, which gave the secretary of the interior broad powers to set up a comprehensive program for the protection, conservation, and propagation of endangered and threatened species of wildlife throughout the United States and its possessions. Under this landmark act, species listed as endangered were those in imminent danger of disappearing throughout their entire range, or a large portion of it. Those listed as threatened were those likely to become endangered in the near future. Killing, taking, or harming any of the listed species, or doing anything that would alter or destroy their critical habitat, was prohibited.

In the years since, the Endangered Species Act has proved to be one of the most vital and valuable wildlife laws ever passed. Enthusiastically supported by conservationists, it has consistently been attacked by industry as too restrictive, "one that costs American jobs." Up for renewal every four years, the Act has at times been strengthened, at other times weakened, depending on which federal administrators or lobbying groups were in control at the moment. The Act has stood the test of time, however, and traces its roots back to the conservation activism of Secretary of the Interior Udall and the strong support President Johnson consistently gave to environmental issues.

Other Environmental Legislation

Near the end of his presidency, Johnson delivered a special message to Congress, emphasizing the importance of passing still other environmental programs and observing that "Conservation's concern now is not only for man's enjoyment—but for man's survival." Under increasing criticism of the social programs of his "Great Society" and his handling of the war in Vietnam, however, he bowed out of the 1968 presidential race. As a result, the fate of many of his proposals was thrust into limbo.

In a closely contested election that fall, Republican Richard Nixon defeated Hubert Humphrey and was inaugurated as the nation's thirty-seventh president in 1969. Nixon was keenly aware of the threats to our environment and the looming population crisis, about which scientist Paul Ehrlich had warned in his 1968 book, *The Population Bomb*. The president delivered a long message to Congress on the subject, and the following year he addressed the General Assembly of the United Nations, declaring that "one of the greatest threats to the well-being of mankind is the burden of excessive population growth. . . . The world is already experiencing a population explosion of unprecedented dimensions. We are, in short, in a rush toward a Malthusian nightmare." Congress responded by establishing a Commission on Population Growth and the American Future.

In 1969 the National Environmental Policy Act (NEPA) was passed, requiring each federal agency to prepare an estimate of the environmental impact before commencing any action which might possibly do harm to the environment. That same year the Council on Environmental Quality (CEQ) was established, as was the Environmental Protection Agency (EPA), with William D. Ruckelshaus as its first administrator.

As his secretary of the interior Nixon had selected Walter Hickel, a former governor of Alaska. Hickel had a hard-nosed reputation as a builder, developer, and friend of big business—a reputation which made many environmentalists wary. But, as secretary of the interior, he offered several welcome surprises: he strengthened and enforced oil pollution policies, blocked the building of a mammoth jetport in the Everglades, banned the use of most toxic pesticides, and strongly supported the Wilderness and Wild and Scenic Rivers acts. After two years in office, however, he was forced to resign and was succeeded by Roger B. Morton.

The First Earth Day—April 22, 1970

The support for environmentalism—"respect for nature"—had been gaining strength steadily since World War II, as ordinary citizens, especially the younger, postwar generation, became aware of what was happening to our land, waters, air, and wildlife as a result of misuse and reckless exploitation. "Environmentalism has roots in conservation: the preservation and careful use of natural resources," wrote Victor Scheffer in his 1991 book *The Shaping of Environmentalism in America.*

The environmental movement reached its greatest height to date on the nation's first "Earth Day," April 22, 1970. On that heady and stimulating first Earth Day, conceived and spearheaded by Wisconsin's Senator Gaylord Nelson, more than twenty million

Americans, from grade-school and preschool youngsters to college students and older citizens of all classes and backgrounds, celebrated the beauties of the earth and the actions needed to safeguard it in rallies and parades at more than fifteen hundred colleges and ten thousand schools in all fifty states. From that date on, the movement gained strength and spawned countless new organizations devoted to promoting programs to preserve the environment and protect our natural resources. As a result, the 1970s came to be known as the environmental decade.

The movement, however, has always been opposed by those who view environmentalism as a threat to jobs and the free-enterprise profit system, and by those who believe that technology alone can solve all of our problems in an increasingly artificial world.

Management of Public Lands

In 1974 President Nixon resigned under the threat of impeachment because of the Watergate scandal, and his vice president, Gerald Ford, took over. During Ford's term of office, Congress passed two acts of vital importance to the future fate of the nation's public lands and the preservation of wildlife habitat. The first of these was the Federal Land Policy and Management Act of 1976—also known as the BLM (Bureau of Land Management) Organic Act—which spelled out how the nation's 337 million acres of public lands would be managed. "The Act was a compromise," asserts Victor Scheffer. "The Senate favored more protection, the House more exploitation." The fate of many wildlife species hung on how the provisions of the law would affect their vital habitat.

That same year Congress passed the National Forest Management Act, which required each of the 120 national forests to prepare a fifty-year management plan—a blueprint for future logging, mining, road building, oil and gas drilling, and other activities.

Democrat Jimmy Carter succeeded to the presidency in 1977 and was quickly embroiled in the politics of conservation versus exploitation. During Carter's first year in office two important acts affecting the environment were passed: the Surface Mining Control and Restoration Act and the Federal Water Pollution Control Act of 1977, dealing with sewage disposal. An oil crisis occurred the next year when countries of the Persian Gulf banned oil exports to the United States. In response, Carter instituted a vigorous fossil fuel energy conservation program, with emphasis on research to develop alternate sources of energy. With just 5 or 6 percent of the world's population, the United States was using a disproportionate percentage of its energy, and demands for power were increasing every year.

In 1978 Carter was faced with another crucial controversy concerning the use and fate of public lands, this time in Alaska. Ever since Alaska had become a state in 1959, the ownership and use of its public land had been disputed by the federal government, the state government, and the Native Americans who had been in Alaska long before it became part of our country. The U.S. House of Representatives finally passed an Alaska Lands Act in 1978—an Act which would have spelled out the divisions of ownership of some 113 million acres of public lands—but a filibuster in the Senate blocked its passage. President Carter then stepped in and asserted his leadership. Acting under the provisions of the BLM Organic Act of 1976 and the Antiquities Act of 1906, he withdrew the Alaska public lands in question from possible state control and protected them either permanently or temporarily. Two years later Congress finally did pass the Alaska Lands Act, in spite of intense opposition from timber, mineral, and oil interests, and Carter signed it in December 1980. To the nation's preserved lands it added over 103 million acres of national parks and monuments, national wildlife refuges, national forests, and national wild and scenic rivers. Carter hailed the act as "the environmental vote of the century."

The Curious Case of the Snail Darter

But the conservation and wildlife news was not all good. When the Endangered Species Act came up for renewal in 1979, it was weakened by an amendment which, in special cases, permitted

Snail Darter

economic considerations to override biological factors in determining the fate of endangered species. This amendment was the result of the designation of the snail darter (*Percina tanasi*), a tiny freshwater fish, as an endangered species. Found only in a very limited habitat, the Little Tennessee River and its tributaries, the endangered snail darter was blocking the completion of construction of the Tellico Dam, a $120 million project of the Tennessee Valley Authority (TVA)—much to the consternation and anger of many developers, industrialists, and politicians. As a Bronx Zoo education specialist, Elaine Grandjean, noted at the time in the New York Zoological Society's magazine, *Animal Kingdom*, "The snail darter symbolized the complex economic, political, biological, and emotional issues that entangle the whole question of what species should be considered endangered and how to protect them from extinction."

The resultant political and legal battle reached all the way to the Supreme Court, which ruled in favor of the snail darter. But that was not the end of the matter. Congress then weakened the Endangered Species Act by an amendment allowing the secretary of the interior to activate a special endangered species committee—the "God Squad"—to consider "whether the benefits of industrial expansion outweigh the benefits of saving the species." When the new "God Squad" was convened, it voted against any exemption for Tellico. Still, the legal and political maneuvering continued. Representative John Duncan of Tennessee unobtrusively added a rider to a routine energy and water appropriations bill, exempting Tellico from the provisions of the Endangered Species Act—or any other law. The House passed the bill, the rider almost unnoticed. When it came before the Senate, however, the exemption for Tellico was at first rejected. A compromise vote of both houses finally permitted the dam construction to go ahead, and President Carter signed the bill. Politics had at last triumphed over the snail darter.

Reaganomics

In the fall of 1980 Ronald Reagan, erstwhile popular Republican governor of California and, before that, star of many Hollywood movies, won the election for the presidency by a landslide over Jimmy Carter. He took office the following year, with Texas oilman George Bush as his vice president. Both were conservative, and both favored economic growth and the welfare of industry and the gross national product over environmental concerns. As his secretary of the interior, Reagan appointed James G. Watt, an even more fervent promoter of big business.

During his first year in office Reagan cut the nation's support of the United Nations' environmental program from $10 million to $2 million (Congress later restored it to $7.85 million). The next year, when the representatives of 119 nations of the world signed the Convention on the Law of the Sea, designed to safeguard and protect the world's oceans from exploitation, the United States refused to sign because of a dispute over the mining of the ocean floor. "The wealth of the ocean bed should be owned as the common heritage of mankind," urged Arvid Parvo, UN ambassador from Malta. But the U.S. delegation, alone of all the nations at the conference, disagreed. In 1984 the president vetoed a measure designed to create an American Conservation Corps, and in 1987 he proposed opening the Arctic National Wildlife Refuge in Alaska to oil exploration.

Secretary of the Interior Watt was even more ardent in pushing anti-environmental measures. Calling environmentalist goals "extremist," he proposed oil drilling along the California coast and the entire outer continental shelf. He supported ranchers, and oil and mineral developers, in their struggle against federal control and protection of public lands. In 1983 he was forced to resign after the Powder River Basin scandal—the leasing of coalmining rights at a loss of between $60 and $130 million to the federal treasury.

In 1989 President Reagan stepped down after two terms as president and was succeeded by George Bush. During Reagan's eight years in office, his anti-environmental stands had so alienated environmentalists that they were actively fighting back by every means available.

George Bush—the "Environmental President"

When George Bush took over the reins of power, he came in as the self-proclaimed "environmental president." His actions, however, soon belied the title, for he almost invariably supported industrial growth and economic development at the expense of the environment. His vice president, Dan Quayle, his chief of staff, John Sununu, and his budget director, Richard Darman, were all hostile to environmentalists. Manuel Lujan, his secretary of the interior, had little use for the Endangered Species Act and, as quoted in *Time*, declared, "I believe that man is at the top of the pecking order. I think God gave us dominion over the creatures, not necessarily to serve us." It is perhaps no coincidence that harmful secondary activities increased on more than half (63 percent) of our nearly 500 national wildlife refuges, totaling about 90 million acres. These included such activities as mining, military exercises, grazing, logging, hunting, and the use of recreational powerboats and off-road vehicles.

During his four years in office, as recorded by Jeremy and Coral Rifkin in their 1992 book, *Voting Green*, President Bush pushed to open the Arctic National Wildlife Refuge to oil development. He consistently based the nation's energy strategy not on conservation but on the opening up of new areas for fossil fuel exploitation. He proposed dropping nearly one third of the nation's remaining wetlands from protection—this despite the fact that between the mid-1970s and mid-1980s, some 2.6 million acres of this vital but dwindling resource went down the drain. He maneuvered to weaken and dismantle the Endangered Species Act which was scheduled to come up for reauthorization in 1993. He presided over what proved to be—after Iraq deliberately sabotaged and torched Kuwait's oil fields—one of the most environmentally destructive wars in history, the Persian Gulf war. And in June 1992, at the Earth Summit in Rio de Janeiro, the United States was the only major country in the world to reject the biodiversity treaty, aimed at conserving animal and plant species.

The "Wise Use" Movement

In most of these anti-environmental policies and positions President Bush was supported by millions of citizens and four hundred or more organizations nationwide that were loosely involved in the "wise use" movement. These ranchers, miners, lumbermen, oilmen, and industrialists were pro-development, and claimed that environmentalists had gone too far in trying to safeguard our natural resources. "Wise users" worked to weaken the Endangered Species Act, the Clean Water Act of 1972, and other laws that hindered or regulated development and land exploitation.

But the environmental movement was strong, and it had the facts to demonstrate that the world was headed for a crisis situation unless all nations—the United States in particular—worked actively to safeguard this fragile spaceship we call Earth.

At the Second World Climate Conference sponsored by the UN in Geneva in 1990, the United States had been singled out as "the great polluter" by some eighty environmental ministers from around the world. With just 5 percent of the world's population, our country in 1992 was using 25 percent of the world's fossil fuel annually, 33 percent of its paper, and 24 percent of its aluminum, according to a report in *Audubon* magazine. In the United States, the report claimed, during his or her lifetime, a typical middle-class child will drive 700,000 miles by auto, using more than 28,000 gallons of gas, and discard about 110,000 pounds of trash. Could the earth sustain such profligate use of resources—such a lifestyle for all the planet's peoples? Hardly.

Although many believed that President Bush was very skillful in conducting America's foreign policy and global strategy, the majority of United States citizens were deeply dissatisfied and mistrustful of his management of our country's economy and domestic policy. In 1992 the United States was wallowing in the depths of a prolonged recession, with many industrial and business failures and resultant high levels of unemployment. The numbers of homeless persons and those on welfare were soaring. At the same time, the cost of food, housing, and health care was spiraling.

Clinton and Gore

Opting for a change, the voters sent Republican Bush down to defeat in November 1992, and elected Democrat Bill Clinton, governor of Arkansas, as our next president. As his running mate, Clinton chose Senator Albert Gore, Jr., of Tennessee. Gore was known as an ardent and avowed environmentalist, and he had long espoused programs that would safeguard our natural resources. His book, *Earth in the Balance: Ecology and the Human Spirit*, had been published in the spring of 1992 and had quickly become a bestseller.

Environmentalists were heartened by the election victory of Clinton and Gore. Now, perhaps, the worldwide ecological crisis would get the attention it desperately needed. President-elect Clinton, they reasoned, would not have picked Gore as his running mate unless he sympathized with Gore's ideas and supported the environmental cause.

As his secretary of the interior, Clinton chose Bruce Babbitt, a former governor of Arizona and president of the League of Conservation Voters. He also appointed Carol Browner, a former senate aide to Senator Gore, as administrator of the Environmental Protection Agency. He backed her appointment with a pledge to press Congress to make the EPA a cabinet department.

The Endangered Species Act, on the books for the past twenty years, was up for reauthorization by Congress in 1993, early in Clinton's administration. It faced a tough challenge from opposition groups representing timber, mining, and grazing interests, who had prepared amendments to weaken the Act. In a speech to the American Mining Conference in February, however, Babbitt strongly defended the ESA, declaring that it was needed to "maintain the biodiversity that supports the life systems of the water, and the land resources and productivity of this country."

That same month Clinton directed Babbitt to cut grazing, timber, mining, and water subsidies on nearly 500 million acres of public lands, in an attempt, as *The New York Times* noted, "to roll back more than a century of practices that have promoted the development of the West at government expense." There were immediate outcries from western senators who opposed the plan. As a result, in an attempt to get his federal budget approved, the president was forced to backtrack from his original position and compromise.

The politics of dealing with the environment was still alive and well. But the federal government, at long last, was sympathetic to the cause of the envionmentalists. Time alone will tell how successful the administration's efforts to protect America's land, waters, and air will be.

"For civilization as a whole," Gore declares in his book, "the faith that is so essential to restore the balance now missing in our relationship to the earth is the faith that we do have a future. We can believe in that future and work to achieve it and preserve it, or we can whirl blindly on, believing as if one day there will be no children to inherit our legacy. The choice is ours; the earth is in the balance."

Unless such a change in attitude does come about, time is running out for countless wildlife species in America and throughout the world, as the following chapters show.

II

POSSIBLE VICTIMS OF THE FUTURE

The hillside stripped of its tree cover, the air ruined by smog, the animal poisoned by indiscriminate use of insecticides—these are other signs pointing straight to a darkened and dangerous future for all living creatures. Unless man, the giant predator, becomes the farsighted conservator of this planet, he may join the whooping crane, the great blue whale and the golden eagle as a threatened species.

The New York Times *editorial*
(January 26, 1966)

Those discordant serenaders, the wolves that howled at evening about the traveller's campfire, have succumbed to arsenic and hushed their savage music. . . . The mountain lion shrinks from the face of man, and even grim "Old Ephraim," the grizzly bear, seeks the seclusion of his dens and caverns.

—Francis Parkman,
The Oregon Trail

9

THE NEVER-ENDING WAR AGAINST THE PREDATORS

Man, the greatest predator of all, has through the ages waged continuous warfare against all other predators. They hunt wild game that man considers his rightful quarry alone. What's worse, they sometimes prey on man's domestic stock, and occasionally they attack even man himself. Little wonder that he has been their sworn enemy since prehistoric times.

Today, only a few of us have any reasons for fearing the depredations of predators. But old prejudices die hard, and a great many people still think of all other meat eaters as "no-good varmints." The farmer hates the fox, without a thought that it helps to keep rabbits, woodchucks, and other wild rodents on his land in check. Many sheepmen seem to think that coyotes eat only lambs, and cattlemen typically consider any bear or wolf or mountain lion within hundreds of miles an immediate menace to their stock. Many hunters still think of any and all predators as outlaws that kill game that belongs—by some divine right—to the human hunter. "A predator," as a Missouri Department of Conservation pamphlet observes, "is any creature that has beaten you to another creature you wanted for yourself."

Such attitudes persist, despite the fact that ever since the Kaibab deer catastrophe of the twenties wildlife researchers have been piling up more and more evidence to show that predators generally do far more good than harm. They act as natural checks on their prey populations, thus helping to keep these animals in balance with the environment.

For years wildlife biologists have been discrediting the widespread system of paying bounties on predators. They consider bounties as mere trapper subsidies, prone to many different types of fraud and double collecting and with little or no discernible benefit in terms of either wildlife balance or agriculture. Yet, as recently as 1960, thirty-three states paid out more than two million dollars in bounties on predators and other "pests."

Besides the bounty system, predators have had to contend with the relentless war the federal government has waged against them for the past seventy-five years or more. In 1915, at the urging of ranchers, the Bureau of Biological Survey began a campaign of killing wolves and coyotes. The activities of this Predator and Rodent Control Section (PARC) of the bureau soon exterminated the wolf from most of its range in the forty-eight states—but not the coyote. Agents of both the Departments of the Interior and Agriculture continue the campaign against this wily and resourceful species to this day.

In 1931 Congress approved an Animal Damage Control Act, giving the Department of Agriculture more money and authority tto increase the war against predators—mountain lions, bears, bobcats, foxes, and coyotes. Today the Animal Damage Control unit has an annual budget of $30 million or more, and more than six hundred employees who shoot, trap, and poison such predators throughout the country. In 1989 alone, government hunters killed 86,502 coyotes, 1,220 bobcats, 7,158 foxes, and 80 wolves. To many critics, these federal operations appear not just as "control when needed" but as an out-and-out campaign of complete extermination. And in many areas the cost of control is a great deal more than the damage alledgedly done by the predator.

Coyotes have always been the main target. "In 1988 the feds alone killed 76,050 coyotes," writer and ecologist Bil Gilbert has observed. "Private citizens, and state and local agencies rubbed out 352,799 more of them. At a conservative estimate, about 20 million coyotes have been 'controlled' in this century." In spite of this, the coyote's overall population has increased, and the species has in recent years extended its range northward to Alaska, southward to Costa Rica, and eastward to New England and Florida.

Yes, the adaptable coyote flourishes, in spite of all the measures the government and people have taken against it. But the story for most of the other predators is very different.

GRAY OR TIMBER WOLF
Canis lupus

We categorize our universally beloved pet, the dog, as "man's best friend." Yet the wolf, the ancestor of our fireside companion, has from time immemorial been hated and feared. It is cast as a vicious killer and villain in countless stories, legends, and songs. For many centuries humans have hunted, trapped, and poisoned it wherever it ranged, and offered bounties for its pelt. Ranchers, stockmen, and sports hunters in particular trumpet its evils as a killer of sheep, cattle, and deer, and even Teddy Roosevelt, an ardent champion of most wildlife, called the wolf "the beast of waste and destruction."

In pioneer days the wolf ranged throughout most of North America, from the arctic regions to central Mexico. By the late 1920s, however, it had been exterminated almost everywhere in the United States south of the Canadian border. Forty years later, only three or four states still boasted tiny remnant populations. Minnesota had perhaps 300 or 400 eastern timber wolves (*C.l. lycaon*) in northern wilderness areas, and Wisconsin had perhaps 100 of them. Michigan, which finally repealed its wolf bounty in 1961, had about twenty-five wolves left in its Upper Peninsula, and about the same number on Isle Royale National Park in Lake Superior.

Wolves first appeared on Isle Royale about 1949, coming across the ice from Ontario and preying on a herd of about 600 moose that lived in the park. Since that time the number of both species on the island has remained remarkably stable. A continuing study of the moose-wolf relationship on Isle Royale by well-known wildlife expert Durward Allen and several of his graduate students at Purdue University—notably David Mech, who continued the study—indicated rather conclusively that the wolves have been a beneficial, limiting control on the moose. Before the arrival of the wolves, Isle Royale suffered an overpopulation of moose in the thirties, with consequent overbrowsing and deterioration of the island's vegetation.

With the passage of the Endangered Species Act of 1973, the wolf was classified as endangered, and protected in the lower forty-eight states. Today, tiny remnant populations continue to survive in Michigan and Wisconsin, but the wolf population in Minnesota has increased to an estimated 1,500 or more. As a result, the wolf has been reclassified in Minnesota as "threatened," and provisions have been made to recompense stockmen for proven losses to wolves. These losses have been remarkably light; the wolves evidently prefer wild prey.

In our Southwest, the Mexican wolf (*C.l. baileyi*) had been exterminated throughout its range in the United States by the 1920s, except for a few isolated lobos. In Mexico it had disappeared everywhere except in the Sierra Madre, where a tiny remnant population survived. In the late 1970s, seven of these Mexican wolves were captured and taken to the Sonora Desert Museum in Arizona, where they were held for captive breeding. Thanks to this successful program, there are now about thirty Mexican wolves in captivity, and several different sites within the wolf's traditional range in Arizona are being considered for eventual release of some of them. In New Mexico, the White Sands Missile Range, chosen a half-century ago as a testing site for the atomic bomb, is also being proposed as a release area. In both states, ranchers and hunters oppose the idea.

The status of the Rocky Mountain wolf (*C.l. irremotus*) has taken a turn for the better in recent years. Early in the century it was completely exterminated throughout its natural range in the forty-eight lower states, but in 1985 a few wolves wandered down into Montana from Canada. Now an estimated sixty to seventy wolves in six different packs have made themselves at home in their old territory in the state. Two or three naturalized wolf packs now live in the Cascades of Washington as well, and there are indications that wolves have also infiltrated northern Idaho.

By 1926 wolves had been exterminated in Yellowstone National Park. The Endangered Species Act, however, requires that the species, historically part of the park's fauna, be reintroduced. In 1991 a House of Representatives vote directed the Fish and Wildlife Service to reintroduce them, and an environmental impact study of such an action is presently under way, with a final report due in 1994. As usual, ranchers and stockmen in the area violently oppose such introduction, while most park visitors and private individuals favor it. Only in time will we know whether such a reintroduction can succeed. Perhaps wolves infiltrating from Canada will solve the issue on their own. In March 1993 the Fish and Wildlife Service reported that a ninety-two-pound animal shot the fall before in the Teton wilderness just south of Yellowstone had been identified through DNA tests as a purebred wolf.

Wolves are still plentiful over much of Canada, with an estimated population of 25,000 or more. They can be hunted legally in most provinces and territories, and 1,500 or more pelts are taken yearly for the fur trade.

Alaska today has a population of perhaps 7,000 wolves— little more than half their numbers in 1980. Here they are still frequently made the scapegoats for any decline of caribou, moose, deer, or mountain sheep populations, despite a great deal of wildlife research to the contrary. Until the law forbade it, wolves were bountied in Alaska, and as late as 1966 our most northern state paid fifty dollars for each of the 1,350 wolves killed there.

In the years following, private "sportsmen" in single-engine planes were permitted to pursue wolves until the animals were exhausted, then land and shoot them. This "land-and-shoot" killing was stopped just two years ago. The state still permits wolf trapping, and the hides sometimes sell for as much as $500 or $600 to the tourist trade.

In November 1992 the Alaska Board of Game voted to start a campaign of killing at least 300 wolves a year over much of Alaska's wilderness from planes and helicopters. The rationale was that this "predator control" would tip the balance in favor of more moose and caribou to delight big-game hunters and tourists. In the two weeks that followed, the Board and Alaska's governor, Walter Hickel, were literally swamped with protests from conservation organizations and with threats of tourist boycotts. As a result, Hickel in early December indefinitely postponed the proposed wolf killing and said that he would invite wolf supporters, wildlife biologists, and conservation groups to Fairbanks in January 1993 for what he termed an "Alaska wolf summit."

RED WOLF
Canis rufus

Intermediate in size between the gray wolf and the coyote, the red wolf once ranged from Florida to Texas and northward as far as Indiana and North Carolina. Occurring in two color phases, rufous and black, it has long since been exterminated through most of its former range. By 1970 it survived in greatly reduced numbers only in the Gulf Coast region of southeastern Texas and southwestern Louisiana.

Although the red wolf had always been considered a distinct species, recent studies by animal geneticists indicate the possibility that it may be merely a genetic strain of coyote, or a gray wolf-coyote hybrid. To this day scientists disagree with one another about the matter. One fact that has not been disputed is that the red wolf in the wild frequently crossbreeds with the coyote. Even when dead it is often confused with its close relative.

In an effort to protect what they considered to be pure strains of red wolf, government scientists began live-trapping the species in Gulf State swamps in 1975. About two dozen were captured and sent to breeding facilities at the Port Defiance Zoo in Tacoma, Washington, in an effort to establish a captive breeding stock. Two years later a mated pair was introduced on Bulls Island, Cape Romain National Wildlife Refuge, South Carolina.

In 1980 the Fish and Wildlife Service declared the red wolf extinct in the wild. The captive population continued to breed, however, and in 1987 eight of these were released in the Alligator River National Wildlife Refuge in North Carolina. Two litters were born to this group in 1990, and other captive-born individuals were subsequently released in the area. In 1990 several pairs were taken to installations in the Great Smoky Mountains National Park in North Carolina and Tennessee for acclimatization and eventual release. Another pair was sent to the St. Vincent refuge in Florida, where they produced a litter of two pups to begin another island propagation project.

In years to come, if these transplants take hold, the red wolf may again inhabit some parts of its original range. On the other hand, the successful and spreading population of coyotes may overwhelm it through hybridization.

KIT AND SWIFT FOXES
Vulpes macrotis and Vulpes velox

Hardly bigger than a house cat, the pretty little kit fox of western deserts and foothills has a tawny coat, huge ears, and a black-tipped tail. Digging its burrows in sandy soil, it seldom appears during the day, but comes out at night to hunt for rodents and other small desert animals. A similar but slightly larger relative, the swift fox, inhabits the high plains from Canada to Mexico.

Attractive and harmless, kit and swift foxes have little of the cunning and resourcefulness that enable such other wild canines as the red fox and coyote to prosper in spite of adversity. For many years, kit and swift foxes have been common victims of poisoned bait put out for rodents and coyotes. As a result, both have been exterminated or become rare over much of their former range.

One form, the San Joaquin kit fox (*V.m. mutica*), is in serious danger of extinction. Found only in California's famed agricultural valley, the San Joaquin kit fox is a victim not only of campaigns to poison rodents, but also of illegal shooting, and the transformation of its natural habitat to cultivated crops.

MOUNTAIN LION
Felis concolor

In primitive days the mountain lion ranged through all the forested and mountainous areas of the New World, from northwestern Canada to the Straits of Magellan. Early settlers knew it by many names: panther, painter, catamount, cougar, American lion, mountain lion, puma, and others. Its principal prey was deer and smaller game, but when it had the chance it sometimes fed on domestic stock as well. Pioneers feared and hated the mountain lion and killed it whenever they could.

Long before 1900 the big, tawny cat had been exterminated nearly everywhere in the East. The last certain record of its presence in Pennsylvania, where it had once been common, was in 1893; the last record for New York, 1900. Soon thereafter the eastern race of the mountain lion (*F.c. cougar*) was considered extinct. A small population of another subspecies, the Florida lion (*F.c. coryi*), still survived in the Everglades and neighboring pockets of wild country.

The western race of the mountain lion (*F.c. hippolestes*) was a fairly common and much hated predator in all the Rocky Mountain and far western states, where it was usually classified as vermin. Many of these states offered bounties, and it was hunted and

trapped relentlessly by ranchers, stockmen, and government hunt-ers. As a result, it gradually disappeared, and by the 1950s and 1960s its population had reached an all-time low—perhaps four or five thousand animals in all.

In subsequent years, state after state withdrew its bounties and reclassified the lion as a game animal, protected from all but regulated and limited hunting. In consequence, the population of the big cat rebounded nearly everywhere, and about 16,000 lions now roam our western states. "Today, every state with lions except Texas regulates the killing of the animal," Maurice Hornocker, the country's leading expert on the big cat, stated in 1992. Hornocker began his mountain lion research in 1963, while he was pursuing his doctoral degree at the University of Idaho, and he has added a great deal to our knowledge of the animal. At present he is conducting long-term research on the lion in New Mexico's San Andres Mountains.

California, which paid bounties on the mountain lion until 1963, designated it as a big game animal in 1970. Seven years later the state gave it complete protection, banning all lion hunting until 1986, when a limited hunt was permitted. In 1990, however, voters approved a law banning all sport-hunting of the species. The state's lion population is now estimated at more than 5,000. There have been livestock losses as a result, and an increasing number of encounters with people.

There is no question that the lion can, on rare occasions, be a threat to human beings. In the hundred years between 1890 and 1990, there have been fifty-eight documented attacks on people, ten of them fatal, throughout the animal's range in North America. Thirty of these attacks occurred in British Columbia, twenty of them on Vancouver Island.

On the other side of the continent, the Florida lion clings to survival, with an estimated population of perhaps forty or fifty animals in Big Cypress Swamp and the Everglades. In 1989 the Department of the Interior created a 30,000 acre national wildlife refuge adjacent to Big Cypress National Preserve to safeguard the panther habitat. Threats to the Florida panther's survival are illegal shooting and car kills. Since 1972 eighteen have been struck down by cars on the highway that cuts through the panther habitat.

Some twenty Florida panthers have been captured and fitted with radio collars in order to monitor their travels and activities. Six Florida kittens were captured in 1991 to form the nucleus of a captive breeding stock for eventual release.

To the north, the eastern mountain lion has been considered extinct for the past century, and the Fish and Wildlife Service so designates it on its endangered and threatened wildlife list. However, there have been many reports in recent years of tawny, long-tailed cats sighted in forested and mountainous regions from New Brunswick to the southern Appalachians. Most mammalogists are now willing to concede the possibility that a few individuals may have survived in remote areas. Given protection, these may in time reoccupy remaining wilderness areas of their former range.

GRIZZLY BEAR
Ursus arctos horribilis

A formidable wilderness monarch, the adult grizzly bear weighs anywhere from 500 to 1,000 pounds, is equipped with fearsome teeth and claws, and has an unpredictable temper. A hump on its shoulders and a concave facial profile give it a distinctive appearance. The shaggy fur varies in color from pale yellow to almost black. It frequently has a grizzly frosting, giving rise to the bear's nickname, "Silvertip."

In the days of Lewis and Clark the grizzly bear ranged over most of western North America, from Alaska to northern Mexico and as far east as the Dakotas and Minnesota. Such a huge and dangerous animal could not be tolerated close to man and his settlements and, wherever they established their farms and homes, western pioneers waged war on grizzlies. Great numbers of the bears were killed during the California Gold Rush, for the fortune seekers found their flesh made good eating and their skins warm bedding.

In the old Southwest, Spanish cowboys, or *vaqueros*, with an urge to live dangerously, sometimes lassoed grizzlies from horseback and captured them alive. With ropes secured around each of its legs, the bear was spread-eagled and immobilized. Then it was quickly trussed up and carried triumphantly to town, where it was often chained to a stout post and subjected to the cruel sport of bearbaiting.

Grizzly Adams, a Massachusetts shoemaker who migrated west about the time of the Gold Rush and set up a hunting camp in the Sierra Nevada of California, had many exciting encounters with grizzlies. A fearless hunter, he killed many; but what is more interesting, he captured and tamed several young cubs. He named his first pet Lady Washington, after the territory where he caught her, and taught her to accompany him on hunting trips, carrying packs on her back. Another pet, Ben Franklin, he affectionately called "the flower of his race, my firmest friend, the boon companion of my after-years." Ben Franklin, indeed, once helped to save Adams's life by tackling a wild grizzly that had attacked his master.

As cattle and sheep populated the West, some grizzlies turned to killing lifestock for food. Stockmen feared and hated them, just as they hated wolves, and hunted them just as relentlessly. Renegade bears sometimes wreaked great damage. One of the most notorious was Old Mose, a Colorado grizzly that terrorized a wide range of mountain country for nearly thirty-five years. Two missing toes identified Old Mose, and during his long reign of destruction he was accused of killing at least 800 head of cattle, numerous horses and sheep, and five men. Wily and cunning, he seemed to lead a phantom life as he eluded hunter after hunter out to collect the $1,000 bounty on his head. In 1904 a hunter with his dogs finally cornered Old Mose and pumped eight bullets into him to vanquish the old desperado.

Harried and hounded on every side, the grizzly bear dwindled, then disappeared, in state after state. California, which pictures the bear on its state flag and seal, lost its last grizzly about 1922. Arizona and New Mexico saw their last specimens about the same time. By the 1930s grizzlies were nearly gone south of the Canadian border. The few that were left were making their last stand in the wild country in and around Yellowstone and Glacier National Parks and in the Sierra Madre of Chihuahua. These Mexican grizzlies vanished in the 1960s.

Today there may be 200 grizzlies in and around Yellowstone National Park, and as many as 500 to 700 in the Glacier National Park ecosystem and northwest Montana. Alone among all the states, Montana permits fourteen grizzlies to be killed yearly, from all causes. Between 1981 and 1991, eighty bears were legally shot in the state.

A handful of grizzlies still roams the Selkirk Mountains of northern Idaho, and some wildlife biologists propose that grizzlies should be reintroduced into the Selway-Bitterroot Wilderness of central Idaho, once prime grizzly country. Scientists believe the habitat would support 200 to 400 bears, but there is bitter opposition to the proposal from ranchers, hunters, residents, and others who enjoy the area for hiking and other recreational activities.

In Canada and Alaska the grizzly population seems to be holding its own. Estimates place anywhere from 11,000 to 18,000 grizzlies in Canada, and perhaps 8,000 to 10,000 grizzlies and big brown bears in Alaska. These northern lands still have vast areas of wilderness, and wilderness is what grizzlies need above all else. Who knows, however, how much wilderness will still be there a century from now?

During most of the 1960s two wildlife biologists, John and Frank Craighead, conducted a detailed life-history study of grizzly bears in the Yellowstone area. They captured over 200 bears, either in baited live traps or by shooting them with a temporarily immobilizing drug. The captured bears were measured, weighed, and marked with ear tags and an identifying tattoo on the skin under the foreleg. Some were fitted with tiny radio transmitters on collars, so their travels could be followed.

For many years the Yellowstone Park grizzlies had been accustomed to foraging for food at open garbage dumps, where tourists gathered to watch them as they fed. In 1968 park officials decided that the bears were becoming too dependent on this source of food, as well as too accustomed to people, and consequently unafraid of them. The practice was abruptly shut down, forcing the bears to hunt for themselves. The Craigheads protested, favoring a more gradual weaning of the bears to a wild subsistence, but to no avail. Some of the bears did continue to search for food near lodges and campsites, and there were a number of serious encounters between people and grizzlies. In 1970 and 1971 the Park Service began to drug troublesome grizzlies and remove them to remote areas, or even to shoot them if they were considered dangerous. More than eighty bears were eliminated in this way during that period.

Today the population of grizzlies in the Yellowstone area seems to be thriving, with fifty-seven known cubs born there in 1990. For many people who enjoy camping and hiking in remote areas of Yellowstone, that means too many grizzlies. They say that any animal posing a threat should be eliminated entirely.

Grizzlies are too dangerous and unpredictable to be tolerated by modern man anywhere except in suitable wilderness country. Yet millions of visitors had streamed through Glacier National Park after its opening in 1910, and there had never been a fatal encounter between human and grizzly in the park until one night early in August 1967. Then, in the space of two hours, grizzlies attacked at two different campsites some twenty miles apart, and two people died from grizzly-inflicted wounds. Since then, there have been several other fatalities and serious injuries resulting from grizzly attacks in both the Glacier and Yellowstone ecosystems.

Such rare but tragic incidents make many people wonder whether grizzlies should not be removed from these parks in the interest of public safety. Yet the fact of the matter is that grizzlies ordinarily cause less trouble than "tame" black bears that have lost their fear of humans—and humans their fear of bears.

Those who know the grizzly best advise the hiker in grizzly country to talk or whistle or make some noise. Let the bear know you're coming; give it a chance to avoid you. If you do that, chances of grizzly trouble are remote.

ALASKA'S BIG BROWN BEARS
Ursus arctos middendorffi **and its relatives**

The big brown bears of coastal Alaska and its islands look very much like the inland grizzlies, but on average they are even larger. Record specimens have weighed as much as 1,600 pounds. Their only rivals as the biggest land carnivores on earth are polar bears.

These big brown bears inhabit coastal areas and islands from Unimak and the Alaska peninsula to northern British Columbia. They seem to be in no present danger, although salmon fishermen grumble at their take of fish and vast lumbering operations threaten some of their wilderness range.

All of the various races of Alaskan brownies are huge, but the Kodiak bear is probably the biggest of them all. Kodiak Island National Wildlife Refuge, 1.8 million acres of wilderness domain on Kodiak and Afognak islands when originally established in 1941, provides more than 90 percent of this giant predator's habitat. Some 1,500 bears roam the refuge, and each year hunters have been allowed to take an allotted number to keep the population in balance.

"Inholdings" have become a problem on the refuge in recent years, for the Alaska Native Claims Settlement Act of 1971 gave native corporations the right to select over four million acres throughout the state—including about 320,000 acres sprinkled through the Kodiak refuge. Many of these inholdings are threatened with development, or sale to private investors, because the native corporations or individuals who own the land cannot afford to pay property taxes.

In 1992 the World Wildlife Fund, together with various Alaskan native organizations and several other environmental organizations, started an active program of helping native owners of inholdings to solve their financial difficulties and preserve the bear habitat in its undeveloped state.

The biological relationships of the Kodiak, Alaska brown bears, and inland grizzlies have never been clearly worked out. Mammalogist C. Hart Merriam made a valiant stab at it in 1918, but after a study of all available skulls and skins of North American grizzlies and brown bears, he came up with the awesome total of eighty-seven named kinds, including no less than seventy-seven distinct species. Such taxonomic hairsplitting accomplished nothing except such total confusion that no one has been able to untangle it satisfactorily to this day. Most modern mammalogists consider that the different races of grizzlies and Alaskan brown bears, as well as the brown bears of Europe and Asia, are members of one globe-encircling species.

POLAR BEAR
Ursus maritimus

"Nanook" is the name by which the Eskimos know the great white bear of the arctic ice fields. In the old days of primitive weapons,

killing a polar bear was considered a great feat, and many an Eskimo lost his life in the attempt. Aggressive and dangerous, an adult male polar bear may measure nine feet in length and weigh about 1,000 pounds. One is said to have weighed 1,728 pounds, making it the heaviest bear of any kind ever recorded.

Polar bears range the ice cap and bleak shores of the northern lands all around the North Pole. They spend much of their lives on the drifting ice fields of the Arctic Ocean, where they pursue their chief prey, the seal. Until civilization invaded their realm, they had little to fear except the killer whale.

Whaling and sealing expeditions came into the Arctic ever more frequently in the nineteenth and twentieth centuries, however, and took an increasing toll of the big white bears. In 1924 Norwegian sealers alone killed 714 polar bears for their pelts. After World War II many Eskimos and Indians of the far north became armed with modern, high-powered repeating rifles, enabling them to kill polar bears much more easily. Under such pressures, Nanook's future well-being was increasingly threatened.

In Alaska, pursuit of the white bear shifted in the 1950s and 1960s from a subsistence need of the Eskimos to the promotion of arctic safaris for trophy hunters. These modern polar bear hunters hired expert guides and traveled by plane. The planes often worked in pairs, flying out over the ice fields until a bear was spotted. Then one plane would land while the other circled to help in case of trouble, or to "herd" the bear into rifle range. Such safaris added hundreds of thousands of dollars to Alaska's economy, but they were hardly sporting propositions.

Alarmed by the polar bear attrition in his state, Senator E.L. Bartlett of Alaska convened a polar bear conference at Fairbanks in 1965. This meeting was attended by representatives from all countries with polar bear populations: the United States, Canada, Denmark (Greenland), Norway, and the USSR. Hunters from these five countries had officially taken about 1,325 polar bears during the previous season. Records showed that the USSR led all in polar bear conservation; since 1953 it had given complete protection to the species, except for a few bears taken by special permit for scientific purposes.

No one at the conference knew how many polar bears there were in the world—estimates varied from 8,000 to 20,000—or how much of a yearly hunting toll the species could stand. For these reasons, Russian delegates urged an immediate five-year moratorium on all polar bear kills. After much discussion, the delegates finally adopted a program whereby each nation concerned should take all necessary steps to conserve the polar bear as an international polar resource.

Since then, polar bear research has been intensified. What's more, a second international conference on the species was held in Switzerland in January 1968, sponsored this time by the International Union for the Conservation of Nature and Natural Resources. At this conference, the IUCN formed a polar bear specialist group which meets periodically and keeps a close watch on what is happening to polar bears throughout the arctic world.

In 1973 another five-nation conference on the polar bear was held in Oslo, Norway, and an international agreement was was reached on polar bear conservation. This went into effect in 1976, and its provisions were much the same as those of 1968. All the nations agreed to continued research on the life history of the polar bear and the practices that threaten its well-being.

Canada has been one of the leaders in polar bear research

since that time. One helicopter pilot, Steve Miller, has partici-pated in the tracking down and tranquilizing of 2,600 bears between 1982 and 1992 to gather research data. Bears are spotted and tracked by helicopter, then shot and immobilized with a drugged dart. Landing, wildlife biologists weigh and measure the bear, equip it with a plastic ear tag for identification, tattoo a number on its upper gums, take blood and hair samples, and sometimes equip it with a radio collar so its travels can be traced.

Each Inuit village in the Canadian Northwest Territories is allotted a quota of polar bears that it can take each year. The villagers reserve the right to sell some or all of their bears to outsiders, usually trophy hunters.

Churchill, Manitoba, a small town on the southwest coast of Hudson Bay, has dubbed itself "the polar bear capital of the world"—and with good reason. Every summer, polar bears—mostly males and young bears—leave the melting ice packs in Hudson Bay in July and come ashore, then travel northward by land. They usually reach the vicinity of Churchill between mid-October and early November, where they are joined by females and their young who have spent the previous winter in denning sites on the western shores of Hudson Bay. For a few exciting and exhilarating weeks the citizens of Churchill welcome the coming of the bears and advise the flocks of tourists to exercise caution and common sense. By late November most of the bears have moved out onto the freezing ice packs and headed northward on their own annual tour.

Today, the estimated world population of polar bears ranges from 20,000 to 40,000, and the species seems to be thriving under international surveillance. Alaska now permits native hunt-ers to kill a few bears each year in traditional hunts. An average of 120 were killed in such hunts each year between 1985 and 1990.

With the international cooperation and research that have been undertaken, there is every reason to believe that the well-being and survival of the polar bear has been assured.

Every creature is better alive than dead, men and moose and pine trees, and he who understands it aright will rather preserve its life than destroy it.
—Henry David Thoreau,
The Maine Woods

10

THE HOOFED MAMMALS

Hoofed animals have always been the quarry the human hunter prized most. The flesh of deer, bison, and antelope tastes better than that of most other animals, and their tanned hides make the best leather. Primitive man used horns and antlers as tools or implements, while modern hunters proudly display them as trophies.

Every fall millions of hunters in the United States take to the woods with high hopes of bagging a deer—and they usually have good reason for their optimism. Some nineteen million white-tailed, mule, and black-tailed deer roam the United States these days, perhaps more than in pioneer times. The cutting of the forests and the flourishing of succulent second-growth browse brought about the increase, along with strict hunting regulations, elimination of predators, and modern wildlife management. The hunters regularly harvest two million or more deer every year. If they didn't, surplus deer would starve as they overpopulated available range.

But what of isolated races of deer on ranges that are strictly limited? What of some of the other hoofed mammals such as caribou, musk-oxen, and bighorn sheep? Some of these are not faring so well.

FLORIDA KEY DEER
Odocoileus virginianus clavium

Smallest of all the many different races of whitetails, the Florida Key deer averages less than thirty inches high at the shoulder and usually weighs between fifty and ninety pounds full-grown— smaller than some breeds of dogs. For many centuries these little deer have ranged the tropical thickets of the Florida Keys, moving from one island to another at will and flourishing in the tangled growth of mangrove, buttonwood, palm tree, and red bay.

But when people began to settle and develop the Keys, the Key deer's fortunes gradually began to fall. Poachers preyed on the deer illegally, jack-lighting them at night with torches or driving them into the water to be taken easily from a boat. Bands of dogs harassed the deer and ran them down. So did the increasing number of cars that traveled U.S. Route 1 from Miami to Key West. By 1949 there were no more than thirty or forty Key

deer left, according to best estimates, and it didn't look as though these could survive for long.

Conservationists everywhere were deeply concerned. In 1951, through the joint efforts of the National Audubon Society, the Boone and Crockett Club, the National Wildlife Federation, and other groups, a warden, Jack Watson, was hired to patrol the principal Key deer areas to protect the animals.

A few years later the federal government finally authorized the creation of a national Key deer refuge on leased land, and the future of the Key deer began to look brighter. By the mid-1970s, under protection and management, the herd had increased to about 400 individuals—a high-water mark. Since then, however, the population has slowly declined, in spite of all efforts to safeguard it, and today it totals an estimated 250 deer, most of them on Big Pine and No Name keys. As the Florida Keys have become increasingly popular as a winter resort for tourists, land prices have skyrocketed and great stretches of deer habitat have vanished, chewed up for housing and commercial development. Many deer—forty-three of them in 1989 alone—are killed by cars. Others fall prey to dogs and poaching. Fawns sometimes drown in drainage ditches.

Land acquisitions to increase the refuge are ongoing, however, and at present the refuge includes about 7,000 acres. Thanks to continued efforts, the survival of the Key deer in limited numbers seems reasonably assured.

BIGHORN OR MOUNTAIN SHEEP
Ovis canadensis

Bighorn sheep were abundant in the foothills and on the slopes of the Rockies when Lewis and Clark passed through their domain in 1805. Lewis marveled at their agility on steep slopes and wrote that "These inaccessible spots secure them from all their enemies." He reckoned without man, however. When prospectors and other adventurous souls invaded the Rockies in force a half century later, they shot great numbers of the wild sheep for food. Bighorn populations began to dwindle, dropping even more when stockmen introduced domestic sheep and cattle that competed with the wild

sheep for food. Bighorns retreated higher and higher into the mountains and eventually disappeared entirely from many areas.

As bighorns became increasingly scarce in the early 1900s, state after state passed strict laws protecting them. Still, widespread poaching continued and the wild sheep frequently faced stiff competition from introduced livestock for water and available browse as well. Bunched together in their mountain retreats, they were increasingly susceptible to parasites, especially the scabies mite and other diseases transmitted by domestic livestock.

Today the white Dall's sheep (*Ovis dalli*) of Alaska and northern Canada, and the bighorns of the Canadian Rockies and our northwestern states, seem to be holding their own—but in much reduced numbers from pioneer days. The Audubon, or Badlands, bighorn (*O.c. auduboni*), a race that once ranged over South Dakota's Black Hills and Badlands, has been completely wiped out. The desert bighorn (*O.c. nelsoni*), a pale-colored form, inhabits isolated mountain ranges of our arid Southwest from Utah and Colorado south to Texas, New Mexico, Arizona, and southern California.

Desert bighorn numbers dwindled alarmingly during the last half of the nineteenth century and the early years of the twentieth. Under government protection and management, the population began to increase in the 1930s. Permanent waterholes and water "guzzlers," which collect and store rainwater, were established in many areas where the desert bighorn had to compete with feral horses and burros and other animals for the vital water supply. In the 1950s state and federal wildlife biologists began a successful program of trapping desert bighorns and transporting them to historic bighorn ranges for restocking. More than 1,500 individual sheep were moved to new areas under this program by 1985.

Today the population of desert bighorns totals more than 15,000. Centers of population include four federal refuges: the Cabeza Prieta and Kofa Game Ranges in southern Arizona; the San Andros National Wildlife Refuge in New Mexico; and the Desert Wildlife Range, about 1.5 million acres of desert and mountains near Las Vegas, Nevada.

In recent years Arizona, Nevada, and Utah have permitted strictly supervised and limited hunting seasons for desert bighorn rams. Big game hunters consider the animal one of America's most prized trophies.

MUSK-OX
Ovibos moschatus

Although the musk-ox's scientific name, *Ovibos*, means "sheep-ox," this shaggy mammal is neither a sheep nor an ox. Its closest relative is the takin, a large, goatlike animal native to the

Himalayas and the mountains of China. Eskimos call the musk-ox *oomingmak*, "the bearded one."

Snow, ice, and frigid cold are its natural environment. When great ice sheets covered much of the northern hemisphere during the Pleistocene, this species ranged as far south as Pennsylvania and Kansas. But when the ice receded the musk-ox followed it back to the Arctic. In those prehistoric days it ranged throughout far-northern regions around the globe.

Admirably adapted to its rugged environment, the musk-ox resembles a small brownish-black ox with long shaggy hair. Bulls weigh from 500 to 900 pounds, cows somewhat less. Both are equipped with broad horns that sweep downward on either side of the head, then hook upward to a sharp tip. Threatened with danger, a musk-ox band forms a circle with calves in the center. The adults face outward, threatening the intruder with a ring of hooked weapons. This defensive tactic works well against wolves and other natural predators but makes it easy for hunters with rifles to shoot the animals, picking them off one by one.

By 1865 the species had been completely exterminated in Alaska and was becoming increasingly scarce everywhere else. But still the slaughter continued. The Hudson's Bay Company alone bought more than fifteen thousand musk-oxen robes between 1862 and 1916.

Canada finally extended complete protection to the musk-ox in 1917, and in 1927 the Thelon Game Sanctuary, northeast of Great Slave Lake, was established as a refuge for the species. By this time there were probably no more than 500 of them left on the North American mainland. Most of the rest of the world's remaining musk-ox population lived on arctic islands farther north and along coastal areas of northern Greenland.

In 1930, with the idea of reestablishing musk-oxen in Alaska, the U.S. government purchased thirty-four Greenland musk-oxen and transported them to an experimental station at the University of Alaska, near Fairbanks. In 1935–36 the herd was taken to Nunivak Island, a national wildlife refuge off the Alaskan coast, and released. There the musk-oxen flourished and their numbers increased between 15 and 20 percent every year until the population totaled 700 or more—too many, along with the reindeer and caribou that are there too, for the limited vegetation on the island to support. In severe winters the musk-oxen suffered severe losses, with as many as 150 dying annually.

As a result, the Fish and Wildlife Service and Alaska's Department of Fish and Game agreed in the 1960s "to maintain a nucleus herd of approximately 500 musk-oxen on Nunivak Wildlife Refuge for restocking and restoring the musk-ox to its traditional range in Alaska." Under this plan 230 animals were shipped from Nunivak to a number of other sites in the state, including nearby Nelson Island, the Arctic National Wildlife Refuge, and the Seward Peninsula. By 1985 the Arctic refuge herd numbered 387 animals and the Seward Peninsula herd about 275. Since 1975 the state has allowed about seventy animals to be killed yearly in native subsistence hunts on Nunivak. In recent years a few permits have also been granted for trophy hunters on Nunivak and the arctic refuge.

A herd of about 100 domesticated musk-oxen is maintained at Palmer, Alaska, for the production of *qiviut*, the thick underwool native weavers and knitters use to make luxury articles of clothing for sale to tourists. Qiviut, which is shed each spring, is said to be as soft as cashmere and as warm as alpaca. This domestic herd got its start through the efforts of a Vermonter, John J. Teale, Jr., who was president of the Institute of Northern Agricultural Research during the 1950s. He demonstrated the feasibility of keeping musk-oxen in captivity on his New England farm. Ten years later, with the cooperation of the University of Alaska, he established the domestic herd at Fairbanks. The herd was eventually transferred to Palmer, where it provides the material for a thriving business.

Under a half-century and more of protection, the Canadian musk-oxen population has rebounded dramatically. The mainland herds now number at least 15,000, and Banks Island, in the Arctic Ocean, is home to an estimated 20,000. The story of the musk-ox in North America during the twentieth century provides wildlife conservation with one of its brightest chapters.

CARIBOU
Rangifer tarandus

Hundreds of thousands strong, the great herds plodded northward every spring to traditional calving and feeding areas on the treeless tundra of Canada's Barren Grounds. From time immemorial northern Indians and Eskimos waited for them in passes and at river crossings, armed and ready to stockpile supplies of caribou meat and hides for the months ahead.

Stocky deer with white manes and broad, snowshoe hooves, caribou get their common name from a Micmac Indian word meaning "shoveler"—evidently because of their habit of pawing through deep snow to get at lichens and other forage. They are unique among all deer in that both sexes have antlers. In primitive days the population of caribou in North America totaled at least several million, and a few naturalists even believe that they rivaled the bison in numbers.

Today all caribou are considered to be races of one cosmopolitan species, which also includes the Old World reindeer. In America there are two main types: the Barren Ground caribou and the woodland caribou. Mammalogists split the former into a number of different races, including two that are usually known simply as Barren Ground caribou (*R.t. groenlandicus* of northern Canada and *R.t. granti* of Alaska). Woodland caribou (*R.t. caribou*) inhabit timbered areas to the south.

At one time woodland caribou roamed the forests of many of our northern states from Maine to Washington. But they have long since disappeared from most of these, victims of overshooting or the destruction of the forested wilderness habitat they need. Before 1963 the last reliable report of caribou in Maine cited fourteen animals observed near Mount Katahdin in 1908. Then, fifty-five years later, the state game department obtained twenty-four caribou from New Brunswick and released them on the slopes of Mount Katahdin in Baxter State Park. Within three years they had all disappeared.

In 1986 a second attempt was made to bring caribou back to Maine, when twenty-seven Newfoundland caribou were shipped to the state and held in enclosures at the University of Maine in Orono, as nursery stock. These caribou bred and seemed to be doing well, and in 1989 a dozen of them were released in Baxter State Park. Within six months most of them were dead, victims of bears, coyotes, or disease. Another twenty were released the following year, with similar results. Discouraged, officials discontinued the attempt to bring caribou back to Maine.

A very few woodland caribou lingered in northern Michigan and Minnesota until the early 1940s when they disappeared completely. A private group, the North Central Caribou Corporation, is presently conducting a feasibility study regarding the reintroduction of caribou into northern Minnesota, bringing animals in from Canada's Slate Islands in Lake Superior.

The only native woodland caribou that have survived south of the Canadian border is a tiny band that wanders down from Canada at irregular intervals into Washington and the Selkirk Mountains of northern Idaho. By 1984 only a couple of dozen of these caribou were left, and they faced a bleak future, due to habitat loss and kills on the highway that cut through the center of their remaining territory.

In an attempt to bolster the herd, two dozen woodland caribou from British Columbia were released in the Selkirks in 1987, two dozen more in 1988, and another two dozen in 1989. It is too soon to forecast the success of these transplants, for there have been some losses. In 1991 the Selkirk herd numbered some fifty to sixty animals.

The great herds of Barren Ground caribou in northern Canada and Alaska have experienced a number of steep ups and downs during the twentieth century. From an estimated total of two million animals in 1900, the Canadian population had fallen to less than 700,000 in 1948–49, when a census was taken. A second census in 1954–55 was even more disturbing, for it tallied only 280,000 animals—a decrease of more than 50 percent in six years. The Canadian Wildlife Service immediately instituted an intensive study to find out what was wrong. Barren Ground caribou have been the mainstay of far-northern natives for thousands of years, and their disappearance would spell disaster for them.

Many people blamed wolves for the decrease, but research showed that these predators actually benefited the herds by culling out weak and disabled animals. Extensive forest fires that destroy their shelter and principal food—slow-growing lichens—work against the caribou. So do lumbering operations in their wintering grounds. Probably the most serious handicap, however, is the fact that for years the caribou have been victims of wasteful overshooting. In 1955, for example, when the total population numbered only 280,000, about 73,000 were shot—more than the annual increase in calves. Modern repeating rifles made the slaughter easy, and many more animals were killed than was necessary. Canada continued to uphold the right of treaty Indians and Eskimos to hunt caribou. With the hope of checking the deer's downward trend, however, the government prohibited the killing of females and calves and abolished sport hunting of the species.

In recent years Canada's herds of Barren Ground caribou have increased in numbers very encouragingly—but there have been some reverses as well. In 1984, for example, some 10,000 to 20,000 migrating caribou were drowned in northern Quebec as they tried to cross a swollen river. Many Cree Indians and other people native to the region blamed a hydroelectric company, Hydro-Quebec, for releasing too much water through one of its many new dams built as part of a massive hydropower complex. The utility, for its part, blamed the disaster on torrential rains.

By 1993 Hydro-Quebec had inundated 4,000 square miles under Phase I of its James Bay master plan. Now it is pressing ahead with plans to build hundreds of other dams on eleven rivers in Quebec. These dams would flood a wilderness of 6,000 square miles, effectively destroying vast areas of wildlife habitat, the culture of the native people, and the traditional migratory routes of the caribou herds. If completed as planned, the Natural Resources Defense Council, a U.S. organization dedicated to protecting America's endangered natural resources, warns, "The entire James Bay hydroelectric project may well cause more ecological damage than any other single development project in American history."

In southern Canada, the numbers of woodland caribou have decreased recently and in many areas have been eliminated completely due to human activities and pressures.

Most of Alaska's main herds experienced encouraging increases in the 1980s. The Western Arctic Herd had suffered a rapid decline during the 1970s, falling from 240,000 animals in 1970 to 60,000 six years later. In the next ten years, however, it largely recovered, with a population of 170,000 in 1987. The Porcupine Herd, which migrates yearly from rangeland in Alaska's Arctic National Wildlife Refuge to wintering areas in arctic Canada, numbered about 180,000 in 1987. In that year the United States and Canada signed a caribou conservation agreement, designed to safeguard and preserve the herd in both countries.

*. . . the moot point is, whether Leviathan can long
endure so wide a chase, and so remorseless a havoc;
whether he must not at last be exterminated from the
waters, and the last whale, like the last man, smoke
his last pipe, and then himself evaporate in the final
puff.*

—Herman Melville,
Moby-Dick; or, the Whale

11

WHALES, VANISHING GIANTS OF THE SEA

By the late 1960s, after centuries of exploitation, whales had
become so scarce that the world's whaling industry was on
the verge of collapse. Only three nations—Norway, Japan, and the
USSR—still engaged in whaling on the high seas. The United
States had withdrawn from the business almost completely. Instead of killing whales, scientists of the U.S. Bureau of Commercial Fisheries marked them by "shooting" numbered ten-inch
projectiles of steel into their blubber. This operation did not harm
the whales. But if a marked whale was killed later and the tube
recovered, it provided scientists with one more bit of information
on whale migration, longevity, or mortality. A far cry from the
mid-nineteenth century, when the United States was indisputably
the foremost whaling nation in the world.

During the Golden Age of Whaling—from about 1825 to
1860—hundreds of square-rigged American ships sailed the seas
in pursuit of the great ocean mammals. New England was the
center of the industry, with Nantucket, New Bedford, New London,
and Mystic the capitals. The sturdy whaling ships were often away

from home port for three or four years at a time as they pursued their quarry. They charted scores of hitherto unknown South Sea Islands in the process and opened the whole Pacific to American trade and influence.

The most prized quarry in those days was the sperm whale, or cachalot, which belongs to the group known as the toothed whales. The fifteen-foot lower jaw of the sperm whale is armed with conical ivory teeth that are used to seize the whale's food, usually giant squid or octopus. With a harpoon in its side, an aroused sperm whale often proved to be a formidable and unpredictable adversary. "A dead whale or a stove boat!" was the motto, and many a whaleboat was splintered and sunk by a mighty sweep of the flukes, or crushed between the huge jaws. Once in a while the whaling ship itself was the victim of an attack. Such was the whaler *Essex*, of Nantucket, which sank in the Pacific in 1820 after being rammed by an infuriated sperm whale.

For the whalers, however, the quest for the great toothed whale was worth the risk. Every sperm whale had a huge reservoir, or hollow, in its head filled with waxy spermaceti, a superior grade of oil that brought the highest prices. Sperm whales were the only species that yielded ambergris too, a potent-smelling, cheesy substance sometimes found in the whale's intestine and highly valued as a fixative for perfumes.

Although the sperm whale was the species hunted most eagerly during the Golden Age, three other kinds of whales were also pursued relentlessly: the right whale, the bowhead, and the gray whale. All of these were comparatively easy to kill, and all except the gray whale had plenty of blubber that could be rendered into oil. Instead of teeth, they had fringed plates of a flexible horny, substance called baleen, or whalebone, which hung in rows from either side of the whale's upper jaw. Whalebone had a variety of commercial uses, from stays in ladies' corsets to the flexible cores of buggy whips.

For the whale itself, the baleen serves as a food strainer. Opening its mouth, a baleen whale rushes through the water and takes in great quantities of plankton, or krill —tiny fish, crustaceans, and other marine organisms. Then the whale closes its mouth and forces the water out through the fringed plates of baleen. These plates hold back the krill, which is swallowed. In this way a big baleen whale may gather a ton or more of food every day.

As the nineteenth century drew to a close, the old style of whaling gradually became obsolete. Kerosene was replacing whale oil as the principal fuel for lamps, and the hunt became less rewarding as populations of sperm whales, right whales, bow-heads, and gray whales were depleted. Three- and four-year whaling voyages were simply not commercially viable anymore. The old whaling fleets dwindled, then disappeared altogether in the early years of the twentieth century.

Whaling in the Twentieth Century

Another style of whaling was coming in, however, based on new methods and equipment. Probably the most important development was the invention of the harpoon gun, which shot a heavy harpoon into the whale by means of an explosive charge. With such weapons mounted on powered boats, whalers could success-fully pursue and kill such whales as the blue, humpback, and finback, which had not been hunted much because they were too swift and unpredictable, had comparatively thin coats of blubber, and usually sank when killed. This last problem was finally solved by pumping air into the victim as soon as it was dispatched.

With the tropical oceans largely depleted of whales, the center of whaling operations shifted to Antarctic waters in the 1920s. The concept of mother, or factory, ships came into vogue at this time too. These huge ships were floating warehouses and industrial plants that could take care of all the processing of the whales and also supply and give comfort to a group of small steamer-whaler or catcher ships, each about 100 to 150 feet long. New methods of processing also brought new uses for whale products. Now the blubber was used in the manufacture of soap, face creams, paint, explosives, and edible fats. The flesh was processed for human consumption—mainly in Japan—or ground up to be used as food for domestic stock and pets, and the skeletons ended up as bone meal and glue.

By the 1930s an average of 40,000 or more whales were being killed in the Antarctic every year. At that rate, the whaling industry was spelling its own doom, for the world's whale populations could not stand up indefinitely to such prolonged attrition. By this time the United States had bowed out of the running as an important whaling nation, and the principal fleets came from Norway, Japan, Great Britain, the Netherlands, and the USSR. And since whaling was an industry of the high seas, with many different nations engaged in it, there was no regulation of the kill. The urgent need for an international whaling treaty was amply demonstrated by the 1937–38 season, when about 55,000 whales were killed worldwide.

The whales gained a much-needed breather during World War II. Afterward, the first serious attempt to regulate the industry was made with the establishment of an International Whaling Commission (IWC) at a meeting in Washington, D.C., in 1946. Under this commission, the signatory nations established their own regulations and catch limits each year. Usually these were all too clearly set with an eye on how many whales *could* be taken, not on how many *should* be. The commission listened to advice from a scientific advisory committee, but until the 1960s it set whale-catch quotas that were higher than those recommended.

In the meantime, advancing techniques increased the odds against the whales. Helicopters flew out from the mother ships to search for whales, and the ships themselves were equipped with sonar gear to trace whale movements underwater, and radar and two-way radio, to make spotting them on the surface easier. Each catcher ship had a powerful harpoon-cannon mounted on a platform at the tip of its bow. The harpoon had a barbed shaft and an explosive head designed to go off inside the whale. Despite the effectiveness of such weapons, the great sea mammals usually died slowly after being mortally wounded.

With these methods, more than 1.6 million whales were killed worldwide between 1925 and 1964. By this time—and little wonder—whales were becoming noticeably scarcer in the Antarctic. As a result, much of the hunting began to shift to the North Pacific. A total of 18,000 whales were killed there in 1963—more than the Antarctic take for the first time in the era of modern whaling.

In 1964–65 there were fifteen full-scale whaling expeditions to the Antarctic. Two years later there were only nine, and of those, the Japanese quit before the end of the season. There were just not enough whales to make it worthwhile to stay.

Soon the only major nations still engaged in whaling on the high seas were Japan, Norway, and the USSR. The North Pacific became a principal whaling area, and every year the whale populations continued to dwindle. A number of species, including the blue whale, the finback, the bowhead, and the humpback, were threatened with imminent extinction.

With that distinct possibility, preservation measures and programs began to appear at last. In 1970 eight kinds of whales were placed on the endangered list by U.S. Secretary of the Interior Walter Hickel, and in 1971 the United States called for a ten-year moratorium on all commercial whale killing. The following year, Congress passed the Marine Mammal Protection Act, which prohibited the taking of any marine mammals by U.S. citizens, except for scientific or educational purposes, or by Eskimos and Indians in traditional subsistence hunts. In 1974 the International Union for the Conservation of Nature and Natural Resources (IUCN) also called for a ten-year moratorium on whale killing. Japan and the Soviet Union still had sizable whaling fleets, however, and in the 1973–74 season nearly 30,000 whales were taken worldwide by these and other whaling nations.

At the International Whaling Commission meeting that year thirteen member nations gave their support to a selective moratorium, to begin in 1976, on endangered species of whales. When the USSR and Japan refused to participate, the United States offered as an alternative a quota system based on the "optimum sustainable yield" for each species. This idea was accepted. Three years later the IWC cut the whale quota by 36 percent, allowing fewer than 18,000 whales to be taken for 1978. Even so, the populations of most whale species were perilously low.

In 1982 the IWC voted a five-year moratorium on *all* commercial whaling, to start in 1986. The moratorium went into effect over the strong objections of Japan, the Soviet Union, and Norway. The Soviet whaling fleet was aging and poorly maintained, however, and in 1987 the Soviets discontinued most of their whale hunting. Japan, Norway, and Iceland continued to kill whales for "scientific research," but the end of large-scale whaling seemed to be in sight.

In 1991 the five-year moratorium on whaling was extended for another year. In retaliation, Iceland withdrew from the IWC and Norway announced that it would resume whaling in 1992. Japan continued its practice of taking several hundred whales yearly, supposedly for research.

Still, with the support of nonwhaling nations worldwide, the future for whales seems brighter today than it has at any other time in this century.

NORTHERN RIGHT WHALE
Eubalaena glacialis

The right whale is so named because it was the "right" kind of whale to hunt in the old days. Rich in oil, it was relatively slow and easy to approach, hadn't much fight, and had the added virtue of floating after being killed. It occurs in two population groups, one in the North Atlantic and the other in the North Pacific.

Another population of right whales, considered by some scientists to be a distinct species, lives in the South Atlantic.

Exploited since the Middle Ages, the North Atlantic population had all but disappeared from European waters by the year 1700. Pursued just as eagerly by American colonists, it became scarce in the western Atlantic during the latter part of the nineteenth century. By 1935 the species was so scarce everywhere that the principal whaling nations agreed to protect it completely from commercial hunting.

Today, after many years of protection, the northern right whale's population is estimated to be only about six hundred: about three hundred in the North Atlantic and perhaps the same number in the North Pacific. When a species has been reduced almost to the vanishing point, as the right whale was, its recovery—*if* it recovers—may take a great many years. One encouraging note is that the species is now being sighted with increasing frequency in New England waters, after a century of absence. It is being studied on its summer feeding grounds in Maine's Bay of Fundy, as well as on its calving grounds, which were discovered off the coast of Florida and Georgia in 1984.

BOWHEAD WHALE
Balaena mysticetus

A close relative of the right whale, the bowhead was pursued just as relentlessly. In Atlantic waters it was almost completely exterminated by the end of the eighteenth century, and a century later its North Pacific population was almost gone as well. In 1935, the principal whaling nations agreed to give it, along with the right whale, complete protection from commercial whaling. It was believed that no more than several thousand bowheads were left at that time. Today, the North Atlantic population is very small, perhaps several hundred, but an estimated 7,800 survive in the waters of the North Pacific and Arctic Oceans.

These surviving Pacific bowheads migrate yearly from wintering grounds in the Bering Sea to summer feeding grounds in the Beaufort Sea off Alaska's northern coast. Oil exploration and drilling are being conducted in these waters today, and such

Bowhead Whale

human activities may very well be in direct conflict with whale well-being.

For centuries the Eskimos of the region have pursued the migrating whales in time-honored hunts, and the IWC permits such traditional subsistence hunts by native peoples. From 1900 to 1970, Alaskan Eskimos, using traditional methods and weapons, killed about a dozen bowheads annually.

In the 1970s, however, the Eskimos began using modern weapons and technology—explosive projectiles, CB radios, snowmobiles, and the like—in pursuit of the whale. As a result the kill increased significantly, and many wounded whales were lost. In 1977, for example, twenty-six bowheads were killed and brought in, while another eighty-two were struck, wounded, and then lost. To limit such attrition, the IWC instituted a quota system. From 1989 to 1991 it ruled that no more than forty-four whales could be struck each year, and no more than forty-one landed.

GRAY WHALE
Eschrichtius robustus

Inhabitants of the Pacific Ocean, gray whales spend the summer months feeding in the Bering Sea area. As winter approaches, they migrate southward toward the coasts of Korea in Asia, and

California in North America. Traveling close to shore off southern California, the whales swim into protected lagoons—especially Scammon Lagoon in Baja California—and there bear their young, breed, and spend the winter.

Exploited throughout the nineteenth century, the species was reduced from an original population of perhaps 24,000 to just several thousand by 1930. The western Pacific (Korean) stock is still thought to be severely depleted, but the eastern Pacific (Californian) stock, fully protected since 1937, has made a very encouraging comeback and is now believed to total about 21,000.

Asserting that the gray whale was no longer in any danger, the National Marine Fisheries Service proposed in 1991 to remove it from the list of endangered species. But conservationists opposed such a move. Even though the gray whale would still be protected from hunting, no special permits would be required for commercial activities such as drilling for oil on or near the whale's migration routes along the California coast if its endangered status were removed.

Cabrillo National Monument on Point Loma, San Diego, is one of the best places in the world to watch whale migrations. From December to February the gray whales steam past this point singly or in small pods, often within a mile or so of shore. Thousands of people climb into the lookout tower there every year to watch the whales go by.

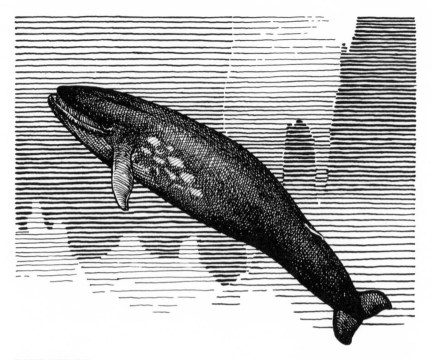

BLUE WHALE
Balaenoptera musculus

The largest mammal that ever lived, the giant blue whale can measure nearly 100 feet long and weigh 130 tons. Once found in all oceans, historically it has been more abundant in Antarctic waters and was little exploited until the modern era of whaling. In this century alone, at least 325,000 blue whales have been killed, with a high of 29,410 taken in the 1930–31 season alone. After that, the yearly take of blue whales tobogganed steadily. In fact, the total population was so small by the 1950s that the annual slaughter, even though severely reduced, was more than the increase by birth. In 1960–61, some 1,700 blue whales were taken by the Antarctic whaling fleets; in 1963–64, only 112; and in 1964–65, just twenty. In 1966–67, when the blue whale was protected in these waters, four were killed. The year before this, however, 594 blue whales were taken by whalers operating from land stations, mostly in Peru and Chile.

Today whaling experts believe that the blue whale population could already be so small that it might have passed the point of no return, even with complete protection. Perhaps 500 still live in Antarctic waters—down from an estimated population of 250,000 in 1920—and a somewhat larger population may survive in the South Pacific and Indian Oceans. No one knows how many there may be in the Northern Hemisphere, but not many. By the end of the present century the greatest animal the world has ever known may be remembered—as are the dinosaurs—only by skeletal remains and replicas in museums.

FIN WHALE
Balaenoptera physalus

The second largest whale, the fin, or finback, sometimes reaches a length of eighty feet. The most common of all the big whales during the era of modern whaling, it has been pursued even more enthusiastically than the blue. From 1947 to 1951 the Antarctic catch was about 18,000 yearly. Then, as the take of blue whales dwindled, the take of fin increased to 25,000 or more each season. Nearly 240,000 fin whales were slaughtered in the single decade from 1950 to 1960. As with the blue whale, the fin population could not stand such slaughter. The annual Antarctic take dropped to less than 14,000 in 1963–64, to about half that total the next year, and to less than 2,500 in 1965–66.

Since the early 1970s the fin has had either partial or complete protection from commercial hunting in most areas, except for very limited takes for so-called "scientific purposes."

Today, fin whales may number as many as 120,000 worldwide, with an Antarctic population of perhaps 10,000.

SPERM WHALE
Physeter macrocephalus

Pursued relentlessly during the nineteenth century, its numbers sharply depleted, the hardy and enduring sperm whale survived. What's more, it rebuilt its population during the twentieth century.

Perhaps its polygamous habits and its movements help to explain its endurance during the era of Antarctic whaling. Bull sperm whales gather harems of cows, and during much of the year herds or pods of the species cruise through tropical waters—bulls, cows, and calves together. For several months each year, however, the bulls take off on a trip to the Antarctic, leaving their mates and offspring in the warmer waters where they have been little hunted until recent years. Some bulls were killed in Antarctic waters, of course, but others lived to return to the Atlantic, Pacific, and Indian Oceans.

In the 1960s, after the center for whaling operations shifted to the North Pacific, the sperm whale was once again hard pressed. Some 20,000 or more were taken annually, and in 1964 the total kill was 29,000. During the 1970s and 1980s, however, the sperm whale gained partial or complete protection in many areas, and today its population worldwide may total nearly two million.

Moby Dick, the most colorful and interesting of all the whales, seems also to have been one of the most persistent. Long may he endure, as in the old whaling song:

> *Oh the rare old Whale, mid storm and gale*
> *In his ocean home will be*
> *A giant in might, where might is right,*
> *And King of the boundless sea.*

It does not seem probable that man, with all his rapacity and all his enginery, will succeed in totally extirpating any saltwater fish, but he has already exterminated at least one marine warm-blooded animal—Steller's sea cow—and the walrus, the sea lion, and other large amphibia, as well as the principal fishing quadrupeds, are in imminent danger of extinction.

—George Perkins Marsh,
Man and Nature

12

OTHER MARINE MAMMALS

Like the great whales, the pinnipeds—seals, sea lions, fur seals, and walruses—were once slaughtered mercilessly by commercial seal hunters worldwide. Those days, fortunately, are largely past, and today few American pinnipeds are commercially exploited to any extent. The northern fur seal is protected by international agreement, and the walrus is usually hunted only by Eskimos and other residents of the far north. Harp and hooded seals, both relatively abundant in American waters, were taken in large numbers until quite recently by commercial seal hunters, but today their take has been sharply reduced.

Our two West Coast sea lions—Steller's and the California species—are no longer exploited for their hides. Some Canadian and Alaskan commercial fishermen consider Steller's sea lion a harmful nuisance, however, claiming that it damages nets and eats salmon and other valuable fish. Under certain circumstances, government regulations allow its destruction when it interferes with fishing operations, although research indicates that its main food consists of fish which are of no commercial value. West Coast fishermen also dislike the common, or harbor, seal for much the same reasons.

Of the other seals found in American waters, the bearded, ringed, and ribbon seals are mainly arctic species. They are locally important to Eskimos but are seldom taken otherwise. The gray seal's center of population is around the British Isles, but there is a population of 20,000 or more in the western Atlantic. Most of these live from the Gulf of St. Lawrence northward, but small colonies inhabit islands off the Maine coast, and a small group hauls up on sandspits off Nantucket Island.

By far the most abundant seal in American waters is the harp, or saddleback, seal (*Phoca groenlandica*), with a population estimated at close to three million in the western Atlantic. This seal gets its common name from the dark harp-like or saddle-like marking on its back. The young are called whitecoats, for at birth they are entirely covered with a soft, thick coat of snowy fur. Sealers once valued this beautiful coat, which had to be taken before the pup was ten days old. After that, the pup started to molt the long white hair and grow a spotted, immature coat.

There are three distinct populations of harp seals, two of them located off the arctic coasts of Europe. The third and largest population lives in arctic waters off Greenland during the summer, then migrates southward each winter to traditional pupping and breeding grounds in the Gulf of St. Lawrence and off the east coast of Newfoundland. Harp seals have been hunted in these waters for over 200 years.

Sealing off the coast of Newfoundland and in the Gulf of St. Lawrence was a rough and risky business in the old days, when ships were often icebound and ran the risk of being crushed by enveloping ice fields. Modern sealing in the 1960s and 1970s was still rugged, but most of the risks were reduced to a minimum. Icebreakers steamed ahead of the sealing vessels to break a path for them, and the ships kept in constant radio contact with individual seal hunters on the ice. Aircraft were used to search out the seal herds, and helicopters ferried men, equipment, and hides back and forth between the floes and the ships. All in all, at least 300,000 seals, most of them whitecoat pups, were taken in these waters every spring. Canada and Norway were the principal harvesters.

In the 1970s Greenpeace, a newly formed conservation organization, began an active campaign to stop the killing of the appealing whitecoat pups, which were simply clubbed to death and immediately stripped of their white coats. Protests grew and spread, and the campaign proved very effective. In 1983 the European Common Market effectively ended the harvest of whitecoats by barring any seal imports, and two years later the commercial killing of the seal pups came to an end. Adult harp seals are still killed in limited numbers in Canada, Greenland, and Norway for their meat and hides, but the take is only a small fraction of what it was twenty-five years ago. Today tourists head for the Magdalen Islands and other nearby areas in the Gulf of St. Lawrence on seal-watching expeditions. There they have the rare pleasure of observing whitecoat pups and their mothers in their natural habitat.

We humans, however, are causing the deaths of countless seals, dolphins, porpoises, and other marine mammals in many ways besides hunting. Worldwide, thousands of dolphins and porpoises die from bacterial infections and other diseases caused by the untreated sewage and industrial wastes we dump into our polluted rivers and coastal waters. Our oceans and shores are becoming increasingly cluttered with discarded nets, plastic, and other debris which entrap and kill untold numbers of sea mammals and birds each year. In 1991 volunteers picked up 2.5 million pounds of trash as they cleaned 3,800 miles of U.S. coastline.

Every year commercial fishing nets cause the deaths of thousands of marine mammals, sea turtles, and birds. Drift nets, sometimes forty or more miles long, ensnare everything down to a depth of thirty feet. According to the Center for Marine Conservation, more than 200,000 ocean mammals are caught accidentally and die in such nets each year. Japan and Korea, the chief offenders, have agreed to discontinue the use of these nets by 1993. Gill nets, used to catch sharks and halibut off the California coast, also ensnare and kill countless sea lions, porpoises, harbor seals, sea otters, and ocean birds.

For the past thirty or forty years the prized yellowfin tuna of the eastern Pacific has been taken commercially by means of purse-seine nets, and this method of fishing has resulted in the deaths of literally millions of dolphins over the years. Purse-nets, up to three-quarters of a mile long and about 200 feet deep, are used to surround schools of tuna. Once the net is in place, its bottom is pursed up, effectively imprisoning the tuna as well as schools of dolphins which frequently travel with the fish.

In the early days of purse-seining for tuna most of the dolphins, as well as the tuna, died when the nets were hauled in. In the 1970s a maneuver called "backing down" was developed whereby careful captains could free most of the entrapped dolphins by jerking the net out from under them without freeing the deeper-swimming tuna. In spite of all efforts and regulations, however, many dolphins still become entangled in the nets and die.

The National Marine Fisheries Service has set up a quota system under which U.S. tuna boats are allowed to kill only a certain number of dolphins, and "countries that want to export tuna products to the U.S. are required to conform to the same kill per ton regulations imposed on the U.S. fleet." In 1989 twenty-nine U.S. tuna boats killed 12,643 dolphins under this system, less than the quota of 20,500 allowed by the NMFS. Ninety-three vessels of other countries killed 84,000 dolphins.

WALRUS
Odobenus rosmarus

In Colonial times the Atlantic walrus (*O.r. rosmarus*) occasionally appeared as far south as the coasts of Maine and Massachusetts, and in the 1630s and 1640s vessels of the Massachusetts Bay Colony made yearly visits to Sable Island off Nova Scotia to kill the "sea horses" for their tusks and oil. Under constant exploitation, the big tusked pinnipeds had retreated far to the north by the end of the eighteenth century.

There, whalers and other commercial hunters continued to hunt them and, in the early days of the twentieth century, they were still plentiful enough that the Hudson's Bay Company was able to export about 175,000 walrus hides in the six-year period between 1925 and 1931. Soon thereafter, the Canadian government restricted the hunt to Eskimos and other permanent residents of the far north. In the old days, the walrus was as important to many Eskimos as the buffalo was to the Plains Indians. The meat and blubber were food for both humans and their sledge dogs; walrus oil was fuel for lamps and stoves; hides served as covering for boats and summer huts; and the ivory of their tusks could be made into tools and other implements or fashioned into carvings for sale or trade.

Today the population of the Atlantic walrus is estimated at about twenty-five thousand in two main groups: north of Russia to eastern Greenland, and from western Greenland to Canada's arctic islands.

The Pacific walrus has longer and less diverging tusks than the Atlantic walrus and is considered a distinct subspecies (*O.r. divergens*). Today it ranges through the Bering Sea and along the coasts of western and northern Alaska to the shores of arctic Siberia. Traditionally hunted by Eskimos as well as by commercial sealers and whale hunters, the population dwindled steadily during the late nineteenth century. In the Pribilof Islands alone, up to 12,000 pounds of ivory were taken yearly before 1890. By the 1950s, no more than an estimated 40,000 to 50,000 walruses remained.

Protected from large-scale commercial hunting for most of

Walrus

the time since then, the Pacific walrus has rebounded very encouragingly. Population surveys and other research activities are undertaken on a regular basis in cooperation with the Russians. In a 1985 census, the Fish and Wildlife Service counted a total of 234,000 walruses. Alaskan and Siberian Eskimos and Soviet harvesters killed 10,000 to 12,000 of them that year in regulated subsistence hunts.

GUADALUPE FUR SEAL
Arctocephalus townsendi

Somewhat smaller than the California sea lion and with a more pointed muzzle, the Guadalupe fur seal originally ranged the coasts of southern and Baja California and could be found year-round on such islands as the Farallons, off San Francisco, and Guadalupe, off Baja California. No one knows how many of them there once were, but the population must have been large. In 1810 alone, eight men are said to have killed a total of 33,740 fur seals on the Farallon Islands. The Russians maintained a sealing station on these islands until about 1840, and every year they took a big harvest of skins. Eventually there were so few Guadalupe fur seals left that it was no longer profitable to hunt them.

When Dr. Charles H. Townsend of the American Museum of Natural History visited Guadalupe in 1892, his party saw only seven fur seals. Two years later, one specimen was taken off Baja California. For the next sixty years the species was considered extinct, or so close to it that the question was academic. In 1954, however, fourteen fur seals were sighted on Guadalupe, and two years later ninety-two of them were observed. Protected, the population now numbers about 1,600.

CARIBBEAN AND HAWAIIAN MONK SEALS
Monachus tropicalis and *Monachus schauinslandi*

A warm-water species with a gray-brown back and pale- yellowish underparts, the Caribbean monk seal, unlike some other seals, never occurred in huge aggregations. It was usually taken wherever sealers discovered it, and it was a rare animal as early as 1850. In 1886 a small herd was spotted on the Triangle Keys off Yucatan and forty-nine of them killed. A few more were discovered and killed in the same area in 1911. Dr. William T. Hornaday, one of the crusading conservationists of that time, believed that the species had been wiped out.

Eleven years later one lone seal was seen off Key West, but after that there were no official reports of the Caribbean monk seal for the next quarter-century. In 1949, however, two individuals were reported in the vicinity of southern Jamaica. Since then, despite hearsay and several unverified reports of sightings by fishermen, the species has been considered extinct.

A close relative, the Hawaiian monk seal, is in somewhat better shape. Hauling up on the atolls of the Leeward chain, north and west of the Hawaiian Islands, this Pacific species was also on the way out a century ago. Under protection it has started the slow road back from extinction and today may number as many as 1,500 animals. Most of these live within the boundaries of the Hawaiian Islands and Midway Atoll National Wildlife Refuges.

FLORIDA MANATEE
Trichechus manatus latirostris

With drooping lips and bristly jowls, paddle-like front limbs, and a broad, platter-like tail, the manatee is a distinctive-looking beast. Along with the Old World dugong and the extinct Steller's sea cow, it belongs to the order *Sirenia*, or "sirens," named for a supposed resemblance to the legendary mermaid. But sailors would have to have been separated from feminine companionship for a long time before they could mistake a manatee's face and rough dark hide for that of a mermaid.

At one time the Florida manatee, a northern race of the West Indian manatee, ranged from the coastal lagoons and brackish rivers of North Carolina to the Texas Gulf Coast. Other races range the Caribbean and coastal areas of northern and eastern South America. Feeding exclusively on aquatic vegetation, the manatee is an inoffensive creature, very easy to capture or kill once spotted. Unfortunately for its survival, it has flesh that tastes like fresh veal. Indians, explorers, and settlers all killed it so enthusiastically for its meat and oil that by the early years of the twentieth century it had disappeared over much of its range and was rare nearly everywhere. Florida passed a law to protect it as long ago as 1907.

During the warm summer months many Florida manatees roam the waters of the Gulf of Mexico and the Atlantic coast. As cold weather approaches, they seek warm-water retreats in shallow, slow-moving rivers and warm springs that have constant temperatures above 68 degrees F. Some gather in areas where the waters are artificially warmed by the effluent from power plants and factories. The total population is estimated at about 1,200 animals. Every year more than 100 of them are found dead from all causes—216 in 1990 alone. Such a high rate of attrition makes some wildlife biologists believe they will all be gone by the year 2000.

Cold weather always poses a serious hazard for the manatee, and a record cold spell from December 1989 to January 1990 killed at least forty-nine. Collisions with powerboats and propeller injuries take an even higher toll. About 85 percent of all manatees bear propeller scars.

In 1978 the state passed a Florida Manatee Sanctuary Act, designating the entire state a refuge for the species and regulating powerboat speeds in many areas. Even so, the danger increases every year. Today, more than 700,000 boats are registered in Florida, up from about 100,000 in the early 1960s, and an additional 300,000 transient boats visit the state's waters every year. With a constantly increasing human population in Florida and a consequent loss of natural habitat, the future of the Florida manatee does not seem bright.

But if goodwill, research, and education succeed, the manatee will survive. Boats are specifically barred from a number of areas where manatees live. One of these is Homosassa Springs Wildlife Park, north of Tampa, operated by the Florida Department of Natural Resources. Manatees live here year round, and are successfully breeding.

For a number of years Miami Seaquarium and Sea World of Florida's manatee-rehabilitation facilities have rescued sick and wounded manatees and rehabilitated them for eventual release back into the wild. To date, at least eight manatees have been born in captivity at the Seaquarium. In 1992 the Lowery Park Zoo in Tampa opened a new multimillion-dollar aquatic exhibit for the manatee, complete with large display pools, a manatee hospital, rehabilitation pools, and a research lab.

There be three things which are too wonderful for me,
Yea, four which I know not:
The way of an eagle in the air;
The way of a serpent upon a rock;
The way of a ship in the midst of the sea;
And the way of a man with a maid.

—Proverbs 30:18–19

13

HARD-PRESSED BIRDS OF PREY AND PARROTS

Blue Mountain, in Schuylkill County, Pennsylvania, is one of the best places in the nation to observe the migration of birds of prey. Sometimes singly, sometimes in loose flights of several dozen or more, broad-winged hawks heading for wintering areas to the south ride the thermal currents of September between the mountains. In October, swift falcons sweep by, sometimes within a few feet of the summit of the mountain, and then a great eagle soars overhead in regal majesty. Birds of prey have been using this route for thousands of years, and in the first third of this century it was a favorite spot for gunners too. They would gather at the summit on brisk fall days to engage in a favorite pastime—hawk shooting. This was great fun—and to some minds it was also providing protection for other wildlife too. After all, hawks and eagles were the feathered equivalents of wolves, foxes, and other "varmints," weren't they?

But in the early thirties a more enlightened attitude was

beginning to come to the fore. For years scientists had been trying to pigeonhole birds of prey into "good" and "bad" species, according to whether they did more economic good than harm. Aldo Leopold, however, scorned such reasoning. "The basic issue transcends economics," he stated categorically. "The basic question is whether a hawkless, owlless countryside is a livable countryside for Americans with eyes to see and ears to hear. Hawks and owls are a part of the land mechanism."

A lot of people agreed with him. One of these was Rosalie Edge, a militant conservationist, who decided in 1934 to do something about the slaughter of hawks and other birds of prey at Blue Mountain. She obtained a lease of the mountain for one year, with an option to buy, and secured the services of Maurice Broun, an ardent young ornithologist, as a warden to protect the flights of migrating birds. In this way the world-famous Hawk Mountain Sanctuary was started.

As related in his book *Hawks Aloft*, Broun had some pretty tense moments during the first several years as he was repeatedly confronted by indignant and defiant hunters bent on a day's sport of hawk shooting. But gradually the idea that he was there to protect the hawks—and meant to do so— took hold. More and more people, some of the former hawk shooters among them, came to watch the big predatory birds sweeping overhead.

Hawks and eagles are still frequently victims of trigger-happy hunters, but modern wildlife research has demonstrated their true value in nature's overall scheme. Today, the vast majority of people who travel to the mountaintops during hawk migrations come only to observe and admire the grace and beauty of the birds in the air. Most of the species are now protected by law, whereas they were once bountied in many states.

In spite of the changed viewpoint, many birds of prey are becoming increasingly scarce across the land. Shooting is still one of the factors working against them. Even more serious, however, is the effect upon the hawks of mankind's changing the land and tampering with it—not only with ax and saw and bulldozer but also with pesticides and poisons.

BALD EAGLE
Haliaeetus leucocephalus

A regal-looking bird with a wingspread of close to seven feet, the mature bald eagle has dark brown body plumage and a contrasting white head and tail. Long-lived, it usually mates for life and uses the same bulky nest year after year. A fish eater, it is more often than not a scavenger as well, feeding on dead fish cast ashore instead of hunting for live prey.

Once the bald eagle ranged over most of the continent and was fairly common in many areas, especially along the Pacific coasts of Alaska and Canada, where it gathered to feed on dead and dying salmon after the spawning runs. From 1917 to 1952 the territorial government of Alaska paid bounties on eagles and killed off about 128,000 of them during that period. Since then, the eagle has been protected in our far-northern state, which today boasts a breeding population of an estimated 15,000 pairs of bald eagles.

In the lower forty-eight states, however, the numbers of bald eagles declined steadily during the first seventy years of the twentieth century, for a number of reasons. Young, all-brown birds—it takes four or five years before they develop the white head and tail—were frequently shot as big "chicken hawks." Lumbering operations often destroyed nest trees or so disturbed the breeding birds that they abandoned their nests. By 1940, the eagle population in the lower forty-eight was so reduced that the federal government stepped in with laws to protect its national emblem. In spite of this, the decline continued.

The traditional nesting centers for bald eagles south of Canada are Maine, the Great Lakes states, the Chesapeake Bay area, and Florida. It was in Florida that a retired businessman, Charles L. Broley, began to band nesting southern bald eagles as a hobby in 1943. From 1947 onward he noted that the eagles' nesting success was declining rather alarmingly, and soon other ornithologists began to observe the same trend. By 1963 only 230 active nests could be located in the whole U.S. Atlantic coast region, including Florida. And many of these had clutches of eggs that never hatched. Something was very wrong with the eagle population, something even more serious than attrition by shooting and destruction of nesting areas.

The principal cause of the trouble was the widespread use of DDT and other hydrocarbon pesticides in the years after World War II. Spread over great areas to combat agricultural and forest pests, such poisons were ingested by insects and microorganisms at the base of the food pyramid. These in turn were eaten by fish and larger animals, and the hydrocarbon residue collected with ever-increasing concentration in their tissues. Sometimes it killed the animal outright; sometimes it merely rendered it sterile, or acted to prevent or reduce the production of calcium carbonate, the material from which eggshell is made. This dangerous accumulation was taking place in eagles and many other birds of prey, for laboratory tests showed such residue in both their bodies and their eggs.

Noting the bald eagle's plight, the National Audubon Society in 1960 began a long-range study to find out what could be done to help the species, which by then was in desperate straits. A census conducted early in 1968 could find only 2,772 bald eagles in all of the United States south of Canada. Recognizing the seriousness of the situation, the National Audubon Society, the Department of the Interior, and many state and private organizations joined in a national campaign of publicity and education to save the surviving eagles.

Finally conceding the harmful effects of DDT, the federal government restricted its use in 1969 and three years later banned its use entirely in the United States. Many states had long since lost all of their breeding eagles. Soon, an imaginative and successful program was instituted to restock them.

In 1974 a couple of eaglets were transferred from nests in Wisconsin to nests in Maine. Here they were fledged by foster parents that had been unsuccessful in hatching their own eggs. The next year four Wisconsin eagle eggs were put into Maine nests, and the eggs they replaced were incubated artificially at the Patuxent Wildlife Research Center. These young in turn were placed in Maine nests and fledged by foster parents.

Soon young eagles were being introduced into many other areas in this way. "Hacking," a technique first developed by falconers, was also used. The fledgling eagles were "hacked" by placing them in artificial nests on towers built in areas where the eagles were to be released. They were fed and cared for by human attendants who were hidden from the fledglings by curtains. When the birds were ready to start flying, the bars that had caged them were removed and the young were free to make experimental flights and begin to learn how to hunt food for themselves. They returned to the tower to be fed until they were ready to take off permanently on their own. This technique has been used in many areas, and so far more than 1,000 young bald eagles have been returned to the wild in this way.

Such programs to restore the bald eagle have been so successful, in fact, that the Fish and Wildlife Service considered changing the bird's status from "endangered" to "threatened" in 1990. Many conservationists considered the proposal premature. The species was still missing or rare in parts of its former range, and many were still being shot or poisoned illegally, especially in the western states.

Overall, however, the future for the bald eagle looks bright. The 1991 winter census counted 13,574 eagles in the lower forty-eight states (some of these were migrant Alaskan birds), and a breeding census later that year listed more than 3,000 nesting pairs south of Canada.

AMERICAN GOLDEN EAGLE
Aquila chrysaetos canadensis

Eyes blazing with fierce courage, deep-brown plumage glinting with dull gold on the crown and nape, the golden eagle is one of the world's most beautiful and majestic birds of prey. One of the bestknown as well, it ranges across North America, Europe, North Africa, and Asia. In the United States its center of population is the mountainous West. Occasionally it eats carrion, but it usually captures live prey.

Sheepmen call the golden eagle a lamb killer, and indeed it does occasionally feed on a dead lamb or kill a weak one. Extensive studies carried out years ago by the Montana Cooperative Wildlife Research Unit, however, indicated that jackrabbits accounted for 37 percent of its food, cottontails another third, while the remainder included a number of other small animals. No eagles were observed attacking sheep during the several years of the study. Subsequent research has generally upheld these findings.

But sheep raisers have considered the golden eagle an enemy for a long time, and it is hard to convince them otherwise. Many golden eagles winter in the Southwest, and stockmen in this region have waged war on them for years, killing many thousands of the birds, especially from 1940 to 1962. Shooting from his plane, one Texas pilot alone killed over 4,800 eagles in six years. Under such pressure, golden eagles dwindled rapidly until alarmed conservationists in 1962 goaded Congress into protecting the species. By this time its U.S. population was no more than 10,000, and perhaps as low as 3,000.

Today the golden eagle's population, estimated at 100,000 to 200,000 birds, is relatively stable. Despite legal protection, however, many are still poisoned or shot every year under the guise of protecting sheep or other domestic stock.

PEREGRINE FALCON
Falco peregrinus

A beautiful, worldwide species, the peregrine falcon, also known in America as the duck hawk, was a resident breeder in most of our northeastern states before World War II. Some even nested on towering New York skyscrapers. During the 1950s and 1960s, however, it disappeared as a resident bird everywhere south of the St. Lawrence River—another victim of the widespread use of chlorinated hydrocarbon pesticides.

But, as with the bald eagle, new knowledge and new techniques that were perfected in the 1970s have resulted in a dramatic comeback for the peregrine falcon. In 1972 Tom Cade of Cornell University's Laboratory of Ornithology first raised young falcons hatched from eggs fertilized by artificial insemination. That same year Heinz Meng, another Cornell graduate, then on the faculty of New Paltz State Teachers College in New York, bred captive peregrines by natural means and raised three chicks. In 1973 three pairs of captive peregrines at Cornell raised twenty young by natural breeding.

Taking the process one step further, Meng raised two fledglings by hacking, placing them in a platform eyrie where he fed them and eventually introduced them to the wild. In the meantime, Cade was testing another method of reintroduction into the wild—transferring fledgling captive-bred falcons from Cornell to the nests of Rocky Mountain peregrines.

As the program gained momentum, Cade established a peregrine fund and expanded the reintroduction program countrywide. One result was the establishment of a World Center for Birds of Prey at Boise, Idaho, which began a continuing program of raising not only peregrines but other species of birds of prey for introduction into the wild.

By 1992 more than 4,000 captive-bred peregrines have been released. There are now 100 breeding pairs in the wild in the East and more than 700 pairs nationwide—a remarkable success story for an endangered species. The only discouraging note is that the ghost of DDT seems to have surfaced once again to haunt the resident falcons in certain New Jersey marshes. DDT was once used heavily for mosquito control in this area, and twenty years later the marsh mud is still evidently laced with DDE, formed by the chemical breakdown of DDT.

OSPREY
Pandion haliaetus

The osprey, or fish hawk, is another cosmopolitan species whose population plummeted after World War II. Exclusively a fish eater, the osprey lives near coasts or inland waters throughout the Northern Hemisphere, where it can catch its finny prey. From the

1950s through the 1970s its numbers declined rapidly, not only in North America but in Europe as well—and the cause again was insecticides.

Ornithologist Roger Tory Peterson noted that there were at least 150 active osprey nests within a ten-mile radius of his home in Old Lyme, Connecticut, in 1954. Ten years later there were only seventeen nests, and by 1971 there were only three. Pesticide residue was found not only in samples of fish taken from the nests but in eggs as well. Ornithologists noted a similar decline in active nests along the New Jersey coast.

In 1968 a Cornell graduate student, Paul Spitzer, started an osprey egg-transfer experiment, switching eggs and nestling ospreys from a relatively uncontaminated osprey population in Chesapeake Bay with the eggs of Long Island ospreys. The Long Island eggs showed no better results in Chesapeake Bay nests than they did at home, but the Chesapeake eggs hatched successfully in the Long Island nests. A similar program was conducted in New Jersey.

After DDT was banned in 1972 the osprey population in both areas rebounded strongly. Nationwide the story was the same, and today 8,000 or more pairs of ospreys hunt for fish from Maine and Florida to the West Coast. To compensate for the scarcity of suitable nesting trees in many areas, conservationists have erected

Osprey

man-made nesting platforms, which the birds have readily adopted.

EVERGLADE SNAIL KITE
Rostrhamus sociabilis plumbeus

The Everglade snail kite is the northernmost race of a widespread tropical species found from Cuba and Mexico through parts of Central and South America. The Florida subspecies was fairly common in the 1920s, but by the 1960s it was considered to be the rarest bird in the United States. From all best counts, there were perhaps no more than twenty of them left—all in the Lake Okeechobee region of southern Florida.

With blood-red eyes, orange feet, and a broad white band on the base of its tail, the snail kite hovers over the sawgrass of Florida's watery wilderness searching for the big, freshwater apple snails that it eats to the exclusion of almost everything else. Spying a snail, it snatches it up and flies to a perch. Then, holding the shell in one claw, the kite expertly extracts the meat with its slender hooked beak and gulps it down.

The kites are found only in areas where the snails flourish— and that is where the main threat to their existence comes. Many of Florida's freshwater marshes where the snail was once found in abundance have been drained for agriculture. In addition, much of the water that normally flows from Lake Okeechobee into the

Everglades has been diverted in recent years for agriculture and domestic use, causing widespread drought conditions in the region. All of these factors have worked against the snails and consequently against the kites. The birds have been decimated by shooting too, and by the increasing use of pesticides.

The kite's nest is a flimsy platform, often built in low bushes or marsh grass and easily destroyed by rainstorms or high winds. This disadvantage has been partially offset by a successful program of relocating nests to artificial structures—woven metal baskets mounted on pipes.

In 1965 and 1966 a number of South American snail kites were brought to Patuxent with the hope that successful methods of breeding the birds and raising the young in captivity could be learned. Over forty young were hatched in captivity, but just one survived longer than six days. That one was reared successfully in 1974 when one evidently vital ingredient—calcium carbonate—was added to its diet. Soon afterward, the program was phased out, for the birds in the wild were faring somewhat better than they had ten years before. By 1983 the Florida population had surged to about 700 birds.

In 1985 the number dropped to 400 as a result of a prolonged drought, but increased to 560 the next year. In 1990 the Fish and Wildlife Service reported the species status as stable, with a population of 464 kites counted in 1989.

The Everglade snail kite is still in serious jeopardy from wetland degradation, loss of suitable habitat, and diversion of fresh water. Kite habitat is protected, however, in the 30,000-acre refuge for the Florida panther, and on some 28,000 acres of breeding habitat leased by the National Audubon Society on the western shores of Lake Okeechobee.

NORTHERN SPOTTED OWL
Strix occidentalis caurina

Strictly nocturnal, the northern spotted owl is found only in forests of dense, old-growth conifers—especially Douglas fir and redwood—from British Columbia to northern California. It is in peril throughout its range because much of its critical habitat has been

destroyed by logging. Its estimated population on federal land in the United States is about 3,000 pairs. A much smaller number live on private lands.

Canada listed the owl as endangered in 1986, but the U.S. government waited until 1990 to list it as threatened—and then only after a legal challenge from conservation organizations. By this time, logging had reduced its preferred forest habitat in the United States to 10 percent of its original extent. With further prodding, the Fish and Wildlife Service in mid-1991 designated 11.8 million acres (later reduced to 6.9 million) as critical habitat.

In the subsequent political and legal battle, there were immediate cries of outrage from lumbermen, whose lives depended on cutting timber; from the large timber corporations, which were busy cutting some 60,000 acres of old-growth timber every year; and from the Forest Service, which for some years had been selling the nation's timber below cost to these same corporations. To conservationists, it was not just the northern spotted owl at stake in the struggle; it was also the preservation of the last remnants of ancient forests that remained uncut in the Northwest.

In September 1991 Secretary of the Interior Lujan convened the Endangered Species Committee—the "God Squad"—to rule on the matter. This committee has the power to overrule the Endangered Species Act if "severe economic hardship" is involved—in this case the timber industry. Meanwhile, in May 1992, a panel of scientists, the Northern Spotted Owl Recovery Team, organized under the provisions of the Endangered Species Act, issued a draft recovery plan outlining measures necessary to protect the owl. In response, Lujan's office immediately proposed a much weaker measure to Congress, providing less protection for the owl, and the "God Squad" voted to permit logging on thirteen federal timber tracts—some 1,700 acres—which had previously been designated as critical owl habitat.

As the 1992 presidential campaign got underway, the battle raged hot and heavy. "It is time," said President Bush, "to put people ahead of owls." Bumper stickers appeared on cars throughout the Northwest stating: "Save a logger, kill the spotted owl." The Weyerhauser Timber Company proclaimed "Going overboard for the owl will hurt people" in advertisements in the *Seattle Post-Intelligencer*, Washington's leading newspaper.

In July 1992 a federal district court issued a ruling that "banned any logging in national forests where the spotted owl lives until the [Forest] service files an acceptable plan to protect the owl." In response, the Forest Service adopted a twenty-four-month schedule in which to comply. In September President Bush stated that he would block the scheduled renewal of the Endangered Species Act unless it was amended to take jobs into account. The struggle continues and, as yet, neither the owls nor the lumbermen are out of the woods.

PUERTO RICAN PARROT
Amazona vittata

Twenty or more members of the parrot family, including about a dozen different Amazon parrots and a half dozen macaws, once lived in the islands of the West Indies. All of the macaws and several of the Amazon parrots disappeared long ago. Most of the surviving forms are now rare and threatened with the same fate.

The Puerto Rican parrot, a stout green Amazon with a red

band between the eyes, was abundant when the Spaniards first came to the island five hundred years ago. Its numbers dwindled through centuries of shooting, collecting for the pet trade, and deforestation of its rain-forest habitat. Today, the species is found only in the Luquillo Mountains of eastern Puerto Rico, where it is protected on some 28,000 forested acres which were declared a wildlife refuge in 1946.

The species has been on the verge of extinction for the past quarter-century or more and reached its lowest point in 1975, when only thirteen birds could be counted. Since then, its population has shown a modest increase, with about 100 birds counted in 1989—forty-seven in the wild and fifty-three in a captive breeding program. Six chicks were produced by the captive birds that year, but an estimated half of the wild birds were lost when Hurricane Hugo swept across the island. Wildlife biologists protect the nesting sites of the wild birds in tree cavities and fit their openings with visor-like caps to prevent flooding. Plans have been made to eventually release captive-bred parrots into suitable habitat in the wild.

THICK-BILLED PARROT
Rhynchopsitta pachyrhyncha

This handsome species is found today in very limited numbers in the forests of the Sierra Madre Occidental, Mexico, where it was declared an endangered species in the 1970s. Formerly, it ranged sporadically northward into Arizona and New Mexico—the only continental parrot species that ranged naturally into the United States since the long extinct Carolina parakeet. According to some accounts, as many as 1,500 to 2,500 of them were there in 1918. The birds disappeared from the United States in the 1930s, however, and were not seen again until recent attempts to reintroduce them.

The reintroduction program began in 1986, when a number of thick-billed parrots were confiscated by federal authorities as smugglers attempted to bring them across the border. Some of these birds were kept to start captive breeding programs in St. Louis and Florida, and others were conditioned for a return to the wild. By 1989, almost fifty birds had been released in southeastern Arizona. Practically all of them were soon lost to drought, forest fires, goshawks and other predators, and a scarcity of their favored food, pine seeds. At least one pair was known to have nested in the state.

In November 1991 another eighteen parrots—ten reared in captivity and eight confiscated from smugglers—were released in Cave Creek Canyon, near Portal, Arizona, but again with disappointing results. When only five of the original eighteen survived, they were recaptured until a better way of reconditioning them for a successful life in the wild could be devised. Today, there are about eighty thick-billed parrots in the captive breeding program.

Meanwhile, the illegal smuggling of all kinds of parrots continues on a vast scale throughout the world. A recent Fish and Wildlife Service investigation indicates that up to 26,000 parrots are being smuggled into the United States each year from Mexico and Central and South America for sale to the pet trade. Argentina alone, the Service says, registers more than 175,000 parrots for "legal" export every year. The illegal trade in parrots and their relatives also flourishes in Asia, Africa, and Australia. As a result, many species are now facing extinction in the wild.

This vast parrot trade, both legal and illegal, is carried on in many countries throughout the world, and the profits make the risks worthwhile. Individual birds may sell for thousands of dollars, with rare South American macaws and Australian cockatoos sometimes selling for $10,000 or more.

"Each year at least 14 million birds are captured to supply the U.S. pet market," according to Donald Bruning, chairman of ornithology at the New York Zoological Society (NYZS),* and other experts as noted in the January 1993 issue of the society's magazine, *Wildlife Conservation.* In shipment, the birds are often so crowded or poorly cared for that the majority of them die before reaching their destination. Many of them are parrots. To help stem the attrition, a Wild Bird Conservation Act was signed by President Bush in October 1992, immediately banning the importation of ten birds listed by the Convention on International Trade in

---

* To emphasize its increasing commitment to the conservation of birds and all other kinds of wildlife, and to underscore its many far-reaching programs in their behalf, the New York Zoological Society changed its name to NYZP/The Wildlife Conservation Society in the spring of 1993. Its big zoological park, popularly known as the Bronx Zoo since its opening in 1899, is now officially called the International Wildlife Conservation Park.

Endangered Species of Wild Fauna and Flora (CITES) as most threatened, and gradually including other CITES-listed species. The aim of the act, Bruning observed, "is to replace the U.S. wild bird trade with one that is effectively regulated and based only on captive-bred birds and those harvested from sustainably managed wild populations."

. . . all America has a stake in our migratory birds—
we must establish while we can, islands of natural
habitat and havens where our wildlife can rest and
reproduce.

—Stewart L. Udall,
1961 speech

14

WATERFOWL, GAME, AND WADING BIRDS

Today our federal wildlife refuge system includes nearly 500 different units, covering more than 90 million acres. More than half of these units were established primarily as waterfowl refuges. Situated on all the principal migratory routes, or flyways, they preserve vitally needed waterfowl breeding, feeding, and resting areas. Many state and private refuges serve the same purpose. A number of the federal refuges were purchased with the more than $285 million raised by the sale of eighty-eight million duck stamps since 1934.

Yet, in spite of all these refuges, the populations of many species of waterfowl are declining nationwide. In order to keep their populations healthy, waterfowl need—as never before—both sufficient wetland breeding areas and strict regulation of their harvest by hunters. Overall supervision of these needs today falls to the professional waterfowl biologists of the Fish and Wildlife Service, and to their counterparts in the Canadian Wildlife Service and Mexico's Department of Game.

The services keep a close check on population trends for

each species through frequent censuses—at summer breeding grounds, at resting and feeding areas during fall migration, and at principal wintering areas. Analyses of these counts are used to determine the length of the waterfowl hunting season in various regions the next fall, as well as the bag limits for particular species.

Waterfowl biologists are well aware that while some wetlands are being preserved as refuges, even more are being drained every year to be converted into agricultural or grazing lands. From 1940 to 1964, for example, more than forty-five million acres of duck-breeding wetlands were drained—lost more permanently than by drought to any future use by waterfowl. At the same time the number of duck hunters increased from about a half-million before World War II to at least five or six times that many today. The birds are caught between dwindling habitat and an increasing gauntlet of hunters to fly through every fall.

The lead shot favored by hunters can kill ducks in either of two ways—by shooting them down outright or, more slowly, by lead poisoning. Every year an estimated two million ducks die from eating the spent pellets that fall into their feeding areas.

In the late 1970s the Fish and Wildlife Service began to establish "lead-free" zones in many states, where only steel pellets could be used. This regulation was vigorously opposed by the National Rifle Association and many hunters—with some success. In 1982, at the bidding of Congress, the Service passed the responsibility for regulating toxic shot to the states. Two years later, the National Wildlife Federation sued the Fish and Wildlife Service, claiming that lead shot was killing bald eagles that were eating fish or waterfowl that had ingested the pellets. The bald eagle, of course, is an endangered species and under federal protection. As a result of this legal battle, a majority of states now have designated steel-shot-only areas.

In 1987 the United States and Canada began a joint long-range North American waterfowl management plan, expected to cost $1.5 billion over the next twelve years. The agreement was designated to protect, improve, and restore waterfowl habitat throughout the two nations.

Loss of vital habitat is also affecting many upland game birds. Man's manipulation of his environment, as well as his modern agricultural practices—which favor huge, one-crop areas, chemical control of pests, and utilization of every square foot of land—work to the detriment of all these birds. The prairie chicken, for example, needs large areas of natural tall-grass prairie to flourish, but natural prairie lands, like wetlands, are shrinking rapidly.

A number of species of waterfowl, game, and wading birds are in serious trouble because they have very limited breeding ranges, such as islands, into which new and disrupting factors have been introduced. Still others are threatened by a combination of many different pressures, as the following accounts illustrate.

NENE OR HAWAIIAN GOOSE
Nesochen sandvicensis

Sometime during the Pleistocene, or Ice Age, a few geese—probably ancestral types of the Canada goose or the brant—found their way from North America to the Hawaiian Islands. No one knows how they got there. Perhaps they lost their way in migration from Alaska; perhaps a storm tossed them ashore. But get there they did. Adapting to their new homeland, the geese gave up migrating and developed nonaquatic habits. Over thousands of generations they developed long legs and lost much of the webbing on their toes. In time they became a distinctive species—the nene (pronounced "nay-nay") or Hawaiian goose.

The nene's original range was on the dry lava slopes of volcanic mountains on the two islands of Hawaii and Maui. When Captain Cook came to the islands in 1788, there were probably 25,000 geese there. Native Hawaiians hunted them for food. So did the crews of nineteenth-century whaling ships, who used to salt them down by the barrelful as a welcome change from the monotonous sea diet of salt pork and hardtack. Polynesians and Westerners between them introduced many exotic animals to the islands: goats and cattle, pigs, cats, dogs, rats, and mongooses, among others. All of these worked against the nene by destroying their ground nests, their eggs, and their young.

By the dawn of the twentieth century, the nene population was drastically reduced. It was still hunted in a four-and-a-half-month open season, with six birds per hunter per day allowed. The species was finally protected in 1911, but by this time the nene had practically disappeared in the wild. A few still survived in captive flocks.

In 1918 rancher Herbert C. Shipman of Hawaii obtained a pair of nene, and by 1927 these had increased to a small flock. In 1927 he gave a few of his birds to a territorial game farm on Oahu, and more than thirty geese were subsequently raised there. Many of these were released on islands where the species had never lived in the first place, and they quickly disappeared. In 1946 an earthquake-born tidal wave wiped out all but eleven of Shipman's birds. After that, there seemed little hope for their future.

Hawaii's territorial legislature appropriated funds in 1948 to help preserve the species, however, and ten years later the U.S. Congress voted additional funds for nene research and propagation. In spite of these last-ditch efforts, the total population of wild nene was thought to be no more than fifty birds in 1959, when Hawaii became the fiftieth state. Hawaii promptly designated the nene as its state bird, nevertheless, and intensified efforts to save it— with some justifiable optimism.

Three nenes from Shipman's original stock had been sent to the world-famous Severn Wildlife Trust in England in 1951–52.

There, under the expert eye of ornithologist Peter Scott, the trust's director, the nenes bred readily in captivity and multiplied from three to several hundred birds. Still others were raised at the Hawaiian state game farm and at the Connecticut farm of noted ornithologist Dillon Ripley.

Many of these captive-raised birds were released on the slopes of Mauna Loa and Kilauea Crater in Hawaii, and in Haleakala Crater in Maui. A new captive breeding facility for the species has been established at Olinda, Maui. Today the wild population on Hawaii and Maui totals about 390 to 425 birds. There is also a small feral population of about thirty-five on Kauai.

ALEUTIAN CANADA GOOSE
Branta canadensis leucopareia

Smallest of the various races of the Canada goose, the Aleutian subspecies is also darker than the others and has a broader white collar. It traditionally nested on Amchitka, Kiska, Agattu, and many other islands of the remote volcanic Aleutians, which stretch in a long chain from the Alaska peninsula more than a thousand miles toward Japan. At one time it bred on Russia's Bering and Kuril Islands as well. The Russian population, long since exterminated, wintered in Asia, and the Aleutian Islands birds in California and Oregon.

With the nineteenth- and twentieth-century settlement of Alaska, there came a boom in fur farming, and many arctic foxes were introduced into the Aleutians. They destroyed the nests, eggs, and young of the Aleutian Canada goose whenever they found them, and exterminated the form on many islands. Tiny Buldir Island, just four miles long by two miles wide, was considered too small for the introduction of arctic foxes, however, and was bypassed. By the 1960s it alone was known to harbor nesting Aleutian Canada geese. About 300 breeding geese were found there in 1962—perhaps the world's entire population.

The next year wildlife biologists captured sixteen goslings on Buldir and sent them to the wildlife research station at Monte Vista, Colorado, to start a captive breeding program. Eight of these birds were soon transferred to the new endangered-species station at Patuxent. Meanwhile, a program to eliminate arctic foxes from the Aleutian Islands was initiated in 1965.

The captive-breeding program was a resounding success and, beginning in the 1970s, captive-reared birds were released on many of the Aleutian Islands. In 1976 another breeding facility was constructed at Amchitka and stocked with Patuxent-bred birds. Since then, major efforts have also been made to protect the wintering grounds of the geese in California and Oregon, through inclusion in the national wildlife refuge system or easements on private land.

Today the total population of the Aleutian Canada goose is about 6,000 birds, on eight islands. Buldir alone has about 1,200 pairs. The species has been upgraded to "threatened" instead of "endangered," and in 1992 ten pairs were sent to Russia on permanent loan to reestablish a migrating population that would winter in Asia.

LAYSAN DUCK
Anas laysanensis

Limited in range to tiny Laysan Island, a mere dot in the Pacific on the way from Pearl Harbor to Midway, the Laysan duck is a little, white-masked duck that lives around the island's freshwater ponds. Now uninhabited, the island of Laysan is part of the Hawaiian Islands National Wildlife Refuge. Early in this century, however, it was exploited by commercial guano gatherers, who brought in rabbits to supplement their food as they collected

Laysan Duck

nitrogen-rich phosphates deposited by thousands of generations of seabirds.

Multiplying in their usual swift fashion, the rabbits soon stripped Laysan of most of its vegetation, leaving it practically a desert. As one result, bird species unique to Laysan—a rail, a miller bird, and a honeycreeper—became extinct, and the Laysan duck barely escaped the same fate. An expedition sent out in 1922 by the Bureau of Biological Survey found only ten Laysan ducks on the island. Another expedition in 1950 counted only thirty-three. A few individuals were captured and shipped to zoos and aviculturists to establish several captive breeding stocks. In the meantime the rabbits were cleared out and the protective vegetation grew back. At last count, there were about 500 ducks on the island, plus others in captivity.

ATTWATER'S GREATER PRAIRIE CHICKEN
Tympanuchus cupido attwateri

Of the three races of the greater prairie chicken, the typical form—known simply as the greater prairie chicken—is presently greatly reduced or completely exterminated over most of its former

range in the middle prairies. The eastern form, known as the
heath hen, has been extinct since 1932. And the third subspecies,
Attwater's prairie chicken, seems to be going the way of the heath
hen.

Ranging over the coastal prairies from western Louisiana to
Texas, Attwater's prairie chicken probably numbered over a million birds in 1900. Parties of hunters used to shoot them by the
hundreds, just for target practice. During those same years, more
and more of the vital prairie-grasslands habitat of the birds was
disappearing forever under the plow, or giving way to oil and gas
activities and residential development. The twin pressures—overshooting and reduction of habitat—proved too much. By 1941
there were only a few thousand Attwater's prairie chickens left,
and the population was becoming smaller every year.

A census in 1965 counted less than 1,000 individuals. By
this time the original coastal-prairie habitat of the bird was almost
entirely gone, and it was restricted to a narrow band along the
Texas coast and a few offshore islands. That same year, the World
Wildlife Fund and the Nature Conservancy raised $365,000 to
purchase 3,500 acres of prairie habitat which supported 300 to
400 birds in Colorado County, Texas. This land, together with
acreage transferred from the neighboring Aransas refuge, became
the Attwater's Greater Prairie Chicken National Wildlife Refuge
in 1972.

An Attwater's Prairie Chicken Recovery Fund has been

Attwater's Greater Prairie Chicken

established to help safeguard and manage suitable habitat, but in spite of all efforts the population continues to decline. In 1990 a spring census counted only about 500 birds. Captive breeding research is underway at Fossil Rim Wildlife Center, in Glen Rose, Texas, with the hope that a way may be found to prevent Attwater's prairie chicken from suffering the fate of its extinct eastern relative, the heath hen.

MASKED BOBWHITE
Colinus virginianus ridgwayi

A distinctive southwestern form, the masked bobwhite is distinguished by the male's blackish head and throat and his almost solid, brick-red breast. Originally found only in the grass-mesquite plains of southern Arizona and the neighboring Mexican state of Sonora, the masked bobwhite disappeared from Arizona about 1900, a victim of drought, overgrazing, and overhunting.

Most ornithologists believed that it was extinct everywhere. Then, in 1927, it was rediscovered in Sonora, reportedly by two naturalists who stopped to eat at an inn and found there a small flock of masked bobwhites that were kept in a pen as potential dinners for customers. A few years later, biologists captured some masked bobwhites in Mexico and brought them back to the United States. These birds were propagated in New Mexico, but releases were not successful.

Two brothers, James and Seymour Levy of Tucson, Arizona, preserved a small captive flock, and in the spring of 1966 they sent four pairs of masked bobwhites to the endangered-species facilities at Patuxent. Five chicks were hatched and reared at Patuxent that same year, and in 1967 forty were raised. A number of wild birds captured in Mexico were added to the Patuxent flock in 1968 and 1970 and the captive breeding program went into high gear, with 3,000 or more chicks produced annually.

The first attempts to return young captive-bred birds to the wild in Arizona were not successful, for they were released in overgrazed and degraded habitat where they could not survive. From 1976 on, releases made in areas where active habitat improvement had been undertaken were more successful. An improved release technique—putting the young birds in family groups with foster parents—was also employed.

In 1985 the Fish and Wildlife Service purchased the Buenos Aires Ranch in Alter Valley, Arizona, as a refuge for the birds. By 1991 some 10,000 young had been released there.

FLORIDA GREAT WHITE HERON
Ardea herodias

This beautiful big bird was once thought to be a distinct species (*A. occidentalis*), but today it is considered a white morph, or form, of the great blue heron. From a distance it resembles a common egret, but at closer range there is no mistaking it, with its huge size and yellowish-green legs. Usually building its nest in mangroves, it is found only in southern Florida—mostly in the Keys—and in Cuba and coastal Yucatan.

Common within its very restricted range in the United States, the Florida great white heron is protected by law. Much of its habitat is also safeguarded in Everglades National Park, and in the Great White Heron and Key West National Wildlife Refuges in the Keys. The number of birds fluctuates from season to season, depending somewhat on hurricanes, which may destroy both nests and birds. After the great hurricane of September 1935, the herons were reduced to an estimated 150 birds. Another great storm in 1960 destroyed an estimated half of the Everglades population. Undisturbed for several years, however, the population quickly recovered. Barring hurricanes, about 2,000 great whites live in the Everglades and the Keys today.

ROSEATE SPOONBILL
Ajaia ajaja

With its long flattened bill, and its pink- and carmine-colored wings, the roseate spoonbill is one of North America's most unusual and beautiful birds. A century and a half ago it was a common breeding bird in Florida and along the Gulf Coast, but for the past seventy-five years or more it has been a rare bird over much of this, the northern edge of its range. The species also lives and breeds in the Caribbean region and along the coasts of Central and South America.

Plume hunters prized the roseate spoonbills and killed them so mercilessly that they had disappeared from Texas by the turn of the century and were very rare in Florida. Finally protected by the abolishment of the plume trade, the spoonbills were then faced with the loss of many of the marshes and shallow bays they needed as feeding and breeding areas. These were being drained for crops or filled in for developments.

By 1930 there were only about thirty spoonbills left in Florida, all of them in one small rookery on Bottleneck Key near Tavernier. Protected by National Audubon Society wardens, the number has slowly increased and spread. Today the breeding birds nest on various small mangrove keys in Florida Bay and along the Gulf coast of the state, and the population seems to be holding its own.

The birds returned to Texas about 1920 and started a breeding colony on the Vingt-et-un Islands in Galveston Bay. The National Audubon Society established a refuge there for the birds in 1932. Today there are a number of other nesting colonies along the Texas coast as well.

With protection and the preservation of sufficient habitat, the roseate spoonbill may in time be induced to occupy even more of its original U.S. range.

AMERICAN FLAMINGO
Phoenicopterus ruber

With its incredibly long legs and neck, its crooked, black-tipped beak, and its bright pink plumage, an American flamingo is a striking bird indeed. It once nested on many of the Caribbean islands, as well as along the coasts of Yucatan and northern South America. Some ornithologists believe that it also nested occasionally on the Florida Keys. It was, in any case, a common bird in post-nesting flights along the Florida peninsula during much of

the nineteenth century. Today, the only flamingoes one is likely to see in Florida, however, are captive or semi-tame birds. The flock at Miami's Hialeah Park is the best known.

In order to breed successfully, the flamingo needs freedom from disturbance—by man or anything else. As early as 1905 the fledgling National Association of Audubon Societies was concerned about the bird's survival in the face of increasing interference by man, and it petitioned the Bahamian government to protect the breeding colonies of flamingoes in the islands. From this came the Bahamas Wild Bird Protection Act of 1905. But poachers still plundered rookeries for eggs and young birds, often frightening adults away so they never returned to their nests. By 1912 William Hornaday, director of the New York Zoological Park and tireless champion of wildlife conservation, was lamenting: "From Florida these birds quickly vanished. The six great breeding colonies of flamingoes on Andros Island, Bahamas, have been reduced to two. . . ."

The flamingoes clung to existence on Andros, however, until the outbreak of war in 1940. Then pilots on training missions from Florida bases used to buzz the breeding colonies just for the sport of seeing the shimmering pink cloud of birds arise. Disturbed too frequently, the birds had abandoned Andros entirely by war's end.

The flamingoes disappeared from many other old breeding areas as well, in the face of increasing disturbances of civilization.

They still nested on Great Inagua Island, however, where the Society for the Protection of the Flamingo in the Bahamas had long been active on their behalf.

In 1966 more than half of Great Inagua Island—the southernmost and one of the most easterly of the Bahamas—was set aside as the 287-square-mile Bahamian National Park. This was done mostly to protect the largest remaining colony of flamingoes—some 3,000 pairs which produced about 2,500 young in 1968.

In the years since, the flamingoes on Great Inagua have prospered. Indeed, the colony increased so much that in the early 1980s a new flock was formed on Aklins Island to the north. In 1991 two new rookeries were discovered on Andros Island as well. The flamingo was reclaiming its old territory.

Today the parent colony on Great Inagua boasts some 40,000 to 60,000 birds.

*Man's use of the land has caused great changes in its
character, and most of them have been detrimental to
bird life. Some species . . . have increased in numbers
as the result of man's conversion of wild land into
cities, farms, and parks. But for many species man's
changes have reduced the population of native birds,
some of them to extinction.*

—Joel Carl Welty,
The Life of Birds

15

EVEN THE FALL OF A SPARROW

Equipped with binoculars, notebooks, checklists, and Peterson field guides, groups of experienced bird-watchers the country over sally forth before dawn one day during the Christmas and New Year's holiday period every year on a special hunt. They are participants in the annual Christmas bird count, a continent-wide census of birds organized by the National Audubon Society and carried out in collaboration with wildlife services of the United States and Canada. Today, more than eight hundred groups—from Alaska and Hawaii to southern California, Key West, and Central America—participate. Each group counts the birds spotted and identified within a fifteen-mile-diameter circle. Compilation of all the lists gives a general picture of the continent's winter bird population, indicating the rise and fall of individual species.

Continent-wide banding operations also help to keep track of American bird populations. A private organization, the Bird Banding Association, started this work in 1909, but in 1920 the Bureau of Biological Survey (now the Fish and Wildlife Service) took over supervision of the program. Today it does the job in cooperation with the wildlife services of Canada and Mexico. As a result, more than 52 million birds of over 600 species had been banded by 1993, and close to 2.8 million bands have been recovered from birds which were retrapped or picked up when they died. Each bird carries a light aluminum band on its leg marked with a serial number and the stamp of the Fish and Wildlife Service. The records of these recoveries are kept up to date at the Bird Banding Laboratory at the Patuxent Wildlife Research Center in Laurel, Maryland. They are of inestimable value in indicating movements, ranges, nesting habits, and lifespans of American birds.

No one knows, of course, just how many birds there are in North America. Drawing on all available data, including census and banding records, ornithologists estimate that there are probably between five and ten billion birds in the United States today. Ornithologist Roger Tory Peterson believes that, in late summer, just after the nesting season, the total may be as many as 20 billion birds for all of America north of the Mexican border.

That would seem to be enough birds to satisfy anyone. And indeed, there may very well be more birds in the United States at the present time—the hordes of passenger pigeons notwithstanding—than there were in Colonial days. But although the total numbers may be greater, the variety of species in most areas is less than it used to be. A large portion of the bird total is made up of a very few highly successful species that have profited enormously from man's clearing and changing of the wild land. Two examples are the introduced Old World house sparrow and starling. Others are grackles, blackbirds, and cowbirds, which often flock together at roosts millions strong. Judging from recent Audubon counts, the starling and red-winged blackbird may be the most abundant bird species in America today.

Often called pest or "locust" birds, such species prosper because of our modern system of agriculture, which for economic reasons favors vast areas devoted to a single food crop. Descending in darkening clouds on a great expanse of rice or other grain field, the pest species may—and often do—cause great devastation. Farmers and wildlife biologists fight the pest birds with sprays, nets, chemicals, guns, and noisemakers—but still they proliferate. Scientists are striving to develop new methods to limit such pest species. In the long run, however, perhaps the best way to deal with them would be to diversify our collective agricultural methods. While these few bird species are too successful for comfort, many others are declining rapidly.

Every spring the Fish and Wildlife Service conducts a breeding bird survey at about 1,700 different locations across the country. Since 1968 this survey has shown a steady decline in the populations of many of the more than 300 species that breed in North America, then migrate south to winter in Mexico and Central and South America.

Among the hardest hit are many of our songbirds—warblers, vireos, tanagers, kingbirds, thrushes, and peewees. Seeking the cause of this decline, scientists point to several possibilities: widespread destruction of tropical rain forests and other natural areas needed by these migrants as winter habitat; the extensive use of various deadly pesticides—now illegal for use in the United States—in many Latin American countries; parasitism of nests by cowbirds; and the steady loss of suitable nesting habitat in North America because of agricultural and other human activities. "Saving our migratory songbirds," wildlife writer Les Line declares, "may be the most daunting task ever faced by American conservationists."

Today the Fish and Wildlife Service and many private conservation organizations have banded together in a cooperative effort known as "Partners in Flight" to study the reasons for this decline in songbird species and promote practices to end it. Unless this is successful, many species face eventual oblivion.

KIRTLAND'S WARBLER
Dendroica kirtlandii

A pretty little warbler with a yellow belly and a gray back streaked with black, Kirtland's warbler winters in the Bahamas. Its known breeding grounds are only a few counties in Michigan's Lower Peninsula.

Within its limited breeding area, Kirtland's warbler further requires a very specialized nesting habitat. It will build its nest

Kirtland's Warbler

only on the ground under stands of young jack pine trees with undergrowth of a certain density. And jack pine reseeds itself only when fires sweep through its stands, when intense heat makes the cones pop open and scatters the seeds. This worked well when natural fires swept periodically through the forests of the Lower Peninsula. Today, however, most of these forests are state- or federally-owned and close fire-control watches are maintained. Without fires, there are no young jack pines. And without young jack pines, no Kirtland's warblers.

It seems strange to help preserve a species by setting fires, but that is exactly what was done in the warbler's nesting areas. The U.S. Forest Service set aside 4,010 acres in Huron National Forest as a Kirtland's warbler management area, and the Michigan State Conservation Department set aside three similar areas of four square miles each on state forest lands. On these, carefully controlled fires were periodically set and allowed to burn through stands of jack pine, freeing the seeds and starting new seedlings to shelter Kirtland's warbler nests.

During the late 1980s the Fish and Wildlife Service acquired about 6,000 additional acres for the warblers, and just recently instituted an extensive tree-planting program to provide the birds with more nesting habitat. In 1991 alone more than a million trees were planted. In spite of this, some authorities say that, because of forest management policies, suitable nesting habitat for the warblers is only about a third of what it was in the 1960s.

Through the years the Kirtland's warbler has been increasingly victimized by the parasitic brown-headed cowbird which lays its eggs in the nests of other bird species. The cowbird eggs hatch before those of the warbler, and the foster nestlings, larger and more aggressive, get the lion's share of the food. As a result, few of the warbler young survive. In 1971 an ongoing program to trap and control the cowbird was instituted and has proved quite successful. In 1990 more than 7,500 cowbirds were removed from colonies of breeding warblers. Before the program started, about 75 percent of warbler nests were parasitized; today that has been reduced to about 5 percent.

Every year a Kirtland's warbler census is carried out by recording the number of singing males. The count in 1992 was 396 birds, indicating a total population of 800 or more. That is the highest population for the species since the 1960s.

BACHMAN'S WARBLER
Vermivora bachmanii

Very possibly the rarest songbird in the United States, the Bachman's warbler was first described in 1833 by the Reverend John Bachman, Audubon's collaborator, who discovered the species near Charleston, South Carolina. A rather inconspicuous little bird, it has an olive-green back and yellowish underparts. The male is distinguished by a black crown and throat.

For about fifty years after Bachman discovered it, the species was not seen again. Indeed, it has been observed so rarely at any time that we know very little about it. Its only known wintering area is Cuba and the Isle of Pines, and it is thought to nest in thickets of canebrake in swampy bottomlands along our southeastern rivers. Early in this century, it was seen much more frequently than at any time before or since—even though the number of birdwatchers in those days was only a fraction of the number today. There have been a few sightings of the species in Cuba over the past ten years, but the last confirmed sighting in the United States occurred in 1962.

How has man affected this species, already rare when it was first discovered? No one really knows. Some ornithologists believe that cutting the forested bottomlands along the southeastern rivers early in this century may have taken away much of the special breeding habitat it needs. Human activities in Cuba may have affected its winter habitat as well.

GOLDEN-CHEEKED WARBLER
Dendroica chrysoparia

Bright yellow cheeks and a black line through the eyes distinguish this pretty little warbler. The male has a black back and bib and black-streaked sides, but the female's colors are mainly dark olive-green. The species breeds only in mature Ashe juniper woodlands in central Texas, then migrates south to Guatemala, Honduras, and Nicaragua for the winter.

Land-clearing operations for Texas agricultural and housing projects are destroying more and more of its critical nesting habitat every year, and similar human activities in Central America are damaging its wintering areas. As a result, the numbers of this endangered species are declining every year. Today the total population is thought to be no more than 4,600—perhaps only half that many.

In the fall of 1992 Texas voters approved a $22 million bond issue to acquire land for the Balcones Canyon Land Conservation Plan, which would set aside 29,000 acres of habitat used by the golden-cheeked warbler and another endangered species, the black-capped vireo (*Vireo atricapillus*). Under this Habitat Conservation Plan (HCP), developers would be allowed to develop other similar terrain in the area, given Fish and Wildlife approval.

In spring 1993 Interior Secretary Babbitt worked out a similar compromise agreement with developers to preserve vital coastal scrub habitat for the imperiled California gnatcatcher (*Polioptila californica*).

DUSKY SEASIDE SPARROW
Ammodramus maritimus nigrescens

Restricted to salt marshes near the Kennedy Space Center on Florida's Cape Canaveral, the dusky seaside sparrow, a dark-colored bird with streaked underparts, declined in recent years because of changes in its salt marsh environment brought about by flooding and the pesticides used in mosquito-control operations. As both the rocket-launching pads and the human beings increased on Cape Kennedy, so did efforts to control the pestiferous mosquitoes. As a result, the population of this little bird shrank from about 900 dusky males counted in 1968 to just 54 in 1973. By 1980 biologists counted seven males only. Six of these were captured and attempts were made to crossbreed them with a close relative, Scott's seaside sparrow (*A.m. peninsulae*). Several hybrid sparrows were reared successfully, but the last pure dusky, an old male, died in 1987. The race is extinct.

CAPE SABLE SEASIDE SPARROW
Ammodramus maritimus mirabilis

Found only in freshwater and brackish marshes on the southwestern edge of the Everglades, the Cape Sable sparrow's fortunes rise and fall with what happens to its very restricted habitat. A small species with olive-green upperparts and almost white underparts, it has become endangered because of changes in its salt marsh breeding habitat brought about by droughts, fires, and hurricanes. Particular threats to its survival in recent years have been drainage projects and real estate developments as well as the use of insecticides and the flooding of marshes for mosquito control. All of these activities have further reduced its specialized living area. Best estimates put its present numbers at about 6,600 birds.

IPSWICH SPARROW
Passerculus sandwichensis princeps

Breeding only on Sable Island, Nova Scotia, the Ipswich sparrow, a sand-colored race of the Savannah sparrow, winters among coastal sand dunes southward to Georgia. The Ipswich sparrow is already a very rare bird, and its decline may be due not only to the washing away of much of its beach-nesting habitat on tiny Sable Island but also to the construction of housing along much of its shoreline wintering habitat.

THREATENED HAWAIIAN BIRDS

Scientists have long known that species of wildlife and plants native only to particular islands have a much higher extinction rate than mainland species. Because of their limited living space, they are much more vulnerable to changes in habitat or to outside forces that invade their island homes. On Guam, for example, at least nine species of native birds disappeared after the accidental introduction of a single species of snake, native to Australia and New Guinea, that systematically destroyed the birds' eggs and their young.

More species of birds have become extinct within historic

Maui Nukupu'u

times on Pacific islands than in all the rest of the world put together. And of the many island groups in the Pacific, the Hawaiian Islands have perhaps the sorriest record of all.

About seventy kinds of native birds lived in the beautiful Hawaiian archipelago before civilization descended upon it. At least twenty-three of these birds are now extinct, including four different honeyeaters, eight kinds of honeycreepers, and the Hawaiian rail, last seen in 1884. Natural disasters such as fires, hurricanes, and volcanic activity may have hastened the downfall of some of these, but most of them were doomed by human activities. Some were reduced in days past by overshooting, and never recovered. More of them, however, probably died because their specialized or limited habitat was destroyed by pigs, goats, sheep, and other domestic stock, or by drainage and agricultural and lumbering operations. Still others were unable to cope with competition from hardy and aggressive introduced bird species, or from such introduced predators as dogs, cats, rats, and mongooses.

Of the native birds that still survive, no fewer than twenty-eight are now listed as either endangered or threatened. Seven of them have populations of less than a hundred surviving individuals.

One bright spot in this sad story was the rediscovery in December 1967 of the Maui nukupu'u (*Hemignathus lucidus*)—a honeycreeper—that had last been seen in 1897 and had long been considered extinct. About thirty individuals of this species still live in the forests of the Kipahulu Valley in Maui, where they cling to survival by the slenderest of threads.

Reptiles are a part of the old wilderness of earth, the environment in which man got the nerves and hormones that make him human. If we let the reptile go, it is a sign we are ready to let all wilderness go. When that happens we shall no longer be exactly human.

—Archie Carr,
The Reptiles

16

ENDANGERED REPTILES AND AMPHIBIANS

In his 1963 book *The Reptiles*, herpetologist Archie Carr sadly prophesied, "If the world goes on the way it is going it will one day be a world without reptiles. Some people will accept this calmly, but I mistrust the prospect." Today he would probably say the same of amphibians—frogs, toads, and salamanders. They too are rapidly disappearing in many regions worldwide.

Reptiles face the same overriding threat these days that all other wildlife does—the loss of much of their vitally needed habitat through changes brought about by man. But that is not all they face. Throughout the world, many of the crocodilians, sea turtles, and big lizards are being systematically exterminated for profit—slaughtered just as ruthlessly as were the bison and passenger pigeon in their day. Many other reptiles, snakes especially, have age-old fears and prejudices working against them.

Snakes, Carr believed, may be disappearing faster than any other group of vertebrates. In the United States, automobiles take an ever-increasing toll of them on our vast network of highways. The kill is especially high when snakes lie on the pavement to warm themselves, or when they haul up on roads to escape rising floodwaters. And no one knows how many snakes are bludgeoned to death every year for no other reasons than prejudice, or fear, or "sport." But the total must be astronomical.

Every year thousands of beneficial and harmless species are killed by people who think they are venomous snakes. Every spring or fall, gangs of snake-haters travel to areas where rattlesnakes or other venomous snakes are known to hibernate, and kill or collect them by the hundreds, just for "sport." That is one of the reasons why the timber rattlesnake, the largest—and now the rarest—reptile in New England, survives only in small numbers in a few remote pockets of its original habitat in the eastern United States.

For those who put the value of wildlife on a dollars-and-cents basis, it might be well to reflect that snakes, whether harmless garter snakes or poisonous rattlesnakes, are among man's most potent allies in helping to control rodents. And for those who fear poisonous snakes it may be comforting—although it probably won't be—to know that more people die of bee and wasp stings in the United States every year than from snakebites.

Apart from the hazards mentioned above, man's changes in the landscape can be particularly serious for reptiles that have restricted or specialized habitats. One of these is the San Francisco garter snake, a subspecies that lives only in the vicinity of reservoirs in the San Francisco area. It is threatened because its natural habitat is fast disappearing before subdivisions, water-control alterations, and agricultural changes in the land. The blunt-nosed leopold lizard of the San Joaquin Valley also faces extinction for much the same reasons.

We hold no prejudices against turtles as we do against snakes, but even so, we are recklessly killing off sea turtles, as already noted, for their flesh, eggs, shell, oil, and leather. Most of the smaller freshwater turtles are not endangered for the same reasons, although the diamondback terrapin, the snapping turtle, and several other species are hunted for their flesh or to make turtle soup. Formerly, many thousands of newly hatched painted turtles and red-eared sliders were sold in the pet trade yearly. Most of them faced a lingering death in a small bowl.

As with other forms of wildlife, some turtles face extinction because of the destruction of their habitat. The desert tortoise, which inhabits dry and desert areas of the Southwest, is threatened because of rapid residential development in many areas and overgrazing of its habitat by livestock. The bog, or Muhlenberg's, turtle, a small species with a large orange or yellow patch on each side of its head, lives in isolated colonies in marshes and wetlands from southwestern Massachusetts to North Carolina. It has become rare in many areas in recent years because much of its best habitat has been drained or filled in. The diamondback terrapin faces possible extermination not only because it is highly prized for its succulent flesh but also because its coastal habitat is threatened by pollution and development. Mortality on coastal highways is especially high in some areas.

The crocodilians are an ancient group, tracing their lineage back hundreds of millions of years to the time when reptiles ruled the world. But today the populations of many of them are fast dwindling the world over. If their fortunes continue downhill for another century as they have the past century, they may very well disappear completely. Despite legal protection, the American crocodile has almost lost its precarious clawhold in southern Florida and the Keys. It faces the same fate throughout the rest of its range in the Caribbean, Central America, and northern South America, largely because of human persecution. The American alligator, however, once threatened with imminent extinction in the wild because of illegal hide hunting, has recovered strongly under federal protection and regulation.

Where Have All the Amphibians Gone?

Most North American amphibians—frogs, toads, and salamanders—are tied to water for at least some portion of their lives. As wetlands and marshes disappear, as ponds and streams become unlivable because of pollution—so go the amphibians. And those with localized ranges may be wiped out very quickly if something happens to alter or destroy their environment.

Eight salamanders are presently listed as endangered in the United States. One of these, the Santa Cruz long-toed salamander, is known only in two localities in midcoastal California. Another, the Texas blind salamander, a ghostly white species with external gills, lives only in deep wells and underground streams in the caves of Hays County, Texas. All are endangered by changes brought about by man in their limited and specialized environment. Several have also been the victims of overly enthusiastic collecting by biologists.

One way to save these and other threatened species would be to preserve a portion of their breeding areas as national wildlife monuments. The Endangered Species Act makes provisions of this sort for saving threatened wildlife with limited ranges. Some years ago, the Texas chapter of The Nature Conservancy acquired Ezell's Cave in Texas to preserve the habitat of the Texas blind salamander. If other amphibians and reptiles with equally restricted ranges are not protected in some such manner, they will in all probability become extinct within the next few years.

Many populations of amphibians the world over—not just those with restricted habitats but a number of once common and wide-ranging species as well—are also in serious trouble. During the past twenty years, herpetologists have noted with alarm the massive decline or total disappearance of many frog, toad, and salamander populations in at least sixteen different countries and five continents. They had long noted the destructive effect of acid rain on salamander eggs and developing embryos, but this global decline was affecting amphibians that lived in seemingly pristine or wilderness areas as well. What was the cause?

In 1990 a herpetological conference on "Declining Amphibian Populations—a Global Phenomenon?" was held at the University of California to investigate the problem. Many suggestions and theories about what was causing the die-offs were presented: acid rainfall, global warming, an increase in ultraviolet radiation, pesticides and herbicides, destruction of tropical forests and other critical habitat—or perhaps a combination of all these, indicating a general environmental degradation worldwide. But no one had the ultimate answer.

During the conference, University of California biologist David Bradford declared, "A declining amphibian population of the extent and magnitude we are seeing signals a growing level of pollution worldwide and serves as an early warning system of environmental crisis." As a result of the meetings, a Declining Amphibian Populations Task Force was formed to collect and correlate existing and future data—with the hope of eventually pinpointing the cause and coming up with solutions to reverse the trend.

There is no mystery, however, to the widely fluctuating fortunes of two large and well-known reptiles—the American alligator and the green sea turtle. For centuries, their populations have been at the mercy of human activities, either for or against them.

AMERICAN ALLIGATOR
Alligator mississippiensis

"Behold him rushing forth from the flags and reeds. His enormous body swells. His plaited tail, brandished high, floats upon the lake. The waters like a cataract descend from his opening jaws. Clouds of smoke issue from his dilated nostrils. The earth trembles with his thunder." This rather inflamed and smoky description of America's biggest reptile was written nearly two centuries ago by William Bartram, who was usually an accurate and trustworthy naturalist.

Alligators were abundant in Bartram's day, and many of them grew to huge size. Only eight or nine inches long when first hatched, they grow at the rate of a foot or more each year until they are five or six feet long, then at a slower rate. Alligators seldom live long enough to attain giant size any more, but in Colonial days many of them measured twelve to fifteen feet. The record is nineteen feet and two inches.

The alligator's main food is fish, but turtles, birds, and small mammals are eaten too. Even pigs, dogs, deer, and cows occasionally fall victim to big gators. Under exceptional circumstances they have been known to attack human beings.

After mating in the springtime, the female alligator builds a huge mound of mud and vegetation in which she lays twenty to sixty eggs. She then stays close by, guarding the nest until the young hatch. Unlike most other reptiles, she usually remains near the young during the first critical year and protects them by her presence. Full-grown gators excavate deep pools for their headquarters, with an underground den in one bank. Such pools are lifesavers for fish and other swamp life in times of drought, when other sources of water dry up.

In Bartram's time, the alligator ranged rivers and coastal marshes from North Carolina to eastern Texas. By the 1960s, it had disappeared from great portions of this original range— principally because of unremitting persecution at the hands of man. Since the time of the American Revolution, millions of alligators have been killed for their hides, which were fashioned into expensive suitcases, handbags, and other luxury leather products. During the nineteenth century an estimated two-and-a-half million gators were killed in Florida alone. This figure is probably much too conservative when compared with reliable records of 1,475,000 skins taken in Florida in the ten-year period from 1929 through 1938.

Florida is the center of the gator population, but the bayous of Louisiana are a close second. An estimated half-million hides were taken here between 1940 and 1957. A great many of them came from three- or four-foot alligators which had not yet reached breeding age. Under pressure like this, the Louisiana population declined by an estimated 90 percent from the late forties to the late fifties, reaching a point where a couple of dry years in a row could finish the gators off. In dry years alligators concentrate in the diminishing wet areas and can be taken easily if not protected.

But gradually the southern states wakened to the fact that their alligators were fast disappearing. Florida outlawed all gator hunting in 1961, and most of the other states took similar steps to protect their remaining populations. In 1967 the federal government declared the alligator an endangered species, fully protected everywhere. But poachers continued to kill the gators in defiance of the law.

Alligator poaching was big business in those days, with hide hunters often using high-speed boats equipped with two-way radios to warn each other of approaching wardens. The lawbreakers ran little risk of being caught, for there were not enough law-enforcement officers to patrol all of the areas of the alligator habitat. In response, state and federal game protectors increased the penalties for poaching and stepped up their campaign against the violators of the law. They finally won the war against the poachers and almost at once alligator populations began to increase. By 1987 the alligator had recovered so well that the Fish and Wildlife Service changed its listed status from endangered to threatened.

Sea Turtles

Worldwide in distribution, the sea turtles are the most valuable reptiles of all, as far as man is concerned. There are eight species: leatherback, loggerhead, olive ridley, Kemp's ridley, hawksbill, black (sometimes considered an eastern Pacific race of the green), flatback, and the green sea turtle. All of them except the flatback, which lives in the waters off northern Australia, are presently endangered and face ultimate extinction because of human activities. The green (*Chelonia mydas*) is considered the most valuable. As a consequence, it is the most exploited. Humans eat green-turtle eggs and flesh, use the calipee (the cartilage connecting the undershell plates) for making the best grade of turtle soup, and

Atlantic Green Turtle

value the leather of the back and flippers for making high-grade pocketbooks and other leather products.

Green turtles inhabit warm seas around the world. The females come ashore on sandy beaches to dig nests where they lay their eggs, then crawl back to sea. When the young turtles hatch sixty days later, they immediately head for the sheltering waters and swim away—no one knows where—to grow to maturity. Years later the mature females start coming back to the ancestral nesting grounds to lay their eggs. This is when most of them are captured.

Green turtles were abundant in the waters of the middle Atlantic in Colonial days, laying their eggs on many beaches in southeastern states and warm-water islands. As early as 1620 the Bermuda Assembly passed "An Act agaynst the Killinge of ouer Young Tortoyses," proclaiming it illegal to take any of "so excellent a fishe" with a shell breadth less than eighteen inches. The Colonial administrators had the right idea, but in the long run they failed. By the 1950s green turtles no longer laid their eggs on Bermuda beaches. Nor did they nest on Cape Hatteras, where in Colonial times a turtle hunter could sometimes kill as many as 100 turtles a day, nor in Florida, where one collector alone gathered 2,500 of them in the vicinity of Sebastian in 1886. In fact, green turtles no longer nested on beaches anywhere in the

United States, and they were facing extinction throughout the Atlantic community unless effective conservation measures could be applied in time.

A twenty-two-mile stretch of beach at Tortuguero ("Place of the Turtle"), Costa Rica, was the only known remaining nesting grounds for green turtles in the western half of the Caribbean Sea. In 1957 the Costa Rican government moved to protect this turtle nursery by law. Florida herpetologist Archie Carr, who had been studying sea turtles for years, then promoted the creation of a private conservation organization, the Brotherhood of the Green Turtle, in 1958. The brethren in turn founded the Caribbean Conservation Corporation, dedicated to the study and preservation of the sea turtles. Under the sponsorship of this and other organizations, the nesting beaches at Tortuguero were patrolled and guarded against poachers and a long-term, wide-ranging study of the turtle was undertaken. It continues today.

In recent years many thousands of hatchling green turtles and eggs have been flown to many different localities in the Caribbean and along the coasts of South America, Mexico, Florida, and Texas, with the hope that they would return to these release points when they were old enough to breed. If such restoration projects prove successful, and if the green turtle is properly protected, it can once again become a valuable resource of the Caribbean, as it was in bygone days.

The breeding grounds of the rare Kemp's ridley sea turtle (*Lepidochelys kempii*) remained a mystery until the 1950s, when herpetologists discovered and reviewed an old film taken in 1947 that showed an estimated forty thousand female ridleys coming ashore to lay their eggs on an isolated stretch of beach near Rancho Nuevo, on the Gulf Coast of Mexico.

Over the years, the species has been exploited so ruthlessly for its eggs and flesh that it is now in serious danger of complete extermination. Today only a few hundred females haul out on the nesting beaches of Rancho Nuevo to lay their eggs, even though the area is patrolled and the turtles protected.

During the ten years between 1978 and 1988, some 12,000

Kemp's ridley eggs were taken to Padre Island National Seashore, near Corpus Christi, Texas, in a continuing effort to help the species and try to establish it on other breeding grounds. There the eggs were incubated and hatched, with the hope that the young would be imprinted with the distinctive smells and chemistry of the beaches and waters around Padre Island. The hatchlings were then taken to Galveston, where they were raised until the age of nine or ten months in the laboratories of the National Marine Fisheries Service. They were then released in the waters off Padre Island. It is still too soon to know whether they will come back as adults to Padre Island beaches to lay their eggs.

There have been several very positive developments in the efforts to safeguard the various species of sea turtles in recent years. In 1990 Mexico outlawed the killing of all sea turtles and the harvesting of their eggs. That same year, the United States instituted new regulations requiring shrimp trawlers to install turtle-excluder devices (TEDs) in their shrimp nets as an escape hatch for sea turtles. Before this, many thousands of turtles had died when they became ensnared in the nets.

Finally some 500 acres of Florida's Atlantic coast were established in 1991 as the Archie Carr National Wildlife Refuge. Today some 600 to 800 green turtles lay their eggs along the Florida coast, and about 40 percent of them use the beach on the Archie Carr refuge. So does the largest nesting colony of logger-head turtles (*Caretta carreta*) in the western hemisphere.

And an ingenious Spaniard says, that rivers and the inhabitants of the watery element were made for wise men to contemplate, and fools to pass by without consideration.

—Izaak Walton,
The Compleat Angler

17

CLEAN WATERS AND FISH

As badly as man has treated the American land and its re-sources, he has been even more reckless in the way he has treated its waters—not only its freshwater rivers, streams, and lakes, but its coastal estuaries and marine wetlands as well. "Water today has the dubious distinction of being America's most misused resource," according to the 1965 Conservation Yearbook of the Department of the Interior. "With nearly all our waterways befouled by sewage, silt, industrial wastes and pesticides, and in spite of every readable sign pointing to the absolute necessity for recycling and reuse, we continue to squander our bank account with water capital. Science has given us knowledge; who will teach us wisdom?"

Rivers and streams that once abounded with fish now run polluted and lifeless, their waters choked with sewage and indus-trial wastes. Long-abandoned mines seep acids into many streams, making them death traps for aquatic life. Deadly pesticides drain into innumerable other streams with similar results. Many millions of fish are recorded as having been killed by identifiable pollution in the United States in recent years. These, however, were just a small fraction of the numbers that died from pollution but were not counted.

Reckless lumbering and improper agricultural practices have laid many watersheds bare to erosion from quick drain-off. The resultant silting and sedimentation bar many species of fish from their traditional feeding or spawning areas. Dams pose insurmountable barriers to others that must travel upstream to spawn. Atomic power plants that use water for cooling are another threat. The rise in water temperature that results from the operation proves fatal to many kinds of fish.

Our five huge inland seas, the Great Lakes, once supported a vast and flourishing fishing industry. In recent years, however, the harvest has deteriorated, partially because of overfishing of particular species; partially through depredations of the sea lamprey, which invaded the upper lakes by way of the Welland Canal; but principally because time and events have caught up with our habits of using these same lakes as convenient cesspools and sewage-disposal areas. Today the Great Lakes states are all working to reverse this trend.

Great Lakes fish, however, are not the only ones in serious trouble because of pollution and other human activities. *The New York Times* reported in 1990 that "Fisheries biologists estimate that more than one third of the approximate 1,000 native freshwater fish species and subspecies are endangered, threatened, or of 'special concern,' meaning that even minor environmental disturbance could jeopardize them."

Man needs clean, fresh water too, and in recent years our country has begun to waken to the dangers of pollution of our lakes, rivers, and streams, and to demand that the trend be reversed. The costs of collecting and treating municipal and industrial wastes adequately are staggering, and some people question whether we can afford to do it. It would be more sensible by far to ask ourselves whether we can afford *not* to do it.

The saltwater fisheries of the United States are our country's greatest single wildlife resource. Many of the commercially important species of marine fish come into shallow waters near shore to breed or feed. Our coastal bays and estuaries also support crabs and lobsters and vast resources of shellfish. Yet we continually treat these coastal waters as dumping grounds for sewage and wastes of all sorts. We destroy natural coastal environments by dredging, or by filling in saltwater marshes for housing and industrial developments.

Partly as a result of this contemptuous policy, partly as a result of over-harvesting of particular species over long periods, the production of our commercial marine fisheries is also threatened. The National Marine Fisheries Service notes that 65 of the 153 species it is charged with overseeing are being overfished in U.S. waters. These include cod, salmon, haddock, flounder, swordfish, red snapper, tuna, and many others. The Atlantic bluefin tuna has been pursued so relentlessly by commercial fishermen using super seiners and giant drift nets that the number of adults of breeding age in the western Atlantic has decreased by 90 percent in the past twenty years. A few more years of such attrition could spell the end of the species.

One of the world's richest fishing grounds is Georges Bank, off Cape Cod. This area produces 40 percent of the fish eaten in the United States, about 12 percent of the entire world's commercial catch. In the 1960s oil companies began to prospect on the ocean floor of Georges Bank for offshore oil, an activity that posed a serious threat to the vital fish resource of that area. If an accident were to befall an oil line, releasing a flood of oil against the northeast coast, the consequences could be catastrophic. The New England Fisheries and Conservation Committee expressed its concern early in 1968 by asking the governors of the New England states to support a bill in Congress to protect this important fishing ground. "In this age of population explosion, when more than half of mankind goes to bed hungry every night," the chairman of the committee warned in his report, "endangering a resource that has fed man for five centuries seems foolhardy."

In spite of such warnings, the Georges Bank fisheries have deteriorated badly in recent years because of another danger— overexploitation. Overfishing has caused the stocks of cod, haddock, and other commercially desirable fish to shrink alarmingly. Populations of dogfish, sharks, and rays, on the other hand, have increased, and the pressures these species exert may make it impossible for the others to recover.

Today our marine fisheries are under the continuous surveillance of the National Marine Fisheries Service (NMFS) of the Department of Commerce, which controls the harvest regulations. NMFS research biologists constantly seek new ways to safeguard and improve this vital resource. In its 1992 report on the status of U.S. marine resources, the Service notes that commercial fisheries produced $3.9 billion in revenue to fishermen at U.S. ports in 1991, and that 17 million American anglers enjoy saltwater fishing each year, catching more than 230 million fish.

For inland waters, each state regulates the sport fisherman's catch; and state, federal, and private fish hatcheries all work to keep as many of our streams and lakes as possible supplied with stocks of trout, bass, and other fish species favored by anglers.

ATLANTIC SALMON
Salmo salar

Acknowledged as a noble adversary by fly fishermen, just as fervently acknowledged a royal food by gourmets, the Atlantic salmon is one of earth's best-known fishes. In the Old World it once inhabited all the principal rivers from northern Spain to

Norway and eastern Russia. In the New World it could be found in rivers from northern Labrador to Connecticut.

The salmons are anadromous fish—except for land-locked forms, they grow up in the sea, then ascend rivers to breed. Atlantic salmon lay their eggs in late fall in shallow, swift-moving streams. After the young hatch the next spring, they spend the next two to four years in fresh water. Then, as silvery five- to eight-inch smolts, they pass downstream in spring to the sea, where they feed and mature. Recent tagging research indicates that American salmon congregate in waters off western Greenland, while those from Europe head for the waters around the Faeroe Islands, between Iceland and Scotland. At maturity the fish is sleek and beautiful, with a steel-blue back and silvery sides. Virgin migrants usually weigh about ten to twelve pounds, and repeat spawners may weigh twenty pounds or more. Some mysterious homing instinct guides the salmon back to the river and stream of its birth. It fights its way past falls and rapids before finally reaching the spawning grounds where it hatched years before. Unlike Pacific salmon, which die after spawning, many Atlantic salmon survive to return to the sea, eventually to come back and spawn again.

There are still a number of good salmon streams in eastern Canada, although they do not support the big runs of former years. In the United States, however, the Atlantic salmon had all but disappeared by 1900. Only several small rivers in eastern Maine still supported salmon runs of any size.

In Colonial days the salmon fishery was an important industry in the northeastern United States. At least twenty-eight coastal rivers and their tributaries supported flourishing salmon runs. Indians speared the fish at falls and rapids and took them in quantity in circular fenced traps or weirs. For many years the Colonials continued this abundant harvest of fish. The industry was especially important along the Connecticut River and Maine's Penobscot.

Once it started, though, the downfall of the salmon fisheries came fast. Thrifty New Englanders began to dam their streams in order to get water power for mills and other industries. As early as

1798 a sixteen-foot dam was built at Miller's Falls on the Connect-icut—without any fish ladder or other provision for the fish to pass through. At one stroke the salmon were barred from all their upstream spawning grounds. Soon other dams were being built downstream as well. Mills and factories began to line the banks of the river, and towns and cities sprang up, all of them spewing sewage and industrial wastes into the water. By 1810 salmon fishing in the Connecticut River was almost unknown.

A few years later the same sequence of events was repeated in Maine. Here the lumbering industry swept over the vast virgin forests in the mid-nineteenth century, destroying the protective cover around the watersheds of salmon streams and leaving them wide open to erosion, silting, and pollution from logging debris and pulp mills. By 1880 only eight Maine rivers still maintained appreciable salmon runs. The take dwindled yearly, and by 1950, to all intents and purposes, salmon fishing in the United States was almost a thing of the past.

In 1948 a major effort to reestablish the Maine salmon fishery got under way with the organization of the Atlantic Sea-Run Salmon Commission, with headquarters at Orono, Maine. The commission hoped to reestablish the species by removing old dams, weirs, and other obstructions, building fish ladders and runs where necessary, and then restocking the streams with hatchery-reared fish. In 1965 Congress passed the Anadromous Fish Act, which made federal funds available to states on a matching basis to help such restoration projects. With this aid, fishways were constructed around six hydroelectric dams on the Penobscot River, and pollution was controlled. Today the Penob-scot and its tributaries have sizable runs of silvery, leaping salmon in them once again. Efforts in recent years have focused on building downstream fishways to enable smolts and spent adults to migrate safely to the sea.

A similar program was carried out in the Connecticut River, which had had no salmon runs for more than a century. After the river's pollution was controlled and fish ladders built around numerous dams, young hatchery-raised salmon were introduced into the numerous historic spawning streams, there to develop and eventually migrate downstream to the sea. Millions of salmon smolts have been introduced into the Connecticut and its tributaries in this way yearly, but so far only several hundred return to the river as adults each spring. Most of these are captured and stripped of their eggs and milt (sperm). The resulting progeny are raised in hatcheries and them released when they attain the proper size. A large percentage of them die as they pass through hydropower turbines at the dams. Many others are victims of river and ocean predators, or end up in nets of commercial fishermen.

The drift net commercial fishery of Denmark, Canada, and other nations took a heavy toll on salmon off Greenland and in the waters around the Faeroe Islands until the 1980s, when an international agreement was reached to regulate and limit the take. Nevertheless, appreciable quantities of salmon continued to be harvested in the North Atlantic. An international body, the North American Salmon Conservation Organization (NASCO), supposedly set quotas for the commercial fishery, but the allowable catch was usually set so high that it wasn't reached. In the summer of 1993 Secretary of the Interior Bruce Babbit hailed the signing of a historic five-year agreement to suspend the wild salmon fishery in the North Atlantic, with Greenland to be compensated for its loss of revenue.

"The total catch of wild salmon is a mere 4,000 metric tons per year," outdoor writer Mike Rosenthal observes, "while more than 200,000 metric tons of the fish are commercially grown every year in nets placed in the ocean, mostly in the fjords of Scandinavia." Perhaps this method of salmon aquaculture points the way for commercial fishermen to raise and harvest salmon profitably. Then the wild fish could be classified as a "sportfish," legally caught only on rod and reel by recreational fishermen.

SOCKEYE SALMON
Oncorhyncus nerka **and its relatives**

At the time of the California Gold Rush, an estimated ten to fifteen million Pacific salmon—sockeye, chinook, coho, chum, and pink—and steelhead trout returned to the Columbia and other nearby West Coast river systems to spawn. Today, the return is

Sockeye Salmon

just 2.5 million fish, about 75 percent of them produced in hatcheries, and the numbers grow smaller every year. According to the American Fisheries Society, 214 naturally spawning salmon stocks in California, Oregon, Washington, and Idaho are either threatened with eventual extinction or are of special concern, largely because of the destruction of the natural environment.

The Columbia River has the world's largest hydroelectric system, with eight massive dams that block the way and force the wild salmon to swim a fearsome gauntlet as they struggle upstream to traditional spawning grounds. Mining and agricultural practices, as well as urban growth, have caused widespread habitat destruction and deterioration of water quality. Excessive logging operations clog waterways and cause erosion which silts up the once-clear spawning streams. As a result, few fish ever make it to their ancestral runs, and a large percentage of those that do fail to reproduce successfully.

The young smolts have a similar difficult migration downstream. Hydroelectric turbines kill or injure many of them so they are easy prey for predators, especially squawfish, that wait below the dams.

In November 1991 the National Marine Fisheries Service reported that only four Snake River sockeye salmon—one female and three males—had returned that fall to their ancestral spawning grounds, and that the fish was to be protected under the

Endangered Species Act. The fertilized eggs of that lone female were being raised under protected hatchery conditions.

Many other Pacific salmon stocks face the same fate in the future, unless immediate and drastic steps are taken to protect their environment. The Endangered Species Committee of the American Fisheries Society observes in the March 1991 issue of its magazine *Fisheries* that ". . . habitat restoration and ecosystem function rather than hatchery production is needed for many of these stocks to survive and prosper into the next century."

CUTTHROAT TROUT
Oncorhynchus clarki

A beautiful, fighting game fish of western rivers, the cutthroat trout gets its name from the pair of vivid reddish markings on its throat. Of the numerous subspecies, several are presently threatened with extinction. The Lahontan cutthroat trout (*O.c. henshawi*), found only in the waters of the Lahontan Basin of west-central Nevada, is vanishing as a result of dams, pollution, and damage to its spawning beds by forest removal and overgrazing. The greenback cutthroat (*O.c. stomias*), which lives in several small Colorado streams, is also threatened. Its status has improved recently, however, and in 1969 hatchery-raised greenbacks were stocked in various lakes in Rocky Mountain National Park.

Two closely related trout—the Gila trout (*O. gilae*), found only in headwaters of the Gila River in New Mexico, and the Arizona or Apache trout (*O. apache*), which lives in tributaries of the White River in Arizona—are both seriously endangered because of their limited numbers, the deterioration of their restricted waters, and competition from introduced non-native fishes.

BLUE PIKE
Stizostedion vitreum glaucum

Up until the 1950s the blue pike, a slate-colored race of the familiar walleye, was one of the most important commercial species in Lake Erie, with annual catches of twenty million pounds or more. Yet between 1956 and 1963 the take dropped from 6.8 million pounds to just 200 pounds, as the blue pike almost completely disappeared from both Lake Erie and Lake Ontario, where it also used to be taken in much smaller numbers. Today it is considered extinct. The speedy extermination of this fish is due mainly to the deterioration of the waters of both lakes because of increasing pollution.

LONGJAW CISCO
Coregonus alpenae

Another Great Lakes fish, the longjaw cisco, formed a major part of the commercial chub fishery of Lakes Michigan and Huron until the 1950s. By the 1960s, however, it had all but disappeared due to a combination of reasons: too-intensive fishing, increasing predation by sea lampreys, increasing competition from other hardier species, and, of course, deterioration of its watery habitat. Only seven longjaw ciscoes were taken during intensive studies of southern Lake Michigan during 1962–64. Today it is considered extinct.

Two relatives—the deepwater cisco and the blackfin cisco—that were an important part of the Great Lakes fishery in former years, have disappeared as well, and for much the same reasons. No specimens of either have been taken since the 1950s.

Fish with Restricted Habitats

Many of the endangered fish of the United States are little-known species or subspecies found only in very restricted areas. Some of them inhabit only one small stream, or a single spring or well. Any specialized form that has such a restricted range is a prime candidate for extinction if anything happens to alter its limited environment, whether that change is brought about by man or through natural causes.

A number of species of Cyprinidae, a worldwide family of

fishes that includes the minnows and daces, are presently in danger of extinction in the United States. The melancholy roll call includes the desert dace, a small minnow living in warm springs of Humboldt County, Nevada; the Little Colorado spine dace, of which probably less than 1,000 still survive in East Clear Creek, a tributary of the Little Colorado River in Arizona; and many others.

The family Cyprinodontidae, or topminnows, includes many small and colorful fish that are popular with aquarists. In America, various members of the family are in present danger: the Devil's Hole pupfish, the Comanche Springs pupfish, the Owens River pupfish, and the Pahrump killifish. Each of these is found only in a single spring, or in several neighboring springs and their outlets, in southwestern states. All of them are threatened with extinction because of tampering with their specialized habitat by man.

Devil's Hole Pupfish

The fish family Percidae includes the darters—small, quick-moving, bottom-living species found only in temperate North America east of the Rockies. A number of them are so rare that they could become extinct almost overnight without anyone even realizing they were gone. One, the Maryland darter (*Etheostoma sellare*), lives only in Swan Creek near Havre de Grace, Maryland, and has not been seen since 1988.

The notorious little snail darter (*Percina tanasi*), whose

imperiled status because of the construction of the Tellico Dam became a cause célèbre in the 1970s, survives today in several small streams. In 1984 the Fish and Wildlife Service upped its status from "endangered" to "threatened."

Many of the fish mentioned above, and other rare species that have extremely limited habitats, might be protected and saved if the centers of their populations were set aside as national wildlife monuments or refuges, as has been done for the Moapa dace (*Moapa coriacea*) and several others.

It is interesting to contemplate a tangled bank, clothed with many plants of many kinds, with birds singing in the bushes, with various insects flitting about, and with worms crawling through the damp earth, and to reflect that these elaborately constructed forms, so different from each other, and dependent upon each other in so complex a manner, have all been produced by laws acting around us.

—Charles Darwin,
The Origin of Species

18

BUTTERFLIES AND OTHER INVERTEBRATES

"The diversity of life forms, so numerous that we have yet to identify most of them, is the greatest wonder of this planet," observes Harvard scientist, writer, and Pulitzer Prize winner Edward O. Wilson. He goes on to note that about 1.4 million different living species of animals and plants have been described so far. Of these, about 250,000 are plants and 41,000 are vertebrates—animals with backbones. All the rest—more than a million—are invertebrates: protozoans, insects and other arthropods, molluscs, sea stars and their relatives, worms, jellyfish, and sponges. More than 750,000 of them are insects alone.

Wilson and other zoologists believe that these 1.4 million living forms that have been described and catalogued are just the tip of the iceberg. All told, they believe that there may be anywhere from five to thirty million different kinds of animals in the world, the vast majority of them still unknown. Practically all of them are invertebrates. The ground we walk on, the air we breathe, the waters of our rivers and seas teem with creatures that we have no knowledge of, have never seen.

The luxurious tropical rain forests, which originally covered about 7 percent of the earth's surface, have always been particularly rich in animal and plant life of all kinds, and zoologists believe that they contain more than 50 percent of all the world's species. For the past quarter-century or more, however, tropical rain forests throughout the world have been under siege—cut down for their lumber, or burned and cleared for agriculture and other human projects. This rain-forest destruction is taking place so relentlessly that many scientists believe they will be mostly gone thirty years from now.

As the forests are destroyed, countless kinds of animals and plants are disappearing too. In his 1992 book, *The Diversity of Life*, Dr. Wilson suggests that 20 percent of all existing species of animals will become extinct within the next thirty years at the current rate of destruction. The vast majority of these, of course, are insects and other invertebrates. In tropical rain forests worldwide, he estimates that "the number of species doomed each year is 27,000. Each day it is 74, each hour three. Clearly," he warns, "we are in the midst of one of the great extinction spasms of history."

For several years after the Endangered Species Act of 1973 became law, the Fish and Wildlife Service focused practically all its efforts on threatened vertebrates—the majority of them mammals and birds. These were the glamor species, familiar and attractive animals that held the most interest for the general public. Little thought was given to the invertebrates until 1975 when the Service proposed forty-one butterflies as candidates for the threatened or endangered listing. "Destruction of habitat is the main reason for the loss of butterflies," declared Dr. Paul A. Opler, head of the newly formed entomological section of the Office of Endangered Species, in a news release announcing the action.

By 1984 the Service had expanded its invertebrate list to more than 1,000 forms—335 of them from Hawaii alone. Practically all of these still wait their turn for public comment and review before they can be given formal protection under the Act. In a 1990 report to Congress on the program, the Service listed eighty-one invertebrates that are currently protected. These include eleven butterflies, seven beetles, ten crustaceans, and thirty-nine clams and mussels. Thousands of other endangered invertebrates remain unlisted and unrecognized.

The main causes of invertebrate disappearance can be traced—as with the vertebrates—to destruction or alteration of their vital habitat at the hands of man. Many freshwater clams and mussels are disappearing because of pollution or the silting up of their watery habitat by dams and drainage projects. Butterflies recede in the aftermath of pesticides, roadside spraying with herbicides, over-collecting of rare and isolated populations, and—above all—their loss of specialized habitat or food plants to agricultural clearing and urban development.

Just as birds are favorite vertebrates because of their beauty and song, butterflies are favorite invertebrate animals with many nature-lovers because of their striking patterns and colors and their fascinating life histories. All of the hundreds of American species are facing an increasingly hard struggle for survival, as the following accounts show.

SCHAUS SWALLOWTAIL
Heraclides aristodemus ponceanus

One of our largest butterflies, the Schaus swallowtail, gets its name from a medical doctor who discovered it on Brickell Hammock near Miami while he was in the area treating Spanish-American war casualties in 1898. A beautiful insect, with broad yellow bands and spots on mahogany-brown wings, the Schaus swallowtail disappeared soon after it was discovered, only to be found again on Florida's Lower Matecumbe Key in 1935.

After a hurricane swept across the Keys in the fall of 1938, it disappeared once more, only to reappear several years later. The butterfly's very specialized and restricted habitat is wild hardwood hammocks—elevated islands of forest land surrounded by marshes—where the larva feeds upon wild lime and torchwood.

Much of that living space has disappeared, destroyed by the commercial development of the Keys, the clearing of the land for

Schaus Swallowtail

housing, highways, and airports. Most of what is left is sprayed with pesticides for mosquito control.

Because of its rarity, the Schaus swallowtail has always been eagerly pursued by collectors and commercial dealers, who in the past have offered perfect pairs for as much as $150. This is now illegal under the Endangered Species Act.

In 1984 Dr. Thomas C. Emmel, a zoologist at the University of Florida who has studied the Schaus swallowtail for years, estimated that the entire population was just seventy individuals. Two years later, however, he found that many on Key Largo alone and estimated the overall population at about 1,000. The survival of the butterfly depends on the preservation of what remains of its wild habitat in Florida.

MISSION BLUE BUTTERFLY
Icaricia icarioides missionensis and its relatives

A subspecies of a little blue butterfly found in many western states, the mission blue survives only in several small and isolated populations of coastal grasslands and scrub in the Twin Peaks area of the San Bruno Mountains on the San Francisco peninsula. Its larva feeds on wild lupine. The wings of the adult male are bright azure-blue above and silvery with black dots on the underside. The female is duller. It is listed as endangered, and its limited habitat is threatened by development.

To help insure its survival, the Fish and Wildlife Service has worked out a Habitat Conservation Plan (HCP) with local governments and private developers in the area. Under the agreement, several hundred acres of critical habitat have been set aside for the butterfly, and some development in the surrounding area is permitted.

A number of other small blue butterflies—Smith's blue, El Segunda blue, lotis blue, Palo Verdes blue, Karner blue, and others—also face imminent extinction because of the destruction of their specialized living space by development. One close relative of the mission blue, the Fender's blue butterfly (*I.i. fenderi*), had been considered extinct for more than fifty years, for it had not been seen since 1937. In 1991, however, Paul Hammond, an entomologist at Oregon State University, rediscovered it in a remote prairie in Oregon's Willamette Valley.

The Xerces Society, an international nonprofit organization

dedicated to the global protection of butterflies and other terrestrial arthropods, was founded in 1971 by Dr. Robert Michael Pyle of the Yale School of Forestry and Environmental Studies. The Society gets its name from the Xerces blue butterfly (*Glaucopsyche xerces*) that once lived in the San Francisco area and became extinct in the early 1940s.

MONARCH BUTTERFLY
Danaus plexippus

We have a national bird, the bald eagle, and a national flower, the rose. Dr. Pyle, founder of the Xerces Society, thinks we should have a national insect as well, and that it should be the monarch butterfly. It is, he says, "the best-beloved butterfly of our land, a living, moving, reproducing wonder whose beauty inspires millions, whose metamorphosis touches thousands of schoolchildren, and whose annual migration binds Canada, Mexico, and the United States as no treaty ever could."

A cosmopolitan species, the beautiful orange-and-black monarch can be seen in North America from southern Canada southward, coast to coast. It is not endangered as a species, since 100 million or more monarchs east of the Rockies migrate thousands of miles south every fall to wintering quarters in the mountains of central Mexico, and ten million or more west of the Rockies migrate to a number of wintering spots along the California coast. In the fall, countless North Americans gaze skyward with delight as monarchs by the score pass above them on their long journey south, or watch as flocks of them settle for the night in the branches of trees.

No, the monarch is not threatened as a species. But its overwintering sites, limited to extraordinarily small areas in Mexico and California, *are* threatened with imminent destruction. If they go, the North American population of monarchs is likely to diminish to few, and the great phenomenon of monarch migration will disappear.

Scientists did not know just where the Mexican wintering grounds were until 1975 when Dr. Fred Urquhart and colleagues of the University of Toronto were led to them by interested Mexicans. The hundreds of millions of monarchs, they discovered, descended to about twenty different forest groves—none of them far from each other—high in the mountains, some sixty miles west of Mexico City. The view of millions upon millions of butterflies clustered in the trees was a spectacle they would never forget.

These vital sites, they quickly realized, were already under siege and in danger of being destroyed by logging, clearing the forested slopes by ax and controlled burning for agriculture, pesticide spraying, and frequent disturbance of the half-dormant insects. Because of this destruction, the International Union for the Conservation of Nature in 1983 designated the monarch migration a Threatened Phenomenon.

In 1986, by presidential decree, the Mexican government protected five of the overwintering sites by designating them as preserves. By this time, however, according to some calculations, at least 80 percent of the overwintering sites had already been damaged or destroyed.

Monarca A.C., a private, nonprofit Mexican conservation organization, became active in trying to preserve the critical habitat and educate the local population to appreciate the butterfly phenomenon as a valuable local asset and tourist attraction. Since 1986 Monarca has bought or leased a number of vital sites. The preservation efforts continue.

In California, practically all of the monarch's overwintering sites are on private land which is threatened by real estate development. A number of legally protected sites have also deteriorated because of human activity in surrounding areas. Pacific Grove, a town some sixty miles south of San Francisco, proudly calls itself "Butterfly Town, USA" and has passed laws to protect its beautiful visitors. But a number of the trees in which the butterflies gather are on private property, and many have been cut down to make way for development. The assumption had been that the butterflies would settle for other nearby trees as their roosts, but for the most part that has not been the case.

In 1987 the California state legislature passed a bill calling for a statewide survey of all monarch habitats, and the next year California voters cheerfully passed a bond issue allocating two million dollars to acquire monarch overwintering sites. In spite of this, the destruction of vital wintering trees continues.

Lincoln Brower and Stephen Malcolm, two members of the Xerces Society's monarch project—a program to save the overwintering habitats of the species—believe that the monarch's plight is very serious. In 1989 they predicted "that its migration and overwintering in North America will be destroyed by the end of this century if extensive overwintering habitat in Mexico and California is not successfully protected."

Man is part of the vast web of life and cannot escape the natural consequences of his actions. . . . The sheer power of the population and technological revolutions may make man himself an endangered species in many parts of the earth.

—Stewart Udall,
quoted in *The New York Times*
(January 26, 1966)

19

HUMANITY, AN ENDANGERED SPECIES

At this moment in history, *Homo sapiens* appears to be one of the most successful species the world has ever known. From humble beginnings human beings have risen to become the dominant form of life on earth, the one species that can alter and manipulate its environment to suit itself. Our superior brain and reasoning power made such a rise possible.

In the beginning, this application of brainpower toward a different kind of life was very slow. For hundreds of thousands of years our distant ancestors lived as foraging and hunting animals. Just one of many different forms of life struggling for survival, they lived with and by the land. Every one of their senses was attuned, as the senses of the other animals still are, to all the rewards and dangers of their natural surroundings.

Very gradually they became herdsmen and tillers of the soil. They invented tools and fashioned weapons. They organized themselves in tribes, settled down in villages, and eventually built great cities and cultivated the arts. Over many thousands of years they evolved into what they are today: creatures increasingly out of touch with the natural world of their beginnings.

During the twentieth century this process of change has accelerated at a dizzying pace, as a result of the explosion of scientific knowledge and the application of that knowledge to medicine, industry, agriculture, and every other facet of modern life. "In the last few decades, mankind has been overcome by the most fateful change in its entire history," Barbara Ward declares in her book *Spaceship Earth.* "Modern science and technology have created so close a network of communications, transport, economic interdependence—and potential nuclear destruction— that planet earth, on its journey through infinity, has acquired the intimacy, the fellowship, and the vulnerability of a spaceship."

But most of us glorify the concept of the spaceship in quite a different way. Today everything seems possible, and we reach for the stars.

Life in the Twenty-first Century

What do the swift tides of change augur for human life in the future? Not surprisingly, opinions vary. Technology advocates wax enthusiastic over their vision of the twenty-first century, declaring that applied science and technology will make all Earth a utopia, with the land transformed so that it can support many times the present population. They envision a brave new world of scientific triumphs: gleaming cities, all enclosed under domes, where the environment will be controlled and purified; people living in mile-high, connected towers, where no one will need to venture outside for weeks or months at a time. If they should, giant rocket-propelled transports will enable them to whisk from New York to London, Moscow, or Beijing within minutes. Food will be produced in chemical nutrients on vast indoor farms. There will be under-seas farms too, where seaweed and plankton and other seafood can be continually grown and harvested. Disease will be conquered, and scientists will be able to manipulate human genes to produce "desirable" types of human beings at will.

All of these marvels are indeed possible—and that very fact profoundly disturbs a great many people. What will be the effect of such a machine-dominated civilization, not only upon our natural environment but upon our soul and spirit as well?

Already there are too many people in the world. Yet, along with the explosion of knowledge, the human population of the world keeps increasing. Every year there are ninety million or more people on the planet Earth than there were the year before: ninety million more individuals that need more food, more homes, more products—and more technology to produce these things.

Little wonder that progress and prosperity in the advanced nations are generally equated with a constantly growing gross national product, and that in the frantic effort to meet the demands of an insatiable economy, we carry the raid on our national resources, the destruction of our natural environment, further and further every day. "With our spanking new toy, technology, we have already done more to disrupt natural things in our own lifetimes than were previously disrupted by all living things, including man, in all previous history," David Brower, now chairman of Earth Island Institute, asserted a quarter of a century ago in *Technology Review*. "Can we go on this way, worshipping growth, confusing it with progress?" How true those words ring today!

To continue blindly in this direction, ecologists warn, is to flirt with the ultimate disaster—destruction of the earth as a fit living place for humans and every other living thing. We have already advanced so far down this path of "more people, more technology" that no matter what programs may be launched to reverse the trend, they will not be enough to prevent a great deal of agony in the world brought about by famines, overcrowding, and the struggle to survive in a deteriorated environment. As Dr. Edward O. Wilson noted in a 1993 article in *The New York Times Magazine*, "On November 18, 1992, more than 1,500 senior scientists from 69 countries issued a 'Warning to Humanity' stating that overpopulation and environmental deterioration put the very future of life at risk."

Tipping the Ecological Balance

Heedless or unaware of such a possibility, most people continue on their accustomed way, demonstrating ever more forcefully that

Homo sapiens, in relation to his environment, is the world's dirtiest and most destructive species. "A case could certainly be made out for the contention that modern man as a race has the death wish," Joseph Wood Krutch observed in a 1967 article. "Otherwise he would not be marching so resolutely toward literal extinction."

Consider:

The Sierra Club Legal Defense Fund notes that "In the United States alone, we dump 2.7 billion pounds of toxics into the air every year, discharge over 500 million pounds of toxic waste into our rivers, and bury 160 million tons of trash. Worldwide, we annihilate 74,000 acres of rain forest a day . . . 17,500 plant and animal species a year."

In similar vein, Al Gore notes that every man, woman, and child in our country produces twice his or her weight in wastes—garbage, sewage, cans, paper, plastic, and many other throw-aways—every *day*.

It is impossible to predict the long-range consequences of our fossil-fuel civilization, based on the vast consumption of coal and oil, which is adding carbon compounds to the atmosphere at a rate more rapid than plants on land and in the oceans can absorb them by photosynthesis. Just one big jetliner, it has been calculated, burns about six tons of petroleum hydrocarbons for every hour of flight and releases into the atmosphere about eight tons of water and twice that amount of carbon dioxide. Multiply this by thousands of planes, twenty-four hours in a day, 365 days in a year. Then add the carbon compounds released into the air from all other sources, and some idea of the extent of the problem can be gained.

By means of photosynthesis, plants utilize carbon dioxide to manufacture organic compounds, releasing oxygen as a byproduct. Animals, on the other hand, breathe oxygen and release carbon dioxide as a waste product of metabolism. The vital carbon-oxygen relationship has remained essentially in balance for some 400 million years of earth history. But now, through our use of fossil fuels, we are increasing the amount of carbon dioxide in the atmosphere, and at the same time, through bulldozer, ax, plow, and pollution, we are reducing the earth's potential for oxygen production. As a result, we are upsetting the earth's carbon-oxygen balance and altering the basic chemical, geological, and biological cycles on which all life depends.

Every year we see increasing evidence of the destruction we are inflicting on planet Earth from the millions of tons of toxic gases we are pumping into the atmosphere. In 1988 alone, we put 5.5 million tons of carbon into the atmosphere by burning fossil fuels. Scientists warn us that the buildup of carbon dioxide and other gases is causing a "greenhouse effect" and consequent global warming, since the opacity of the carbon dioxide inhibits the earth's surface heat from radiating back into space. Temperature increases of anywhere from 2 to 9 percent are predicted for the twenty-first century, with melting of much of the polar icecaps, rising sea levels, drastic climate changes over much of the earth, and other unpleasant and potentially disastrous possibilities.

Scientists also view with alarm the "ozone holes" that are appearing over both the Antarctic and arctic regions. The thinning of the protective ozone layer in the atmosphere allows increased deadly ultraviolet radiation to get through to the earth. It is caused for the most part by the emission of chlorofluorocarbons (CFCs) into the atmosphere, where they break down into ozone-destroying chemicals. In 1989 the United States alone produced 700 million pounds of CFCs, which are used in refrigerants, airconditioners, and aerosol sprays. Another environmentally destructive force is acid rain, caused by sulfate and nitrate emissions into the atmosphere. In the air, the nitrogen and sulfur compounds combine with oxygen to form acids, which are then removed from the air by rain or snow which falls upon our forests and lakes. Acid rain kills or stunts the trees and renders thousands of lakes in the United States and Canada unfit for fish, amphibians, and other aquatic life.

Assessing the continuing deterioration of the environment, the Worldwatch Institute, a Washington, D.C.- based environmental research organization, declared in its annual report, *State of the World, 1993*, that "nothing short of sharp changes in government policies and people's attitudes will rescue the earth's ailing ecosystems from destruction."

One note of hope is that the ecological conscience of many people is slowly changing for the better. After the 1991 Persian Gulf war, a poll taken to find out the attitude of U.S. citizens on the importance of the environment found a remarkable 93 percent in favor of our country using its position and strength to assume a leadership role in a worldwide effort to protect the environment.

The United States had its chance to do just that in June 1992 at the Earth Summit held in Rio de Janeiro. This United Nations Conference on Environment and Development was attended by delegates from 178 nations, and it was undoubtedly the most important international convention ever held on the subject. A treaty to curb carbon dioxide and other greenhouse gases was up for ratification, as was a treaty on preserving biodiversity, and Agenda 21, a plan for industrial nations to help poor countries develop economically without devastating their environment.

But with President Bush calling the shots, the United States played a reluctant and largely negative role at Rio. Alone of all major nations, it refused to sign the treaty on preserving biodiversity. The United States went along with Agenda 21 but took no leadership in its implementation and worked hard to weaken the wording of the treaty to curb emissions of carbon dioxide and other greenhouse gases. It is ironic, *Newsweek* magazine noted in its June 15, 1992 issue, that "the United States has become the black knight of the green movement."

Our Attitude Toward Nature

All of the environmental pollution that threatens to upset the earth's ecological balance follows in the wake of a civilization based on the ideal of making more and more *things* for more and more *people*. In the process, our sense of values has been distorted, and we seem to have lost our feeling of kinship with the natural world that has sustained us for so long. Vice President Al Gore sadly observes that the enshrined political ethic of the age seems to be, "Get it while you can; forget about the future." Years ago, sociologist Richard L. Means, in an article in *Saturday Review*, pointed out that "justification of a technological arrogance toward nature on the basis of dividends and profits is not just bad economics—it is basically an immoral act. And our contemporary moral crisis, then, goes much deeper than questions of political power and law, or urban riots and slums. It may, at least in part, reflect American society's almost utter disregard for the value of nature."

Part of America's arrogant attitude toward nature is imbedded in the mystique of the pioneer spirit: man against nature, rugged individualism, every man for himself. Part of it, perhaps, goes much farther back, to the beginnings of Western culture and ethics. Albert Schweitzer once observed that "The great fault of all ethics hitherto has been that they believed themselves to have to deal only with the relations of man to man."

The root of the crisis, perhaps, lies in the widely held but misleading premise that all of nature exists only to serve our use. For many centuries there has been a general misinterpretation of the passage in the Bible's Book of Genesis in which God told man: "Have dominion over the fish of the sea, and the fowl of the air, and over every living thing that moveth upon the earth." The understanding of this passage has usually emphasized man's dominance, his right to use and deal with all other animals as he wishes. A more enlightened interpretation points out our moral responsibility for safeguarding wildlife and all the rest of Earth's resources, and using them wisely.

Human beings could, of course, survive in a world without whooping cranes or California condors, grizzly bears or blue whales. Our very existence does not depend upon these and some others of our fellow inhabitants of the earth. But if we should ever become indifferent to the question of whether these animals live or not, if we didn't recognize the worth of saving them, then we would no longer be human in terms of spirit and moral essence.

The question of wildlife preservation also could be answered on the level of simple self-interest: the dwindling fortunes of our wildlife serve as warning signals of mankind's possible fate too. If we cannot save endangered wildlife by preserving some of its essential environment and conditions for its survival—then the human race, in the long run, will go under too.

Our intelligence and our potential are too great, however, for us to believe that this could happen.

A Conservation Program and Ethic for the Future

During the past quarter-century, more and more people the world over are recognizing the dangers in what we are doing to Earth's life-sustaining resources and are speaking out about our responsibility toward our natural environment. More and more people are realizing that the only valid option today is to try to live in harmony with nature, instead of trying to conquer and subdue it. "We abuse land because we regard it as a commodity belonging to us," Aldo Leopold observed many years ago. "When we see land as a community to which we belong, we may begin to use it with love and respect."

In order for that to happen, nothing less than a whole new governmental focus and structure, oriented toward the preservation of our environment, must be instituted. The environment must be considered as one entity and not separate units of land, water, air, plants, and animals. Dealing with the environment in this way, environmentalists urge a massive, nationwide assault on pollution and environmental deterioration of every kind, with much tighter controls and stiffer penalties for violation than at present. But to make this plan work, we must develop an "ecological conscience" and a "land ethic."

Today the vast majority of American children grow up with very few of the opportunities their grandparents had for developing a feeling of kinship with the land, a feeling of being part of the living earth. More and more of the younger generation spend their entire lives in urban situations. Their main contact with living things comes from visiting a park or a zoo—from seeing nature controlled, pruned, and tamed. Biology, as it is taught to the coming generation, has more and more left the out-of-doors and become an indoor laboratory science like physics or chemistry. The emphasis today seems to be on biochemistry, the molecular structure of living things, the wonderful properties of DNA. These are indeed of vital importance, but first there should be a grounding in the study of living plants and animals and the relationship of these living things to each other, to the environment, and to us. "Environmental education," Stewart Udall declared, "should be part of every school's curriculum, every family's moral code." Only by instilling an appreciation and understanding of nature in the hearts of the next generations can we hope to keep planet Earth a fit living place, a place where forests and prairies and wetlands and all other natural ecosystems are treasured and preserved.

For such a program to succeed, as most delegates to the Earth Summit in Rio realized, all the nations of the world must ultimately institute similar programs in greater or lesser degree, and humanity as a whole must control and stabilize its increasing population.

The United States and the other advanced industrialized nations must take the lead in this commitment and extend aid to the world's poor and backward nations—both financial and educational. We must help these countries realize a higher standard of living for their peoples, and also help them to preserve and safeguard their natural environmental treasures.

One reason for optimism lies in the fact that the same technology that has done so much to alter and pollute the environment can also be turned to devising new ways to make it clean and whole once more. Wastes can be recycled and reused toward constructive ends. New ways can be discovered for eliminating air and water pollution. Instead of pesticides, new and even more effective biological controls can be used against insects injurious to crops.

New ways of harnessing the power of the sun, the winds, and the tides for the production of clean energy can be discovered. The possibilities are infinite. And so, in the final analysis, the shape of the future depends on us. All that is needed is a resolute moral and political commitment.

It would be tragic indeed if the time ever came when our children—or our children's children—might not have the opportunity of sighting a graceful deer by the shore of a lonely lake, a proud hawk spiraling in the clear sky, a frog sitting on a lily pad, or a butterfly hovering before a blossom. There always should be pockets of unspoiled wilderness where our children can experience a feeling of awe and wonder in their surroundings, and where wildlife has the natural living space it needs for survival.

Primitive people felt such a kinship with nature, such a sense of being part of a great whole. Today, if we are to survive, we must rediscover this natural kinship and take it to heart. When we succeed—and we must, and will—all wildlife too will have a better chance.

SELECTED BIBLIOGRAPHY

The many wildlife and conservation publications of the U.S. Fish and Wildlife Service (Department of the Interior), and the reports of the National Marine Fisheries Service (Department of Commerce) on its administration of the Marine Mammal Protection Act of 1972, have been very helpful in providing both background material and current information for use in the preparation of this work. One of my principal references has been: U.S. Fish and Wildlife Service, 1990, *Report to Congress: Endangered and Threatened Species Recovery Program.*

A number of magazines and periodicals carry articles and news items concerning endangered wildlife in nearly every issue. The following have been especially useful: *Audubon* (National Audubon Society); *National Geographic* (National Geographic Society); *Animal Kingdom* and its successor, *Wildlife Conservation* (New York Zoological Society); *Natural History* (American Museum of Natural History); *Defenders* (Defenders of Wildlife); *Smithsonian* (Smithsonian Institution); *Wings* and *Atala* (Xerces Society); *Greenpeace Magazine* (Greenpeace); and *Focus* (World Wildlife Fund). The Science section published weekly in *The New York Times* also carries many helpful articles on endangered species.

A complete listing of all the sources that were consulted in the research for this book would be of little interest or use to the general reader. Instead, I am electing to list by subject those particular books and articles which are rich in source material, from which I have quoted, and which should also be of especial interest to anyone who wants to pursue a particular natural history subject further.

Wildlife Conservation and Management (General)

Allen, Durward L. *Our Wildlife Legacy.* New York: Funk and Wagnalls, 1954.

Bean, Michael J. *The Evolution of National Wildlife Law.* Prepared for the Council on Environmental Quality by the Environmental Law Institute. Washington, D.C.: U.S. Government Printing Office, 1977.

Beard, Daniel B., and a Committee of the U.S. Department of the Interior.

Fading Trails, The Story of Endangered American Wildlife. New York: Macmillan, 1942.

Belinger, Diane Olsen. *Managing American Wildlife: A History of the International Association of Fish and Wildlife Agencies.* Amherst, Mass.: University of Massachusetts Press, 1988.

Council on Environmental Quality/ F&WS/ FS/ NOAA; Brokaw, Howard P., ed. *Wildlife and America.* Washington, D.C.: U.S. Government Printing Office, 1978.

Di Silvestro, Roger L. *The Endangered Kingdom: The Struggle to Save America's Wildlife.* New York: Wiley, 1989.

————. *Fight for Survival.* New York: Wiley, 1990.

Dunlap, Thomas R. *Saving America's Wildlife.* Princeton, N.J.: Princeton University Press, 1988.

Farb, Peter, and the editors of *Life. The Land and Wildlife of North America.* New York: Time, 1964.

Gabrielson, Ira. *Wildlife Refuges.* New York: Macmillan, 1943.

Graham, Frank, Jr., with Carl Buchheister. *The Audubon Ark: A History of the National Audubon Society.* New York: Knopf, 1990.

Hornaday, William T. *Our Vanishing Wildlife.* New York: New York Zoological Society, 1914.

King, Laura B., Faith Campbell, David Edelson, and Susan Miller. *Extinction in Paradise: Protecting Our Hawaiian Species.* Washington, D.C.: Natural Resources Defense Council, 1989.

Leopold, Aldo. *Game Management.* New York: Scribner's, 1947.

————. *Round River.* New York: Oxford University Press, 1953.

————. *A Sand County Almanac.* New York: Oxford University Press, 1949.

Matthiessen, Peter. *Wildlife in America*; updated and expanded edition. New York: Viking, 1987.

McClung, Robert M. *Vanishing Wildlife of Latin America.* New York: Morrow, 1981.

Reed, Nathaniel P., and Dennis Drabelle. *The United States Fish and Wildlife Service.* Boulder and London: Westview Press, 1984.

Trefethen, James B. *Crusade for Wildlife.* Harrisburg, Pa.: Stackpole, 1961.

————. *Wildlife Management and Conservation.* Boston: D.C. Heath, 1964.

U.S. Department of the Interior, Fish and Wildlife Service. *Report to Congress: Endangered and Threatened Species Recovery Program.* Washington, D.C.: U.S. Government Printing Office, 1990.

————. *Fish & Wildlife '91, A Report to the Nation.* Washington, D.C.: U.S. Government Printing Office, 1991.

————. *Restoring America's Wildlife, 1937–1987.* Washington, D.C.: U.S. Government Printing Office, 1987.

Man and Primitive America

Bakeless, John. *The Eyes of Discovery.* New York: Dover Publications, 1961.

Cruickshank, Helen G., ed. *John and William Bartram's America.* New York: Devin-Adair, 1957.

DeVoto, Bernard. *The Course of Empire.* Boston: Houghton Mifflin, 1952.

————. ed. *The Journals of Lewis and Clark.* Boston: Houghton Mifflin, 1953.

Golder, F.A., ed. *Steller's Journal of the Sea Voyage from Kamchatka to America and Return on the Second Expedition, 1741–42.* Vol. 2 of *Bering's Voyages.* New York: American Geographical Society, 1925.

Macgowan, Kenneth, and Joseph A. Hester, Jr. *Early Man in the New World.* Garden City, N.Y.: Doubleday, 1962.

Martin, Paul S. "Pleistocene Overkill." *Natural History* 76, no. 10 (December 1967).

Osborn, Fairfield. *Our Plundered Planet.* Boston: Little, Brown, 1948.

Parkman, Francis. *The Oregon Trail.* New York: Modern Library, 1949.

Shoemaker, H.W. *A Pennsylvania Bison Hunt.* Middleburg, Pa.: Middleburg Post Press, 1915.

Swift, Ernest. *The Glory Trail. The Great American Migration and Its Impact on Natural Resources.* Washington, D.C.: National Wildlife Federation, 1958.

North American Mammals

Allen, Glover M. *Extinct and Vanishing Mammals of the Western Hemisphere.* New York: American Committee for International Wildlife Protection, 1942.

Allen, Thomas B., ed. *Wild Animals of North America.* Washington, D.C.: National Geographic Society, 1979.

Audubon, John James, and John Bachman. *The Viviparous Quadrupeds of North America.* 3 vols. New York: Lockwood, 1849–54.

————. *The Imperial Collection of Audubon Animals: The Quadrupeds of North America.* Edited and with supplementary notes by Victor H. Cahalane. Maplewood, N.J.: Hammond, 1967.

Bergman, Charles. "A Brave Return from the Brink for an Ice Age Relic." *Smithsonian* 16, no. 11 (February 1986). (Musk-ox)

Bowden, Charles. "Lonesome Lobo." *Wildlife Conservation* 95, no. 1 (January–February 1992).

Burnett, J.A., C.T. Dauphiné, Jr., S.H. McCrindle, and T. Mosquin. *On the Brink. Endangered Species in Canada.* Saskatoon, Saskatchewan: Western Producer Prairie Books, 1989.

Cahalane, Victor H. *Mammals of North America.* New York: Macmillan, 1947.

Conniff, Richard. "Coming to Grips with the Griz." *Smithsonian* 23, no. 8 (November 1992).

Darling, James D. "Whales, an Era of Discovery." *National Geographic* 174, no. 6 (December 1988).

Ellis, Richard. "A Sea Change for Leviathan." *Audubon* 87, no. 6 (November 1985).

Garretson, Martin S. *The American Bison.* New York: New York Zoological Society, 1938.

Gentry, Roger L. "Seals and Their Kin." *National Geographic* 171, no. 4 (April 1987).

Gilbert, Bil. "Coyotes Adapted to Us, Now We Have to Adapt to Them." *Smithsonian* 21, no. 12 (March 1991).

Hornocker, Maurice G. "Learning to Live with Mountain Lions." *National Geographic* 182, no. 1 (July, 1992).

Kellogg, A. Remington, and other mammalogists. *Wild Animals of North America*. Washington, D.C.: National Geographic Society, 1960.

Madson, John. "Can the Caribou Go Home Again? *Smithsonian* 22, no. 2 (May 1991).

McClung, Robert M. *Hunted Mammals of the Sea*. New York: Morrow, 1978.

McCracken, Harold. *Hunters of the Stormy Sea*. Garden City, N.Y.: Doubleday, 1957. (Historic account of sea otter exploitation)

Murie, Olaus J. *The Elk of North America*. Harrisburg, Pa.: Stackpole, 1951.

Norris, Kenneth S. "Dolphins in Crisis." *National Geographic* 182, no. 3 (September 1992).

Peterson, Randolph L. *The Mammals of Eastern Canada*. Toronto: Oxford University Press, 1966.

Rember, John. "Return of the Native." *Wildlife Conservation* 93, no. 5 (September–October 1990). (Wolf)

Scheffer, Victor B. *A Natural History of Marine Mammals*. New York: Scribner's, 1976.

―――. *Seals, Sea Lions and Walruses: A Review of the Pinnipedia*. Stanford, Calif.: Stanford University Press, 1958.

Seton, Ernest Thompson. *Lives of Game Animals*. 4 vols. Garden City, N.Y.: Doubleday, Doran, 1929.

Stackpole, Edouard A., and the editors of *American Heritage*. *The Story of Yankee Whaling*. New York: American Heritage Publishing Company, 1959.

Storer, Tracy I., and Lloyd P. Tevis, Jr. *The California Grizzly*. Berkeley, Calif.: University of California Press, 1955.

Taylor, Walter P., ed. *The Deer of North America*. Harrisburg, Pa: Stackpole, 1956.

Tennesen, Michael. "Ruler of the Canyons." *Wildlife Conservation* 95, no. 6. (November–December 1992). (Mountain lion)

U.S. Department of Commerce/National Marine Fisheries Service. *Endangered Species Act Biennial Report: Status of Recovery Program, FY 1989–1991*. Silver Spring, Md.: Office of Protected Resources.

―――. *Endangered Whales: Status Update, June 1991*. Silver Spring, Md.: Office of Protected Resources.

―――. *Final Conservation Plan for the Pribilof Islands Northern Fur Seal (Callorhinus ursinus)*. Prepared by the NMFS/Alaska Fisheries Science Center/National Marine Mammal Laboratory, Seattle, Wash., for NMFS/Office of Protected Resources. Silver Spring, Md.: 1993.

―――. *Marine Mammal Protection Act of 1972*, Annual Reports 1987/88 and 1988/89. Silver Spring, Md.: Office of Protected Resources.

―――. *Whales, Dolphins, and Porpoises of the Western North Atlantic*, NOAA Technical Report NMFS CIRC-396. Washington, D.C.: U.S. Government Printing Office, 1976.

U.S. Department of the Interior/ U.S. Fish and Wildlife Service. *Administration of the Marine Mammal Protection Act, 1990*. Washington, D.C.: U.S. Government Printing Office. 1991.

Williams, Ted. "Waiting for Wolves to Howl in Yellowstone." *Audubon* 92, no. 6 (November 1990).

Young, Stanley P., and Edward A. Goldman. *The Wolves of North America.* Washington, D.C.: American Wildlife Institute, 1944.
——. *The Puma, Mysterious American Cat.* Washington, D.C.: Wildlife Management Institute, 1946.

North American Birds

Allen, Robert P. *On the Trail of Vanishing Birds.* New York: McGraw-Hill, 1957.
——. *The Whooping Crane.* Research report no. 3. New York: National Audubon Society, 1952.
——. *The Whooping Crane's Northern Breeding Grounds.* A supplement to research report no. 3. New York: National Audubon Society, 1956.
Audubon, John James. *The Ornithological Biography.* 5 vols. Edinburgh: A. Black, 1831–39.
Banko, Winston E. *The Trumpeter Swan.* (North American Fauna, no. 63). Washington, D.C.: U.S. Government Printing Office, 1960.
Brookfield, Charles M. "The Guy Bradley Story." *Audubon Magazine* 57, no. 4. (July–August 1955).
Broun, Maurice. *Hawks Aloft: The Story of Hawk Mountain.* New York: Dodd, Mead, 1949.
Ehrlich, Paul R., David S. Dobkin, and Darryl Wheye. *Birds in Jeopardy.* Stanford, Calif.: Stanford University Press, 1992.
Graham, Frank. "How Fare the Audubon Birds a Century Later?" *Audubon* 89, no. 2 (March 1987). (Plume birds)
Greenway, James C. *Extinct and Vanishing Birds of the World.* New York: American Committee for International Wildlife Protection, 1958.
Harwood, Michael. "You Can't Protect What Isn't There." *Audubon* 88, no. 6 (November 1986). (Ivory-billed woodpecker)
Koford, Carl B. *The California Condor.* Research report no. 4. New York: National Audubon Society, 1953.
Linduska, Joseph P., ed. *Waterfowl Tomorrow.* Produced by the Department of the Interior. Washington, D.C.: U.S. Government Printing Office, 1964.
Line, Les. "Silence of the Songbirds." *National Geographic* 183, no. 6 (June 1993).
McClung, Robert M. *America's Endangered Birds: Programs and People Working to Save Them.* New York: Morrow, 1979.
McNulty, Faith. *The Whooping Crane: The Bird that Defies Extinction.* New York: Dutton, 1966.
National Geographic Society. *Field Guide to the Birds of North America.* Washington, D.C.: National Geographic Society, 1983.
Peterson, Roger Tory. *A Field Guide to the Birds East of the Rockies.* 4th ed. Boston: Houghton Mifflin, 1980.
Schorger, A.W. *The Passenger Pigeon, Its Natural History and Extinction.* Madison, Wisc.: University of Wisconsin Press, 1955.
Stefferud, Alfred, ed. *Birds in Our Lives.* Produced by the Department of the Interior. Washington, D.C.: U.S. Government Printing Office, 1966.
Tanner, James T. *The Ivory-Billed Woodpecker.* Research report no. 1. New York: National Audubon Society, 1942.

Wallace, George J. "Insecticides and Birds." *Audubon Magazine* 61, no. 1 (January–February 1959).

Welty, Joel Carl. *The Life of Birds*. Philadelphia: W.B. Saunders, 1962.

Wetmore, Alexander, and other ornithologists. *Song and Garden Birds of North America*. Washington, D.C.: National Geographic Society, 1964.

————. *Water, Prey, and Game Birds of North America*. Washington, D.C.: National Geographic Society, 1965.

Wilson, Alexander. *American Ornithology*. London: Whittaker, 1832.

North American Reptiles, Amphibians, and Fish

Behler, John L., and F. Wayne King. *The Audubon Society Field Guide to North American Reptiles and Amphibians*. New York: Knopf, 1979.

Carr, Archie. *So Excellent a Fishe; a Natural History of Sea Turtles*. Garden City, N.Y.: Published for The American Museum of Natural History by the Natural History Press, 1967.

Carr, Archie, and the editors of *Life*. *The Reptiles*. New York: Time, 1963.

Cochran, Doris M. *Living Amphibians of the World*. Garden City, N.Y.: Doubleday, 1961.

Conant, Roger. *A Field Guide to Reptiles and Amphibians of the United States and Canada East of the 100th Meridian*. Boston: Houghton Mifflin, 1958.

Curtis, Brian. *The Life Story of the Fish*. New York: Dover Publications, 1961.

Herald, Earl S. *Living Fishes of the World*. Garden City, N.Y.: Doubleday, 1961.

Livermore, Beth. "Amphibians Alarm: Just Where Have All the Frogs Gone?" *Smithsonian* 23, no. 7 (October 1992).

McIlhenny, E.A. *The Alligator's Life History*. Boston: Christopher Publishing House, 1935.

Nehlsen, Willa, Jack E. Williams, and James A. Lichatowish. "Pacific Salmon at the Crossroads: Stocks at Risk from California, Oregon, Idaho, and Washington." *Fisheries* 16, no. 2 (March–April 1991).

Oliver, James. *The Natural History of North American Amphibians and Reptiles*. Princeton, N.J.: D. Van Nostrand, 1955.

Schmidt, Karl P., and Robert F. Inger. *Living Reptiles of the World*. Garden City, N.Y.: Doubleday, 1957.

U.S. Department of Commerce/National Marine Fisheries Service. *Our Living Oceans: Report on the Status of U.S. Living Marine Resources, 1992*. Silver Spring, Md.: Office of Protected Resources.

Yoffe, Emily. "Silence of the Frogs." *New York Times Magazine* (Dec. 13, 1992).

Butterflies and Other Invertebrates

Borrer, Donald J., and Richard E. White. *A Field Guide to the Insects of America North of Mexico*. Boston: Houghton Mifflin, 1970.

Brower, Lincoln P., and Stephen B. Malcolm. "Endangered Phenomenon." *Wings: Essays on Invertebrate Conservation* 14, no. 2 (Summer 1989).

Howe, William H. *The Butterflies of North America*. Garden City, N.Y.: Doubleday, 1975.

Matthews, Downed. "Mountain Monarchs." *Wildlife Conservation* 95, no. 5 (September–October, 1992).

Wilson, Edward O. "The Little Things That Run the World." *Wings: Essays on Invertebrate Conservation* 12, no. 3 (Winter 1987).

The Environmental Crisis

Carson, Rachel. *Silent Spring*. Boston: Houghton Mifflin, 1962.

Chiapetta, Jerry. "Great Lakes, Great Mess." *Audubon* 70, no. 3 (May–June 1968).

Cole, LaMont C. "Can the Earth Be Saved?" *New York Times Magazine* (March 31, 1968).

Gore, Al. *Earth in the Balance. Ecology and the Human Spirit*. Boston: Houghton Mifflin, 1992.

Horton, Tom. "The Endangered Species Act: Too Tough, Too Weak, or Too Late?" *Audubon* 94, no. 2 (March–April 1992).

Kaufman, Les, and Kenneth Mallory, eds. *The Last Extinction*. Cambridge, Mass.: MIT Press, 1986.

Krutch, Joseph Wood. "Epitaph for an Age." *New York Times Magazine* (July 30, 1967).

Means, Richard L. "Why Worry About Nature?" *Saturday Review* (Dec. 2, 1967).

National Geographic Society. *National Geographic* 174, no. 6 (December 1988). (A special issue on man and the endangered earth)

O'Callaghan, Kate. "Whose Agenda for America?" *Audubon* 94, no. 5 (September–October 1992).

Rifkin, Jeremy, and Carol Grunewald Rifkin. *Voting Green*. New York: Doubleday, 1992.

Scheffer, Victor B. *The Shaping of Environmentalism in America*. Seattle: University of Washington Press, 1991.

Smithsonian Assoiciates. *Smithsonian* 21, no. 1 (April 1990). (A special issue on the environment)

Udall, Stewart L. *The Quiet Crisis*. New York: Holt, Rinehart and Winston, 1963.

———. *The Quiet Crisis and the Next Generation*. Salt Lake City, Utah: Gibbs Smith, Publisher; Peregrine Smith Books, 1988.

U.S. Department of the Interior. Conservation Yearbooks no. 1, *Quest for Quality* (1965); no. 2, *The Population Challenge* (1966); no. 3, *The Third Wave* (1967); no. 4, *Man . . . an Endangered Species?* (1968). Washington, D.C.: U.S. Government Printing Office.

Wicker, Tom. "What Can the Next President Do?" *Audubon* 94, no. 5 (September–October 1992).

Wilson, Edward O., ed. *Biodiversity*. Washington, D.C.: National Academy Press, 1988.

———. *The Diversity of Life*. Cambridge, Mass.: Belknap Press of Harvard University Press, 1992.

———. "Is Humanity Suicidal?" *New York Times Magazine* (May 30, 1993).

INDEX

(Asterisks after page numbers refer to illustrations)

Regular loan : 2 weeks
A daily fine is charged for each overdue **book.**
Books may be renewed once, unless **reserved**
for another patron.
A borrower is responsible for books **damaged**
or lost while charged **on his card**